About the Author

Wanting to live a life worth living, Stephen has exhibited a talent for doing research that, more often than not, has been unfunded. Intermittent income, then, was generated by being a ferryboat skipper, wildlife walks and sea cruises leader, local newspaper nature columnist and above all, as the scientific observer aboard Norwegian Antarctic krill trawlers in the Southern Ocean and aboard Japanese and Taiwanese refrigerated cargo vessels collecting tuna from the tropical Indian and Atlantic Oceans tuna fleets. While seal studies have been his primary interest, he has made many smaller studies of the seals' neighbours and also was a pioneer of studies into marine debris impacts on wildlife and wild places. He lives with his lady in Cornwall, had two daughters — one of whom died following a heart operation — and two grandchildren. He continues to study the seals, but is grateful most of all for the love and friendship that underpins everything.

Stepping Stones to the Seal Caves

Stephen Westcott

Stepping Stones to the Seal Caves

Olympia Publishers
London

www.olympiapublishers.com
OLYMPIA PAPERBACK EDITION

A CIP catalogue record for this title is
available from the British Library.

ISBN: 978-1-78830-643-0

First Published in 2021

Olympia Publishers
Tallis House
2 Tallis Street
London
EC4Y 0AB

Printed in Great Britain

Dedication

To those who went before me, those who shared the adventures and to those who will grow familiar with the same stepping stones hereafter; and to the people of my heart.

Foreword

Very little true wilderness survives in the British Isles. Much that does remain has been described elsewhere. Here is a story of one of the least-known surviving 'pocket' wildernesses — but one not less wild and daunting for all that. It is told by someone who has eked out unique and wonderful insights while tiptoeing there, being frightened and enchanted more times than he remembers over the past thirty years and more.

There would have been no such story to tell were it not for the grey seals that use such places for resting between foraging trips to sea, as nursery places for the production and rearing of their young and as places where some assemble to endure the discomforts of the annual moult. Their all-but-secret presence at such places invited inquiry. Inquiry grew to become the work of half a lifetime, in the course of which the neighbours of the secret seals and the life-patterned wallpaper of their dark haunts became known as well, enriching the whole experience.

The pathfinding studies upon which this book is based describe the grey seals that come to the shores of south-west England, Wales, the Isle of Man, Rathlin Island and NE Scotland, as well as off the coasts of Brittany. They have in common that their distribution here is localised. Rather than occurring anywhere along these coasts, they form often small to medium-sized assemblies in specific localities. Typically, such localities contain sometimes few, sometimes many sites where seals may come ashore remote from easy access by humans from the land. They might include islands, islets, skerries, beaches backed by high cliffs or even floating pontoons and boat awnings in estuaries. They use also sea cave sites of varying complexity — the only seal species in the world to use such habitats but for the extremely endangered Mediterranean monk seals — of which less than one thousand remain at this time of writing.

The seal localities inshore also include inshore water resting places. As indicated by the name, seals do not come ashore here but rest in the sea in assemblies of varying size, often — not always — adjacent to a site used for hauling out. As with the terrestrial haul-out sites, they are used mainly during the low water half of the tidal cycle.

Typically, seal localities are found clustered near major headlands protected by sometimes ferocious tidal streams as well as the sea swell and surf action that can be savagely destructive, especially during the winter months. Here are long stretches of cliffs into the base of which may be gnawed the numerous, black-entranced mouse-holes that, closer to, become the occasionally cathedral-high entrances into sea caves. Always, such places have a stark beauty that can be misleadingly mellowed by sunlight during spells of quiet weather. Better you trust the honest savagery of such places in the glooms of a stormy winter day darkened by lowering nimbus clouds. Then, the repetitive, percussive booming of waves rebounding from the back of the mouse-holes paints the brutal truth of these places. It seems to be broadcasting total hostility to life, and yet… and yet. The seals use such places at such times. They use such places to give birth to their pups and there they raise them to weaning time — from the utter dependence of the new-born to the threshold of a danger-strewn independence.

The grey seals have found a way to live with the savagery of the elemental forces with which, quite reasonably, they might be thought to be contending. That they do is often due to the sea cave architecture and attendant natural features above and below the surface of the sea as well as to the wonderful biology of the seals; but more of that later.

Stepping Stones to the Seal Caves: Early Insights

Cornwall

In Cornwall, especially, when sea caves are discussed between people, speculative conversation often turns first to their value as secret storage places used by smugglers, perhaps with secret passageways leading upward from them to the cellars of remote houses. While a handful of caves could have served that purpose, for the vast remainder it would have been wildly impracticable, the swag being certain to be readily flushed from the caves during periods of turbulence.

Some of you may have heard, may have had described to you, the eerie ululating singing of cave-bound seals. When first you hear them, as you walk along the clifftop tracks, it is very easy to imagine that you are hearing the choral song of mermaids, issuing apparently from tiny black mouse-holes at the base of the high cliffs. And, in a way, these are indeed mermaids singing for, most often, it is the sound of a female grey seal forcefully rejecting the overbearing advances of a male while she lies resting at the edge of a beach somewhere deep within the cave.

Among the questions most often posed during the seal studies upon which this story is based has been 'is seal use of sea caves a modern phenomenon connected with the ever-increasing leisure use of the coastal zone'. In effect, has the increasing lack of privacy on open beaches driven them to take refuge in the sea caves in recent times?

The simple answer is no. Two infinitely eloquent confirmations occur in **Carew (1602)**, which to date appears to offer the earliest accounts of seals using sea caves in SW England.

On page 54, he notes: '*The seale, or soyle, is in making and growth not unlike a pig, ugly faced and footed like a moldiwarp; he delighteth in music or any loud noise, and thereby is trained to approach near the shore and to show himself almost wholly above water. They also come on land and lie sleeping in holes of the cliffe, but are now and then waked with the deadly greeting of a bullet in their sides'.*

On page 185, in a chapter devoted to Penwith Hundred (approximately: the land west of a line connecting Hayle to Marazion), he adds: '*During summer season, the seals haunt a cave in the cliff thereby, and you shall see great store of them apparently show themselves, and approach very near the shore at the sound of any loud music or other such noise'.*

Carew used the old rendering of sea caves as 'holes of the cliff'. That rendering remains approximately current, some 'seal holes' being yet marked on Ordnance Survey maps. His reference to seals being shot in sea caves is, likewise, perhaps, the earliest Cornish reference to the killing of seals in what came to be described as 'battues'. The wonderful acoustics would have ensured that shooting in caves would have been extremely noisy. It could also have been a risky business, especially where the cave floor consisted of boulders. Such substrates are often covered by a mucous-like slime or by similarly slippery seaweeds.

Dr William Borlase (1758) wrote in chapter XIV of The Natural History of Cornwall: '*Among the quadruped reptiles we may reckon the seal, or sea-calf, vulgarly called in Cornwall the Soyle, in Latin the Phoca, or Vitulus marinus. It is common in the caves and on shores of Cornwall which are least frequented: it is five feet in length, sometimes seven; his head somewhat like that of a calf. Its pectoral fins resemble the fore-feet of quadrupeds, with five toes connected by a membrane with which, when in danger, it will throw stones very plentifully at those who pursue: the tail is horizontal and supplies the want of fins in the hinder parts. This creature is amphibious; it cannot altogether live in the water, but requires successive intervals of rest and respiration on the land. The poor people on the north coast of this county, in times of scarcity, do sometimes eat the flesh, and indeed the flesh of the seal as well as of the porpoise in former ages was admitted among the dainties at the most luxurious feasts, but in general the seals are killed not for* *their flesh but for the lasting, useful and spotted skins, and the oil and fat which their bodies afford. It is supposed that the fabulous relations of mermaids and mermen might first arise from observing this creature at sea in an erect human-like posture; for whether it delighted with music or any loud voice, as Mr Carew says (page 35) or whether it is to alleviate the toil of swimming, it shews itself almost wholly above water frequently, and near the shore, ibid. Add to this that the great docility of this creature (little short of that of the human species) and his being so easily trained to be familiar with and obedient to man, may make us with some grounds conclude, that this is the creature to which imagination has given the shape of half fish half man, a shape nowhere else to be found. The cunning of this creature to free itself from its enemy is remarkable, if what is related be true: The seals are in great plenty in the Baltic; when the Russes hunt them, they surround sometimes three or four thousand together, which the seals perceiving, pile themselves up in a heap, by that excessive weight striving to break the ice on which they have been surprized, and so escape their enemy'.*

On October 24, 1763, in a letter to Thomas Pennant, the same author added: '*The seals are seen in the greatest plenty on the shores of Cornwall in the months of May, June and July. They feed on most sorts of fish which they can master, and are seen to be searching for their prey near the shore, where Whistling fish, Wraws and Polacks (rocklings, wrasse and pollack) resort.*

'*They are of different size, some as large as a moderate cow, and from that downward to a small calf.*

'*They are very swift in their proper depth of water; dive like a shot, and in a trice rise above 50 yards distance, so that weaker fish cannot avoid their tyranny, but in shallow water. John Roberts of the parish of Sennen saw, not long since, a seal in pursuit of a mullett (that strong and swift fish); the seal turned him to and fro in deep water, as a greyhound a hare; the mullet at last found he had no way to escape but by running into shoal water; the seal pursued, and the mullett, to get himself more surely out of danger, threw himself flat on his side, by which means he shot into shoaler water, than he could have swam in with the depth of his paunch and fins extended, and so escaped.*

'*The seal brings forth her young in caves of the cliff and dessert (remote) rocks about the beginning of Autumn; our fishermen have seen two sucking at the same time their dam, as she stood in the sea in a perpendicular position. Their head, in swimming, is always above the water, more so than of a dog, and above water the heads of the young ones suck at the nipple.*

'They sleep on rocks surrounded with the sea, and on the least accessible parts of our cliffs left dry by the ebb of the tide, and if disturbed by anything, take care to tumble over the rocks into the sea. They are extremely watchful, and never sleep long without moving, seldom longer than a minute; then raise their head, and if they hear or see nothing more than ordinary lie down again, and so on, raising their heads somewhat, and reclining them alternately in about a minute's time. Instinct seems to have given them this precaution, as being furnished only with very small ears, and consequently not hearing very quick, nor from any great distance.

'As to their throwing stones as they fly from their pursuers, some think it is without design, because their forefeet (as they lift up their body and rush forward) naturally throw backward whatever sort of sand or gravel they are going upon'.

It is evident from these earliest commentaries that seal use of sea caves in the seventeenth and eighteenth centuries was at least locally well-known. That being so, it appears certain that coastal dwelling people would have had the same awareness of such seal haunts in the preceding centuries especially as of all the sites they use, it is in the confined spaces of the sea caves that grey seals may be most successfully cornered and slain.

The nineteenth century saw a proliferation in the publication of notes or traveller's tales telling most vividly of 'battues' — the clubbing or shooting to death of seals — in the sea caves.

Perhaps most prolific among these was John Coulson (J.C.) Tregarthen, who also wrote under the nom-de-plume of 'Envernus' — according to Dr F.A. Turk. As such, he wrote an article for the publication Once A Week, published on October 5, 1867. Entitled 'Seal hunting in Cornwall', the events described occurred just to the north of Boscastle where are to be found the highest cliffs and the sea caves that penetrate most deeply into them in all Cornwall:

I know no pleasanter place for a month's autumnal ramble than the north coast of Cornwall. Unappreciated by Cockneys, as being out of the beat of railways, tea-gardens and fashionable promenades, it may yet lay claim to merits of no inferior order, and the lover of the picturesque will do well to follow the writer's example: strap a knapsack on his back, and set to work with all speed to explore its beauties. He will be guaranteed, at all events, magnificent scenery in abundance, air most pure and invigorating, and a stay among unsophisticated, thoroughly genial inhabitants, whose ready wit and quaint sayings are proverbial, and whose courtesy and hospitality to strangers form a striking contrast to usual experience in better-known localities. The style of living, it must be confessed, is rough, and really good inns are few and far between, but perfect cleanliness will be found in the worst of them, and a hearty welcome given, even though the larder may provide nothing better for reflection of the inner man than ham and eggs or the staple food of those parts, conger eel pie. I could expatiate on these topics to any extent with the greatest satisfaction to myself, and not without some, I hope, to others…I rather hope, instead, to give some account in this paper of an expedition made during my stay at Boscastle to the seals' caverns.

Boscastle has been so often described that it would be a work of supererogation to pass any more panegyrics on it here; suffice it to state here that its harbour forms the only break in the long line of frowning cliffs between Bude on the one side and Padstow on the other, so that any boating excursions along the coast must be undertaken from it. The seals' caverns are distant only some few miles, but the passage to them is generally tedious. It is no easy matter, indeed, to get out to the open sea from the harbour; the broken swell, almost invariably to be met with in the Sound almost so soon as the jutting-out 'profile' promontory is rounded, is enough to swamp any boat, and the fishermen have learned from sad experience never to venture outside, even for the purpose of 'lobstering', by which they gain a subsistence, except in periods of settled calm. They thus gain the unenviable reputation of being 'fair weather sailors', and avoid risking their lives, even though their dignity suffers to a certain extent by it. Nor is it easy to blame them for this apparent want of hardihood; the occasions are so rare on which pluck might be exercised with advantage, and so plentiful on which its exercise would certainly end in futile disaster, that its absence seems to arise almost from a wise provision of nature; at any rate anyone who has been lucky enough to see a heavy swell, fresh from the Atlantic, breaking in majestic grandeur over the cliffs, will be loth to condemn the fishermen for preferring to stay at home rather than venture out on any Quixotic attempt at rescue.

Luckily for the peace of mind of all concerned, none of these dangers attend an expedition to the seals' caverns; the slightest approach to rough weather is a fatal objection to making a start, and the attempt has to be postponed to a more propitious season, for the caverns are unget-at-able except in perfect calm, hence it was that I was detained some weeks in Boscastle before an opportunity offered itself; day after day we held ourselves in readiness to no purpose: the blow-hole spouted ominously, indicative of the roughness of the swell, and we were compelled to wait till the morrow. At length the time came; I was awakened from sleep late one night by the noise of the fishermen calling me on their way down to the harbour. To jump out and follow them was the work of an instant, for time is precious, inasmuch as every minute's advantage has to be taken of the tide. The night was magnificent, the full moon was just showing herself over the stupendous cliffs, lighting up here, and there by comparison deepening tenfold the darkness; the sky was cloudless, and perfect quiet everywhere, broken only at times by the pleasant murmur of the water lapping against the rocks. It was a scene of enchantment that baffles description. Everything was in readiness by the time I reached the pier, and we put off at once. The crew consisted of six men, stalwart beings all of them, under the command of a veteran seal-hunter, — whose presence is always so indispensable on such occasions that no boatman will venture out without him, — my brother and myself. Pleasant, indeed, was the row out, a distribution of tobacco warmed the hearts of the crew towards us, the undulating motion was insufficient to disturb the equilibrium of even an ill-regulated landsman, and whether we took a turn at an oar, or sat lost in contemplation in the stern sheets, the scene seemed equally enjoyable. The men, too, were in more than usual spirits; instead of the sullen silence usually preserved, the flow of badinage was incessant, now breaking out in a monotonous chant, now finding a vent in terse, caustic sayings...

With such sinews as these at work on the oars, we were not long in reaching the neighbourhood of the caverns; and here silence was proclaimed, and we rowed as quietly as possible for fear of alarming the seals, whose organs of hearing are remarkably acute, and who leave their caverns and hurry out to sea on the slightest suspicion of danger. Presently we approached the shore, the towering crags frowned sternly overhead, hiding the moon from us. No landing-place was visible; and in the sudden transition from light to darkness we seemed hastening to certain destruction. At length we saw the mouth of the cavern in front of us, and here the necessity for caution commenced. The entrance is so low as to preclude the possibility of entering it, except at low tide, and even then, there is danger, if there be the slightest swell on the sea, of the boat getting bulged in against the roof. Still more dangerous is the coming out. Nobody need venture in unless everything seems propitious and the attendant risk reduced to a minimum; but once inside the boat is caught, as it were, in a mouse-trap, and must make an effort to get out, whatever be the risk. Hence the caution shown by the boatmen in refusing to make the expedition except in settled weather; the slightest breeze getting up while they were in the cavern might prove excessively awkward; and the possibility which there always is of a ground swell savours quite enough of danger for even the most fool-hardy adventurer. We got in without difficulty and, once inside, lit our torches, laid hold of our bludgeons, and otherwise prepared ourselves for the night's work. It was a curious spectacle. Through the narrow entrance we saw moonbeams dancing on the sea, around us the sombre glare of the torches lit up the fantastically-shaped sides of the cavern; while its depths, impervious to light, remained wrapped in apparently impenetrable darkness. The cave, I was informed, stretches for more than a mile inland; but none within the memory of man has ever penetrated its utmost recesses. Indeed, beyond a certain distance, it would seem quite impossible to track out its numerous windings. The water, even at lowest tide, reaches some way in, and the seals are rarely found beyond. They are left on ledges of rock by the receding tide, plunge under water at once when disturbed, and make with all speed for the sea, running the gauntlet of the invaders who, waist deep in the water, try to stun them with a well-directed blow on their most vulnerable part, the nose. The victims rarely attempt to retaliate. When hard-pressed, an old seal will occasionally turn upon his pursuers, and woe be to the unhappy individual who happens to get in his way; but, as a rule, they fully deserve their hard-earned title of 'harmless murdered seals'. Indeed, it goes to the heart to kill them, and in cold blood one can hardly conceive what pleasure can be derived from the sport. In moments of excitement, however, not even the imploring look of their lustrous eyes can ward off the murderous blow; their doom is sealed, and in death they serve to swell the triumph of their captors.

On this particular occasion we were unfortunate. Almost before our torches were lit we heard a distant splash, then another, and another, and directly afterwards a slight ripple in the water beside us showed that our expected prey had escaped to sea. We were discovered. In a few moments the cavern would be tenantless, and our expedition would have been in vain. Without further ado we jumped overboard, two or three of us, against the advice of the others; but it was the only chance. The water proved not so deep as we expected, and nearly up to our shoulders in it we waded along without much difficulty. Of course, on a rocky bottom it was not pleasant walking; many were the unintended plunges into deep pools and many the scars left on our shin bones, by protruding subaqueous rocks. None of these episodes, however, were calculated to distress us much. True, there was danger when we came to the surface again, after being head and heels submerged, of being mistaken by some misguided comrade for a seal and tapped on the nose accordingly; but the glare of the torches proved sufficient to prevent the occurrence of any such awkward mistakes, and we struggled by degrees upward in safety into shallower parts. So far good; but still no seals. Not a ghost of one had been heard or seen since the first few splashes which had raised our spirits, and sent us helter-skelter overboard; and as the chill of the water made itself appreciably felt on us, we began to apprehend the worst.

All had now left the boat, and in water knee-deep were continuing the search with renewed energy. I happened to be in front, and behind followed the others in a phalanx, some carrying the torches, all armed with bludgeons. Presently a curious flapping sound was audible a short distance off; then came the ominous splash, and, almost before the men could give warning or I could recover self-possession, two great brutes, like cows, came swimming down towards us. On seeing me they dodged and avoided my ill-directed blows. After a short skirmish, however, with the rest of the party, both were dispatched and made a good beginning to the game-bag. They proved to be magnificent specimens of their sort — some seven or eight feet long, each of them — ancient veterans, who ought to have known better at their time of life than to be thus caught in a trap; but 'de mortuis nil nisi bonum', more especially since speaking ill of them does us no good. The pleasing recollection, as I write, of the sensation which my bump of destruction experienced at the success must be my excuse for being unable to resist 'having a fling', as the phrase goes, at the sufferers. We continued our efforts for some time longer, but met with no further success; as, indeed, was only to be expected from my experience of previous expeditions of the sort. It may be noted as an almost invariable rule, that whenever sport is expected some unforeseen reason happens to prevent it. We are always within an ace of having it, and never succeed. Such, at least, is my experience; and thus it happened that when the flickering torches warned us that it was time to retrace our steps to the boat, and everybody else was grumbling at the miserable result of our expedition, I alone was as delighted as if we had never left off massacring innocents from the time of our entering the cavern till we left it. It is not uncommon, I was assured, with ordinary luck, to slaughter and bring home in one's train some ten or twelve seals, besides wounding others; but as the seals themselves are of no use except as trophies, it is hard to see the advantage of a wholesale massacre. We took our two in tow, got out of the cavern without much difficulty, although the wind had freshened up so considerably while we were inside that we were glad not to be burdened with anything more, and finally reached the harbour some three or four hours after we had left it, thoroughly tired out with our exertions. It was almost dawn when we hurried off to bed. Next morning, the two unfortunate seals were skinned; and their skins still *adorn my chambers.*

Writing under his own name, **John Coulson Tregarthen (1904)**, chapter XIV is entitled 'A midnight visit to the seal caves':

The wildest of British wild sports is the pursuit of the seal in the almost inaccessible cliff-caves to which it at times resorts. Of its haunts along the north coast of Cornwall — it is but rarely seen on the south — from the Land's End to Tintagel, the caverns of Hell's Bay are perhaps those which it most frequents. More secluded or safer fastnesses it would be difficult to imagine, yet in these they may be surprised by those who do not shrink from the peril the pursuit involves. The nearest homestead to the Black Cliffs, as those skirting Hell's Bay are named, is Reskageage; and to its occupant Mr N., who has led many expeditions against the seals, I owed the opportunity of sharing a bit of sport the wildness of which is beyond my power to declare.

He had promised to send me word when circumstances seemed favourable to our purpose, and one morning towards the end of September 189-, whilst staying at St Ives, I received the following message from him: — 'Come, if possible, tomorrow (Thursday) afternoon. I have just seen three seals under the cliffs, and the chances are we shall find some in the caves, as they have not been disturbed for a long time. One of the light-keepers of Godrevy tells me that he has not seen so many playing about the reef for years. If you sail across the bay and the sea is smooth, land on the north side of the Red River."

After sending a wire that I should come without fail, I made arrangements with a boatman to take me across the bay. It was close on three o'clock the following afternoon when we rounded the pier head and set the bow of our little craft for Gwithian beach. A fair wind filled the brown sail and drove us at a merry pace over the waves of this loveliest of bays, where the Cornish sea displays its vividest hues in a setting of silver sand. Landing was practicable, and the boat was beached near where my friend was awaiting me on the shore.

'You're rather late,' said he, as we shook hands. 'Well now, you had better go and have a good look at the cliffs while it's light. You'll see where I've been whitewashing the rocks. Get the twists and turns of the way down fixed in your mind: that will be helpful later on. In the meanwhile, I'm going to overhaul the whole of the gear.'

I took the direction he indicated and, stepping out briskly across the intervening neck of rising ground between the two bays, soon reached the dizzy edge of the cliffs. A little on my left hand, zigzagging down the steep descent and almost to the edge of the foam, lay a white dotted line that was to guide us in the darkness. The mouths of the caves — there were four — frequented by the seals were some two or three hundred feet below me, but I could not see them.

Bleak and lone are these Gwithian cliffs, merciless the winds that sweep them. Not a tree or a bush is to be seen and even the heather is stunted. No note of songbird meets the ear, nor scream of seafowl, only the sullen sounds of the Atlantic ground-swell in the caves so far below. Along the coast towards Newquay sunlit headlands stretched out into the ocean; and the low promontory of Trevose, dim and unsubstantial-looking, lay on the far horizon. The mellow rays of the sun now and again caught the snow-white plumage of some bird along the coast, and lit up the surf at the foot of the distant cliffs.

Not a gull floated over the bay below me; but a string of cormorants, with black flight, skimmed the heaving surface just beyond the dark shadow of the coastline and disappeared round a jagged point.

I was following the last of these birds with my eyes when my gaze was arrested by the appearance of a seal below me, and as far as I could judge, not twenty yards from the mouth of one of the caves. It carried its head, which looked as black as jet, clear of the surface, and betrayed not the least sign of alarm. After about a minute it sank — it did not dive — out of sight. I remained watching, in the hope that the quaint-looking creature would show itself again; but, as it gave no sign and the sun was nearing the horizon, I left the cliff and made my way across the heather and stubble to Reskageage.

I found my friend in the barn. The light of a candle stuck against the wall fell on the sun-browned faces of the farmhands, who watched him as he overhauled the equipment for our expedition. The various details were displayed on the lid of a big wooden chest that had once held the tin-ore between 'ticketing' days at Wheal Margy. There lay some dozen torches consisting of small branches of elm, about three feet in length, with pieces of white rag wound round one end and secured by bits of string; three small bottles containing oil, a rather heavy hammer with a new haft about three and a half feet long, a powerful gaff, a long-bladed knife, a revolver and cartridges. Near a big coil of rope was a sack of very bulky appearance, which somewhat excited my curiosity. Undoing the string round the neck of it, my friend drew out a rope — ladder ten inches in width and between fifty and sixty feet long. The rungs were of iron, about three-eighths of an inch in diameter and perhaps fourteen inches apart. The strength of the ladder had previously been tried by the tug-of-war test, but now my host carefully examined the rope where it passed through the eyes in the rungs, to make sure that it had not been weakened by friction or by rust. No defects being found, the free ends of the ropes were tied together, forming a triangle with the top rung; and the ladder was again stowed away in the sack. The big coil of rope was next overhauled. It was knotted at intervals of about three feet. 'What's that for?' I asked

'We keep that up in the adit, in case anything goes wrong with the ladder.'

'And the knots?'

'They make swarming up easier.' A vague idea of the mode of approach and of egress from the cave began to dawn upon me: 'There's only one way out?' I inquired.

'By the adit is the only way, unless you swim for it before the tide covers the mouth of the cave.'

'There's some ledge out of reach of the tide, where you can wait till it falls?'

'No, there's scarcely foothold for a shag or a cliff-owl on the walls of the big cave.' I confess to feeling slightly unnerved at the prospect, the perilous character of which was now evident. However, I meant going through with the business, which was of my own inviting; but though I had the utmost confidence in my friend, it seemed to me it would be safer, in the event of accidents, that three rather than two should descend into the 'big cave', as he called it. It is trying enough to a novice to be let down over a cliff in broad daylight to reach a peregrine's or raven's nest, but I could see that was nothing in comparison with the night expedition before me. In the circumstances, it is natural that the idea of sending for the Earthstopper should have

occurred to me. Not only was he accustomed to the cliffs at night, but he was of firm nerve and of ready resource. I lost no time in suggesting it; already I feared it was too late.

'Very well,' replied my friend, 'in case of accident — not that I expect any, mind you — we couldn't have a better man. Fill in a form — you will find some on my table — and Tom there shall take it at once. There isn't a moment to lose.'

A few minutes later the lad was cantering down the lane between the sand-dunes with this message: 'Be here by midnight. Ride or drive. Seal hunt between twelve and one. T- Reskageage, Gwithian.'

My friend was extinguishing one of the torches as I re-entered the barn. Evidently, he was not content until he had tested everything, even the oil. I could not but remark to him on the extreme care of his preparations.

'I like to see to every detail myself in a ticklish job of this sort,' he said, as he laid the torch down by the side of the gaff: 'a weak spot in the rope, a flaw in the haft of the hammer, bad cartridges or wet matches, may mean more than spoiled sport.'

Leaving the barn, we made our way across the rickyard to the house.

A cold wind was rustling the leaves of the wind-clipt elm that had supplied handles for our torches; and, as the air was chilly, I was glad to get indoors. After supper we withdrew into my friend's sanctum and pulled our chairs up to the furze fire which blazed on the wide hearth. Cases of rare birds and curious relics hung against the walls, and the floor was covered with sealskins.

In reply to some question about the seals, my friend told me it was an old man that spent most of his time about the cliffs, egg-collecting, and looking for things cast up by the sea, who had first called his attention to them. This had led to him finding a way to the caves — for the secret had died with the smugglers who used them — and eventually to the animals themselves. The greatest number of seals he had killed at one time was seven, he said, and the heaviest carcase would weigh five or six hundredweight. His opinion was that at least some of the seals remain on the coast all the year round, and that they do not go far out to sea to fish. They fed chiefly on the herring, but he had seen one rise in Hell's Bay with a big flatfish of some sort, probably a turbot, writhing in its mouth. Then, suddenly jumping up in the middle of an explanation why the eye of the seal is big and the otter's small — 'He's coming,' said he.

We went to the garden gate and looked down the road and, sure enough, a light was coming toward us.

'How on earth did you know he was close at hand?' I asked in surprise. 'You didn't hear anything, did you?'

'No, I did not hear the horse neigh nor the sound of its hoofs, for they fell and are still falling on sand; but the dog must have heard, for I noticed him prick his ears and listen. You see, Andrew's time was almost up; and, putting the two together, I didn't hesitate to say he was coming.'

More and more distinct grew the light; then we heard the thud of hoofs where the track is clear of sand; and at last Andrew, seated on a rough pony and holding the lantern in his left hand, emerged from the darkness.

'Good evening, gentlemen. I was a feared I was too late, though I've shogged on as fast as I could.'

The old shepherd having taken charge of the steaming pony, we soon had the Earthstopper before the furze fire.

'That looks cheerful after the black night, tho' et do make ee blink like a cat at fust.'

'You've had a lonely ride, Andrew?'

'No, sir, I'm never lonely, unless maybe when stopping the Land's End cliffs on a wild night. Why, Lelant flats was all alive with curleys and seabirds as I crossed the Caunsway. Never heard such whistlin' in all my born days. It must be gettin' on for low water.'

'Well now, drink up that glass of toddy and we'll be on the move. It's half an hour to low water, and it's time we were on our way.'

Whilst my friend was saying this, I looked at the hands of the clock in the corner. It was seven minutes past twelve. Our equipment having been divided among us, we set out across the fields for the cliffs.

'We've forgotten the sack,' I said, as we crossed the stubble.

'That's all right,' replied my friend.

It was indeed a black night, as the Earthstopper had remarked. A *great bank of cloud hung like a curtain before the western heaven, and shut out the light of half the stars. On our left, Godrevy shot out its warning beams at regular intervals, and far away up channel Trevose light shone bravely in the gloom. The keen, salt wind blew straight in our faces as we breasted the high ground near the sea. By-and-by the sullen roar which reached our ears made us cautious, for we had neared the edge of the cliff; and when we had roped ourselves together, our guide took the lead and we began the steep descent.*

The otter excepted, there is no more wary animal than the seal; so we passed down past the stones, ghost-like in their white shrouds, as noiselessly as possible, and at length arrived at the foot of the cliff. There was no beach, only huge, wet boulders, between which the tide gurgled. We had scrambled — it was rough going — some distance over these rocks before I felt a pull on the rope, and then, peering through the darkness, I saw that our guide was standing at the entrance to a tunnel that proved to be the way into the seals' cave, the mouth of which is unapproachable except by boat. Here we met with an unexpected impediment. The mast of a ship had got wedged into the passage, leaving only a narrow space between its splintered surface and the rocky walls.

'Hand over your lantern, Andrew,' said my friend as he struck a match on his trousers.

'It's all right,' said he, holding the light against the mouth of the tunnel; 'I think we can get through. Now, undo the rope, and follow me as quiet as mice. You've got the hammer, Andrew?'

'Yes.'

This in whispers; and then we squeezed through the cramped space. The passage was some five feet in height and four in breadth. The floor was very irregular, and covered with water lying in pools of varying depths. At the further side of a deep pool our guide paused, and held a light over the water. This enabled me to avoid the holes between the loose rocks at the bottom, and I managed to get through by wading thigh-deep. The old Earthstopper in his fur cap and velveteen coat followed, trying the depth with the long, white haft of the hammer he carried. I noticed he left the water as quietly as an otter would have done. The increasing noise of the waves warned us as we progressed along the tunnel, that we were getting near the seals' retreat. In the great cave in which we soon stood, the roaring at its mouth and the reverberations within produced a noise that was deafening. Three torches were lit; and we advanced over some loose rocks and shingle to a shelving bed of white sand, on which the seals are generally found. Down this, when surprised, they shuffle to face their enemies and meet death. It was disappointing to find none at home.

We then proceeded to explore the inmost recesses, to reach which we had to scramble on all fours between the descending roof and the ascending floor of the cave. In one of these, that reminded me of a chapel in Westminster Abbey, was a baby seal, which judging from its plaintive bleats, seemed to know the danger it was in. It was about a foot and a half long, of a creamy colour, with big, pleading eyes. Leaving the little creature, we returned to the rocky part of the floor, and held the torches high above our heads to try to illuminate the cave. We could see the great walls of rock for about twenty or thirty feet, but the light failed to scatter the gloom which ever shrouds the lofty roof. Here and there in these darker heights projections of rock were dimly visible, looking like spectral faces craned forward to peer at us. It was a weird scene that this great, resounding ocean-hall presented, and one that haunts the memory. There is little wonder that legends and superstitions cluster round these caves.

'Come,' said our guide, 'there's no time to be lost,' and in a few minutes we were again scrambling between the mast and the rock. I was glad to get a glimpse of the stars again. Out at sea, I could discern the light of some vessel going up towards the Bristol Channel. As I climbed the dusky cliff-side on the heels of our guide, and with Andrew behind me, I tried to brace my nerves for the ordeal that lay before us. The approach to the cave for which we were making is fraught with peril. Few attempt it, and of those few scarce one makes the descent a second time. This cave is the securest stronghold of the seals along the wild coast of Cornwall.

We might have made our way up some seventy feet when the guide struck a rude track on the cliff-side, and this we followed until the light of the lantern fell on the old shepherd sitting with the sack containing the rope-ladder. We had arrived at the entrance to the adit, for which we were making, and along this we all proceeded in single file. It was a strange way of reaching a cave the mouth of which lay sixty feet below. We had not advanced thirty yards before we could hear the hollow roar of the waves.

'Be careful here,' said the guide, as he held his torch over a chasm. For some reason, a piece of the partition-wall between the adit and the cave has been destroyed, and with it half the narrow footway. It was a dangerous spot to pass in the lurid, unsteady light; but the shepherd made nothing of it, and as the projecting part of the sack on his back lay over the chasm when he skirted it, he was able to hug the wall on his right. Some thirty yards farther in, the tunnel pierced the wall of the cave, and again the hollow roar of the sea reached our ears. Whether the adit was driven on a vein of copper is uncertain, but there is no doubt that at one time it was used by smugglers. Kegs of brandy, lace and silk goods were probably taken to the mouth of the cave in boats, and afterwards hauled up to the tunnel and, as opportunity offered, distributed thence over the countryside amongst the smugglers' clients, to wit, the magistrates, landlords and tenant farmers.

Projecting from the wall of the cave, about a foot above the level of the adit, is a stout iron bar, over which our guide, by leaning forward, placed the end of the ladder so that the ropes which had been knotted together lay on each side of it, in the acute angle between the bar and the wall. The ladder was then dropped in the chasm. Clink, clink, clink — clink — clink. The seals must surely have been startled by the unusual noise made by the iron rungs striking against the rocky wall of their wild retreat. Vain warning! for some of the big boulders which cover part of the floor of the cave are dry at low water, and effectually prevent their escape. Our guide was the first to descend. I followed him into the dark abyss. The descent down the wooden ladders of a tin-mine is child's play to going down a rope-ladder which lies against a sheer wall. Twice my feet lost grip of the slender staves, and the second time, failing to recover the rung, I had to go down hand over hand to the point where the ladder hung clear of the rock. Here it twisted and turned, adding a little variety to the difficulties of the descent. The Earthstopper, with the hammer slung across his back, followed, coming down hand over hand nearly the whole way.

'That ladder's a rum un,' he shouted in my ear, as we stood on the rock near the foot of it.

Two lighted torches were then fitted in crannies in the walls; and after lighting three others, we moved forward, each holding one in his left hand. Beyond the slippery boulders over which we were creeping, the flare of the torches fell on the heaving surface of a deep, rocky pool.

'Look out!' shouted my friend, 'they're in.'

We drew a little nearer to the water, now lashed into foam as a seal rushed up and down. Two shots were fired as its glistening head showed above the water, but the only effect as far as I could see was to enrage the creature, and make it more aggressive than at first. For, when it reached our end of the pool again, it threw itself out of the water on to a rock, where it rested momentarily, looking more like some antediluvian creature sculptured in black marble than a living seal. Then with a hoarse roar it slid down the face of the rock and shuffled towards us in a most menacing manner.

'Stand clear, and don't fire again!' shouted Andrew as he swung the hammer preparatory to delivering a blow. My friend jumped aside; and, as the huge brute came within striking distance, the hammer caught it full on the head and felled it to the ground. A tremor passed over the body; the seal was dead.

Whilst the battle lasted, angry bellowings came from the shelving beach beyond, where other seals — blurred, restless forms — awaited our attack. But wholesale slaughter was not our object; not another shot was fired. I would have liked to get nearer to the herd, but the danger of crossing the pool was too great.

'For God's sake, don't think of it!' shouted my friend; 'we'll light more torches.' This done, Andrew picked up the one he had laid on the rocks, and we advanced to the edge of the water with a torch in each hand, holding them well up, and forward at full arm's-length. It was the sight of a lifetime. Five huge beasts, two grey, the rest a dirty yellow, mottled with black spots, lay swaying on the sand, prepared to make a rush — they can shuffle down a slope at a great pace — if we entered the pool; and these were not all, for in dark recesses beyond I saw indistinct forms move, and once I thought I caught the gleam of liquid eyes. For several minutes we stood fascinated by the wild scene, but it behoved us not to linger. Once or twice I noticed my friend turn his face *towards the mouth of the cave. In the excitement he had not forgotten that the tide had turned. There was not time to skin the dead seal and remove the blubber; so my friend, who meant coming for this purpose at next low water, went to the foot of the ladder and shouted to the shepherd to throw down the rope. With some difficulty he made himself understood, for the roar of the waves was now greater than ever; and a few moments after the shepherd had shouted 'Stand clear!' down came the coil on to the boulders. One end of the rope was tied securely to one of the flippers of the dead seal — a huge beast — and the other round a rock on which a bigger one rested.*

Andrew and I were taking a last look at the seals when our guide called out that there was no time to lose; and, indeed, the tide was washing the boulders at the foot of the ladder when we got there.

'Take your time, sir,' said Andrew as he held the bottom of it, 'and higher up, press your knees against the wall, that'll clear the stave above.'

When a third of the way up, I looked towards the inner part of the cave. Profound gloom shrouded it, though the lights still flickered on the walls; and the seals, as far as I could hear, had ceased their angry challenges. Having reached the adit, I held a torch over the chasm to light the Earthstopper in his ascent. When he was near the top of the ladder, I saw that his face was spattered with blood. My friend having also reached the adit, the ladder was hauled up and put into the sack, and we made our way again into the open air. Scarcely a word was said as we climbed the cliff and crossed the heather and stubble to the farmhouse. After a wash and a hurried supper, the Earthstopper attached his lantern to the saddle and rode down the track towards Gwithian Churchtown. I could hear him jogging along until he reached the place where the road lies under feet of driven sand. The black clouds had lifted a little, and Crobben Hill was dimly discernible against the stars.

'Pity we can't have spoart without killin',' were the Earthstopper's words as we had stood near the dead seal, and I thought of them as I turned to go indoors.

29

What Were the Slaughtered Seals Used For?

It is probable that the overwhelming majority of battues consisted, as the name implies, of the bludgeoning to death of seals, most likely by a boatload of men who reached the site by rowing from a nearby harbour or by scrambling down a cliff path and working their way to sites accessible by low tide in the intertidal zone. The extent to which shooting was used is surprising, in that it was dangerous and deafening.

In earlier times, sealskins were highly valued and put to many uses. The skins were made into jackets, mitts and boots as well as rugs and wall hangings. Their flesh was eaten especially by poor people in time of need. The seal's blubber, when rendered down, became oil that was used for lighting, but was also 'rapturously accepted' by people suffering from rheumatism for which it was said to be a 'sovereign remedy'. It was also used as a healing ointment for the necks of oxen galled by the yoke.

Stepping Stones to the Cornish Seal Caves: The time of Naturalists and Scientists

At the beginning of the twentieth century in **Hudson (1923)** — a naturalist's impressions in west Cornwall was written without the author feeling the need to participate in nocturnal seal hunts. As with nearly all early descriptions of grey seals, he mistakes the seals he is describing for common seals (now more widely called harbour seals)—which are now known not to use sea caves anywhere in their world range. In chapter XVI, he wrote: *The rocks to the north of St Ives Bay are an ancient haunt of the common seal, one of the few colonies of this animal now left on the south coast of Britain. The ferryman was one day fishing in his boat at this point close to the mouth of that vast cavern in the rocks where the seals have their home, when a loud barking cry or roar made him jump in his boat, and looking round he caught sight of a seal thrusting his head and half of his body out of the water with a conger about seven to eight feet long fastened to his ear. The blood was streaming from the seal's head and he was trying to shake his enemy off and at the same time turning round and round in his efforts to bite the conger; but the black serpentine body wriggled and floated out of his reach. and in a very few moments they went down. Again and again they rose, the seal coming out each time with the same savage cry, shaking himself and biting, the conger still holding on with bull-dog tenacity. But on the last occasion there was no cry or commotion; the conger had lost his hold and the seal had him by the middle of the body in his jaws. On coming up he swam quietly to the sloping rock close by, and half in, half out of the water began tearing up and devouring his victim, the blood still running from his own head.*

Subsequently, he wrote: *In conclusion of this chapter I will go back to the subject of the Cornish seals of that small surviving colony which has its ancestral home in the caves outside the Bay of St Ives. Sportsmen occasionally shoot them just for the pleasure of the thing, but the fishermen of St Ives do not consider that they suffer any injury from the animals and have consequently refrained from persecuting them. Unhappily they are now threatened with extermination from a new quarter: the students at the Camborne Mining School have recently found out a new and pleasant pastime, which is to seat themselves with rifle or fowling-piece on the cliff and watch for the appearance of a brown head above the water below of a seal going out of or coming in to the caves and letting fly at it. When they hit the seal, it sinks and is seen no more, but the animal is not wanted, the object is to shoot it, and this accomplished the sportsman goes back happy and proud of his success in having murdered so large and human-like a creature.*

The following observations of the grey seals in Cornwall were perhaps the most important in the entire record.

George A. Steven was born in Caithness but by 1930, with D.P. Wilson, he was working at the Plymouth laboratory of the Marine Biological Association (MBA) running popular courses for the majority of professional marine biologists and zoologists who graduated through to the advent of the Second World War. The formal position that he held at the laboratory was assistant naturalist.

By the summer of 1932, he had been commissioned to write a report for the Ministry of Agriculture and Fisheries.

In his Introduction **Steven (1934)** wrote: *During recent years Cornish fishermen have been complaining bitterly of the damage wrought by seals amongst their several fisheries. The fishing communities in the Lizard and Land's End areas claim that these animals rob their trammel nets and also that they not infrequently disperse shoals of mullet, a single haul of which in favourable circumstances will often yield a large sum of money — enough to ensure for the inhabitants of an entire village a good winter's livelihood.*

The most serious charges against the seals have been received, however, from the North Cornwall coast. The fishing communities along that shore complain that the seals frequent the herring fishing grounds and remove from the drift nets many of the herring that have become enmeshed therein. The loss of fish thus entailed does not seriously embarrass these men in a good fishing season. But when fish are scarce and catches small it is claimed that the activities of the seals constitute a grave menace to their already precarious livelihood.

According to reports sent in by the fishermen, the Grey Seal is the chief offender in this respect.

At the request of the ministry of Agriculture and Fisheries, the Director of the Plymouth Laboratory of the Marine Biological Association instructed the writer to visit some of the Cornish fishing ports during the present herring season and find out by direct observation with the fishing fleets to what extent these complaints are justified and at the same time to determine — if possible — whether Grey Seals are numerous in the area.

The observations made and the results obtained, form the substance of this report.

He concludes section III, entitled 'The Seal Menace', by writing: *These are all the observations which were made actually with the fishing fleets at sea. More time spent with them would have produced only a needless repetition of the same kind of data without adding in any way to the value of those already obtained — which shows very clearly that seals are numerous on the North Cornwall inshore herring fishing grounds and that they do haunt the nets of the herring drifters.*

What he covers in Section IV is, in effect, the precursor to his subsequent uniquely inspiring research undertaken two years later, in 1934. It is entitled 'Abundance of Seals':

In addition to keeping a look-out for seals on the fishing grounds, two special exploratory cruises were made in search of them. From St Ives on Monday, 21ˢᵗ November, a cruise was made along the shore, eastward from the harbour, as far as Basset Island, where seals are reported to be very numerous. Only four seals were sighted during the entire trip which extended to about 18 miles and occupied approximately three hours. This may have been due to the fact that a heavy ground swell was running, and it is much more difficult to catch sight of a dark object in the water when its surface is very broken and uneven than when it is calm and smooth. It is of particular interest to note, therefore, that on Monday, 5th December, over 100 seals of all sizes were reported to have been seen lying on a sand beach at the foot of a cliff on the mainland immediately opposite Basset Island. The beach is inaccessible except by sea and then only in calm weather.

On Wednesday, 7th December, a visit was made to some caves — locally known as 'seal holes' — about two miles west from Boscastle, in which seals were said by the Port Isaac fishermen to make their homes and to breed. All but one of these caves are inaccessible except by sea and it was just about high water when they were reached by boat from Port Isaac. The caves are four in number, situated close together some hundreds of yards north of Gull Rock (also known as Beeny Island). All have very small openings in the face of high rocks. One of the openings was too small for a boat to enter it but the cave was seen to 'open out' inside to unascertainable dimensions. A second cave had its opening completely submerged so that it became visible only when the water subsided between successive waves. The two others it was found possible — though difficult because of the swell — to enter.

The northernmost cave was penetrated for a distance of about 100 yards. Here further progress was checked by the complete darkness ahead. Even at this distance from its mouth the water in the cave was over 8 feet deep and it was sufficiently disturbed to make an unseen rock a dangerous obstacle in the way of the heaving dinghy. It was possible to make out, however, that at this point the tunnel-like neck of the cave expanded into a vast cavern in which the troubled water made loud and fearsome noises. No seals could, of course, be discerned in the darkness, and, unfortunately, no lantern was available.

On arrival at these caves, not a single seal was to be seen. On emerging again from the first one entered, and in which a commotion had been made by beating empty petrol cans and buckets, a large number of seals were found to have made their appearance. They were in a state of much activity and excitement, diving and re-appearing with great frequency, but always remaining close to the base of the cliffs.

The second accessible cave was then entered but the roof was so low that the rise and fall of the surging sea made it dangerous to *venture far for fear that the dinghy might be crushed against the rocks above and swamped. On coming out, still more seals were in evidence. Loud noises were made at the mouths of the other two caves, which could not be entered because of the conditions prevailing, in order to make the seals come out if any were inside.*

Because of the rough sea a more thorough exploration of the caves was impossible. There can be but little doubt, however, that the seals which made their appearance in the sea at their mouths had emerged from them. Having been disturbed, they came out — as was to be expected — under the water, which was then sufficiently deep in all the caves for them to emerge unseen. One large seal was observed, however, swimming rapidly out of one of the caves on the surface of the sea and two others on being approached disappeared into the submerged opening already mentioned.

At the end of one and a half hours in the vicinity a great many seals had appeared. Their number could not be ascertained with any degree of accuracy as they were in a state of too much activity. Nevertheless, six or seven heads were generally to be seen on the surface at any one time, and in one instance no less than nine different seals were in view near the mouth of one cave at the same moment.

It can safely be stated, therefore, that in addition to the seals scattered over the various herring grounds at this time, there is at least one seal colony of considerable size in the vicinity of Boscastle, on the North Cornwall coast. It is probable there are other such colonies in the same locality and at other places along that county's northern shore. Little evidence has as yet been collected which will support or contradict the view that these seal resorts may also be breeding places. It may be significant, however, that among the seals which were seen near Boscastle, there were several very young individuals present among others which were obviously old adults.

In section V, devoted to the identification of the seal species observed, George Steven describes the difficulties of distinguishing them under the circumstances in which he was working. However, his conclusions were that: *It will be seen in the Appendix that for only five animals are such identifications given (*namely with certainty*). Of these, one is a Brown Seal (Phoca vitulina) and four are Grey Seals. In* *addition, all those seen near Boscastle appeared to be Grey Seals. If these identifications are correct, it would appear that the Grey Seal (Halichoerus grypus) is much the more common of these two species along the shores of Cornwall.*

In the Discussion, section VI, Steven notes that the grey seal was first recorded from the north Cornwall coast in 1883, when Sir E. Ray Lankester found a newly born grey seal on the shore of Pentargon Cove (just north of Boscastle). However, Lankester's belief remained that the grey seal was extremely rare in Cornwall and that the Brown (Harbour) Seal was the more abundant species, as expressed in his *Diversions of a Naturalist*, published in 1915.

Steven continues: *The very opposite appears to be true at the present time… Little is known, and the present author has been able to find out nothing, concerning the breeding places (if any) of seals in Cornwall. Lankester (op. cit., p.33) was of the opinion that whilst 'the Brown Seal produces its young most usually in caves or rock shelters, the Great Grey Seal chooses a remote sand island or deserted piece of open shore for its nursery'. Sufficient evidence is not available to settle the question of whether or not this statement is justified — at any rate as far as the Cornish coast is concerned. Unless the present writer be in error regarding the seal colony at Boscastle, Halichoerus grypus is an inhabitant of caves in that locality. It probably also breeds there.*

In the Summary, section VII, he lists a number of points, the most crucial of which are: *6. Grey Seals are present in considerable numbers and are probably the commonest seals in Cornish waters. 7. Brown (harbour) Seals appear to be few — they may even be rare — around Cornwall. 8. There is at least one seal colony of considerable size in certain caves near Boscastle. This appears to consist of Grey Seals. Probably other such colonies exist on the Cornish coast.*

Subsequent research has substantially confirmed George Steven's findings and speculations, which hold true today. For example, he was first to record that large assemblies of seals occur at two localities in Cornwall in late autumn/winter: the twin capitals of Cornish sealdom. These were north of Boscastle, at Beeny, and west of Portreath, by Bassett Island. A similar partition still holds true at the time of writing. One assemblage yet remains based on Beeny's remote beaches and caves. The other assemblage has moved a few miles westward, currently being based on Mutton Cove, near Godrevy. Additionally, an associated assembly has come to exist more recently at River Cove, near The Carracks. This small westerly drift may be due either to human disturbance or the collapsing of cliffs in localities where erosion has become increasingly commonplace.

The Brown Seal, now internationally known as the harbour seal *(Phoca vitulina),* is present on the shores of SW England only as a vagrant or uncommon visitor, currently not breeding except, since 2019, at a site on the Dart estuary in south Devon.

The research period during which he was active in securing these observations was approximately mid-November to mid-December, 1932. Sea conditions were clearly difficult, hindering attempts at cave entry on a coast where such exploits are rarely easy. He was there and then because it was the herring-fishing season.

Furthermore, the period late-November to early December marks the (current) time of onset of the assembling of grey seals residing in sea caves, there to undergo the annual moult — something he was then not in a position to know. However, it may account for the high numbers of seals he encountered at that time in the sea caves. It could also account for the reported assembly of over 100 seals seen on the beach inshore of Basset's Island. At the same time, the cryptic colouring of the seals would have made them difficult to spot, let alone count, on the cliff-backed sand, gravel and boulder beaches currently used by grey seals north of Boscastle.

With this and the subsequent paper (below), George Steven led and inspired the long, slow march of inquiry into the biology of the seals using the sea caves not only of SW England but also of Wales, the Isle of Man, Rathlin Island, Eire, Caithness, Shetland, Brittany and the Faroe Islands.

During a fortnight in August 1935, Steven developed his initial findings, initially in a report to the Ministry of Agriculture and Fisheries presented in September 1935.

His Introduction **Steven (1936)** is as interesting as any introduction could possibly be made: *It has long been known that there is a* considerable population on the North Cornwall coast. But precise information concerning the species present, the density of the population, and the positions of the rookeries has been almost entirely lacking. In order to obtain data on those points, a detailed survey of the North Cornwall coast was carried out during the fortnight August 7th — 20th (1935) inclusive.

On this coast the seals live in caves. All the caves of any size or possible importance were visited and explored. With only a very few exceptions, direct landings from a boat could not be made in the caves. Because of the narrow and difficult openings of most of them and of the surf which was breaking in them even on what appeared to be 'dead calm' days, it was usually unsafe for a dinghy to go right in and landing had to be made by swimming.

The method employed was to visit the various fishing ports and villages and hire a motor-boat and dinghy with and from which to explore the shores. The places at which boats were hired were St Ives, Portreath, Padstow, and Port Isaac. At all those places the advice and assistance of fishermen and others interested in the work were freely given and gratefully received. Without the friendly counsel and information which they were able to supply, the difficulties connected with the work would have been very greatly enhanced. At all times, such additional observations as were possible from the land were also made in order to supplement those carried out from the seaward side.

While engaged on this work I was accompanied by Midshipman G. P. Blake, R.N., of the Royal Naval College, Keyham, Devonport, who rendered invaluable assistance both ashore and afloat. Because of the danger involved, it was considered unwise for only one person at a time to enter the caves. Mr. Blake therefore accompanied me into every one of them: in fact, he was usually the first to set foot on their beaches and the last to leave.

The precaution was taken always to work difficult caves on a falling tide. Usually, on each day, from the time that the first cave was entered until operations ceased, we had to work clad only in bathing dress. As a consequence of these lengthy periods spent in a damp or wet garment and of extensive exposure alternately to the heat of the sun outside and the damp, dismal chilliness of the cave interiors, both Blake *and myself became afflicted with a disorder of the skin which can best be described as resembling miliaria or 'prickly heat' and which caused us considerable discomfort.*

The interiors of the caves were all so dark, many of them in their inner recesses being in total darkness, that it was necessary to carry lamps in order to explore them... Two Lucas 'Ever-ready' searchlight torches No. 2223, were used. Ordinary pocket flash-lamps were also carried as additional (emergency) units. One of the chief difficulties to be overcome when, as was usual, direct landing could not be made, was the safe transit of the torches from the dinghy to the cave beach. It was found necessary to seal with electrician's insulating tape all apertures in the lamps through which water could enter them. The lamps were then placed in a tin box — a large biscuit tin — which was also sealed with rubber tape. By means of a line attached to this box, with the torches safe inside, it could sometimes be towed ashore behind a swimmer. When conditions made this method impracticable or — impossible — e.g. breaking surf which would buffet the box about too much — one of us entered the cave with a rope by means of which he later hauled ashore the box. In some instances, numerous wholly or partly submerged rocks were serious obstacles in the cave entrance. When these were encountered one of us landed on the nearest rock and the box was thrown to him. The other then swam to the next foothold farther in and in turn received the box, this process being repeated as necessary until the cave beach was reached. Not infrequently a combination of methods had to be used.

In Section II, his classification of caves still remains at least partly valid, except the dates of his fieldwork precluded discovery of the moulting assembly caves or for the occasional cave sites not otherwise used except by moulted grey seal pups having departed the nursery sites and trying to survive the most dangerous first year of life. It is entitled 'The Caves':

Although seals are to be observed from time to time all along the North Cornwall coast, caves which they can and do inhabit are not uniformly distributed along that shore. Where suitable caves do exist, therefore, the seals congregate into colonies (= rookeries). From thence they disperse in all directions to forage for food, residing for the

*time being in temporary or even semi-permanent resting-places —
termed 'seal lodges' in this report (defined below).*

*So far as seals are concerned, there are three types of caves in
Cornwall. These are: (1) Caves in which seals can and do reside
permanently and in which they can successfully bring forth their young.
Such caves have beaches and/or rock-ledges which lie or extend
sufficiently far above high-water mark to ensure their not becoming
submerged in any state of the tide or the weather. For purposes of
reference, these caves may be termed Seal Caves. (2) Caves which the
seals habitually visit, often in considerable numbers, but which cannot
form for them a permanent home, and in which successful breeding
must be difficult or impossible, as no beaches or adequate ledges
remain uncovered during high tide. Such caves may be called Seal
Lodges. (3) Caves in which seals are seldom or never found. Those
which dry out completely to or beyond their mouths at low tide or, for
any other reason, are periodically or permanently easily accessible
from either land or sea are, as a rule, avoided by the seals. Such caves
are referred to as Unused Caves.*

Section III is devoted to 'The Survey': *Seals are common on the
North Cornwall coast, but they are seldom seen along that county's
southern shore. There is, however, at least one seal lodge on the south
coast, situated at Prussia Cove (O.S. 146).*

Steven drew a plan view of the cave while attaching only estimated
measurements. This procedure was repeated for similar sea cave sites
identified as then being used by seals — at Tregea Hill, Portreath, at
Kelsey Head, Trevose Head, Gunver Head and Fire Beacon Point.

Currently, Prussia Cove is a popular focal point for visitors so use
of the site by seals has lapsed.

*Local fishermen state, however, that in their opinion not more than
six to ten seals lodge in the cave…*

*Apart from this small colony at Prussia Cove, seals are seldom
found in Mount's Bay. But immediately Land's End is reached seals
become common. They are frequently encountered in considerable
numbers among the Longships Rocks, and from thence all along the
rocky shore northward to St Ives Head some seals are generally to be
found. Within this area, however, their most favoured haunts are the*

Carrack Rocks (about three and a half miles west of St Ives; O.S. 146)
and their vicinity. But although this part of the shore is much
frequented by seals, presumably for feeding purposes, caves are few,
insignificant and mainly unused.

Beyond St Ives Bay... the next rocks are found at Godrevy Point.
The shores of this headland and beyond to Navax Point, Hell's Mouth,
Deadman's Cove and eastward to Portreath are favourite haunts of the
seals. But although there are numerous caves, large and small, at
Hell's Mouth — all of which were entered and fully explored (in a
footnote, Steven explains these caves received special attention because
before they were explored they were believed to be important breeding
places — a surmise in which he was correct, as he would have
discovered had the survey taken place perhaps 2–4 weeks later). He
continued: '*none of them can serve for permanent residential and*
breeding purposes. Several are well-fitted to act as seal lodges and
apparently are much used as such, though no seals were present in any
of them at the time of our visit.

The first seal cave proper is situated in the tip of the headland —
known as Tregea Hill — on the south side of Portreath Bay, about one
half-mile from Portreath harbour. This cave extends in through the
rock in the form of a long, straight tunnel, which opens out into a large
cavern with an extensive gravel beach. The mouth of this cave is largely
blocked by a big rock which leaves a very narrow channel through
which a small dinghy can only just be coaxed to pass, and that only in
the most favourable weather conditions. When it is too rough to take a
dinghy through — as on all our three visits — landing may often still be
made on the obstructing rock. From this rock, a small part of the cave
beach is discernible in the distance, but in order to land thereon it is
necessary to swim through the intervening deep water — about 70- or
80-yards estimated distance.

When, after a previous unsuccessful attempt, this cave was first
entered (by landing on the rock) two seals could be dimly discerned
lying on the beach inside. Twenty-four seals were later driven out of
this cave and counted as they passed through the narrow channel at the
entrance. In addition, eleven others had been seen outside, making a
total of thirty-five seals counted in or near this cave — all Grey Seals

(Halichoerus grypus). On the same day that this cave was visited one other seal was passed at Godrevy Point and from sixteen to twenty seals were reported to me as having been seen in the vicinity of the Carrack Rocks. All these must have their main base at Portreath although, as explained above, probably occupying suitable lodges elsewhere (e.g. the Hell's Mouth caves) from time to time. As far as can be judged, the Portreath cave is capable of housing a colony of anything up to 150 seals. Having regard to the fact that up to about 100 have actually been seen at one time in its immediate vicinity (vide letter in Western Morning News and Mercury, 7th December, 1932) it seems fairly certain that the strength of this colony exceeds 100 seals with a maximum of not more than 150 animals.

*About midway between Portreath and Porthtowan are two other seal caves which, however, at the time of our visit, were empty. An explanation of this was supplied by Mr Landry, of Factory Farm, Porthtowan, whose land borders that part of the shore in which these caves are situated. Both caves can be reached without very much difficulty from the land at low tide (*in a footnote, he adds one can also be entered through a disused mine shaft). *During the summer months these caves are visited not infrequently by holiday-makers and the seals depart. But in late autumn, when they are no longer disturbed, some seals return to the caves to breed. At the present time they must be attached to neighbouring colonies.*

Steven continued his odyssey north-eastward, marking Kelsey Head, Pentire Point East, Trevose Head and Gunver Head as locally important sites while finding most caves unused and very few suitable to be seal lodges, before reaching just north of Boscastle:

At Pentargon, near Boscastle, there is what appears to be a seal cave. On our visit, three seals were seen in its vicinity but none inside the cave itself. This colony, therefore, if it exists at all, can scarcely exceed ten individuals.

Just beyond Pentargon Cove are the Beeny High Cliffs in which there are numerous small, unused caves. But just inside the rocks called Beeny Sisters at the place known as Fire Beacon Point, there are three exceedingly large residential caves. Although it was found impossible to fully explore these caves, they appeared to be the largest of any we had seen. Their openings are all close together and not unduly large. The northernmost cave — i.e. the nearest to the Beeny Sisters — consists of a long and narrow, but high, corridor extending inwards for a long way and curving towards the right. Its width, which remains fairly uniform for as far in as we were able to penetrate — an estimated distance of from 80 to 120 yards — was just sufficient to allow the free passage of a dinghy. Eventually, however, the passage narrowed and we could proceed no farther. As far as we went in, and beyond for as far as we could see — this distance being limited by the curve of the cave — there was deep water. By the light of our torches we could see numerous seals swimming about in the water inside of us, while others could be seen and heard plunging from high ledges. It was impossible further to explore and examine this cave. To do so, it would have been necessary to swim farther in. This was considered too risky as, once beyond reach of light from the dinghy, the swimmer would have been in total darkness and might have found it difficult or even impossible to find his way back. Nevertheless, we were able to satisfy ourselves that this great cave is well-provided with ledges at all heights and houses many seals.

A little farther along, in the direction away from Beeny Sisters, there is another cave which was also entered for a short distance. Further progress was completely barred by a sudden constriction of the cave to a narrow slit, too narrow even to swim though in the conditions prevailing at the time of our visits. The narrow part continues only for a short way and through it the cave could be seen to open out again beyond. Still farther along, but around a small bend in the cliff, is a third large cave which runs into the rocks roughly at right angles to the other two. The entrance is narrow but quickly opens out into a large, pitch-dark subterranean cavern in which there is room to row about quite freely. From this cavern, two extensions continue inwards, but because of the low roof of the one and the narrowness of the other it was impossible to enter them. For reasons similar to those mentioned above, it was also considered undesirable to swim into them in the hope of finding a beach. They appeared, however, to continue towards — and almost certainly join up with — the two other caves already described. No live seals were seen in this cave but some could be heard in the distance, the sounds coming from somewhere near where we judged cave number one to be. A dead seal, a small grey, was picked up, however, and taken on board for examination.

Along the base of Beeny High Cliffs, inside of and extending northwards from the Beeny Sisters, is a fairly extensive beach consisting largely of massive boulders. A landing was made on this beach and all the caves in the cliffs behind fully explored. None of them are suitable for either seal caves or seal lodges.

Beyond this beach, still proceeding northwards, is a small bay having on its northern side, and close to the shore, an islet called Beeny Island or Gull Rock. Hard by this island, to northward, in the small headland called Buckator, are three large caves which previously I had thought to be important seal caves. All three were entered and fully explored. They proved to be all seal lodges only. The floors of all of them must be fully covered at high tide, and they are all devoid of ledge accommodation.

It can now be stated definitely, therefore, that the seal colony, well-known to fishermen to be situated somewhere near Beeny Sisters — on which seals are often seen basking in the sunshine — is situated in the caves at Fire Beacon Point and not, as many of them had supposed, in the caves hard by Beeny Island. Seals are therefore much more likely to be observed in them than in impenetrable caves at Fire Beacon Point, which are their true residences. It is thus easy to understand how the Buckator caves came to be considered more important than they really are.

As explained above, it was found impossible to fully explore the caves at Fire Beacon Point, or even to count the seals which were seen in them. As far as could be made out, at least a dozen different individuals came within range of our torches. How many more were in the caves at that time is not known. When we emerged from the caves, however, a large number of seals had appeared outside. Although an exact count was difficult to obtain, the number arrived at was twenty-six individuals. That is to say approximately thirty-eight live seals were counted in addition to one dead one. From these numbers and the nature of the caves — as far as this could be ascertained — I arrived at the conclusion that the seal colony at Fire Beacon Point is of approximately the same numerical strength as that at Portreath — i.e. one hundred to one hundred and fifty seals. Three fishermen, with long experience of this part of the coast, and all unaware of the figure at which I had arrived, separately and independently gave 'about 150 seals' as their estimate of the number having their headquarters in that area. It would appear, therefore, that this figure is reasonably reliable.

There are no seal caves further north than Fire Beacon Point.

Section IV sees Steven providing the first-ever grey seal population estimate offered for Cornwall, sub-divided by the localities upon which he believed them to be centred. Probably it would be fair to assess the estimates as conservative as he was not in a position to know that the 7th to 20th of August survey was a period preceding or marking the beginning of the season of pup production. Current studies show seal caves to be little-used in this period compared with the late summer/early autumn peak use for pup production and the late autumn/winter peak used by the great moulting assemblies. In this, the locality north of Boscastle was the exception, being still more heavily used than elsewhere:

North Coast. It can now be stated that the seal colonies on the North Cornwall coast are situated at Portreath (Porthtowan), Kelsey Head, Pentire Point East, Trevose Head, Gunver Head (?), Pentargon (?) and Fire Beacon Point in Beeny High Cliffs. As far as can be ascertained the numerical strengths of these several colonies are as follows:

Portreath	*100 – 150 seals*
Kelsey Head	*20 – 30 seals*
Pentire Point East	*10 – 20 seals*
Trevose Head	*20 – 30 seals*
Gunver Head	*10 – 15 seals*
Pentargon	*5 – 10 seals*
Fire Beacon Point	*100 – 150 seals*

Allowing a fairly generous margin for errors and omissions it can safely be stated that the total seal population of the North Cornwall coast is not less than about 300 and probably not more than 500 individuals... Although these numbers fall far short of an estimate of 2000 seals put forward by the Fishery Officer to the Cornwall Sea Fisheries Committee, they are extremely large... If, to the present population of, say, 500 seals, be added the 177 seals which were shot last year (see below, Fishery Officer's Report, 1934), *the total seal population at the beginning of 1934 must have been roughly 700 animals...*

It has not been possible in this survey to collect any data which will indicate whether — apart from interference by man — the seal population of Cornwall is increasing, decreasing or static. Nor is any light thrown on the highly important possibility of an influx of seals from other localities at certain times — e.g. during the herring-fishing season.

South Coast. There are but few seals on the south coast. Only the small colony at Prussia Cove was visited. There may possibly be one or more additional small colonies in the vicinity of Lizard Point, but this locality was not investigated. No estimate of the number of seals on-Cornwall's southern shore can therefore be given, but it certainly is very small.

In section V, he returns to the species of the seals seen: *Every seal seen was, without exception a Grey Seal — Halichoerus grypus. Not a single Brown Seal — Phoca vitulina — was encountered. There can be little doubt, therefore, that the Brown Seal, if present at all, is extremely rare around these shores. It would seem that recent references to this species of seal in Cornwall must, almost certainly, have been due to faulty identification.*

Finally, in Section VI, he concludes: *Seals of all sizes and (presumably) of all ages from about one year old upwards were seen. But no seal pups were observed. The breeding season evidently had not begun.*

Between George Steven's two seal surveys, in 1934 the Cornwall Sea Fisheries Committee (CSFC) began a seal culling effort that was to continue annually until 1951. In a letter dated September 1961, addressed to Ray Fordham (see below), the Clerk of the CSFC wrote: *In the interests of preventing damage to Cornish fisheries, for a number of years, we undertook shooting of seals on the North coast and I attach, for your information, a list of the numbers killed.*

46

Entitled 'Eradication of Seals on the North Coast of Cornwall':

Year	Number of seals killed
1934	177
1935	15
1936	89
1937	72
1938	62
1939	33
1940	30
1941	27
1942	40
1943	38
1944	17
1945	No shooting organised
1946	24
1947	28
1948	34
1949	No shooting organised
1950	24
1951	34

Having explained prior approval by the Ministry of Agriculture, Fisheries and Food was required, the following conditions had to be observed: *That only expert marksmen should be engaged. That only rifles of .303 calibre should be used. That, wherever possible, the dead bodies should be recovered and the heads and stomachs sent to the MBA, Plymouth, for scientific examination That not more than £50 should be spent on the work each year*

In the interest of accuracy, all shooting was undertaken from the shore but this, of course, made it almost impossible to recover the bodies of the seals at the time they were shot. However, by arrangement with the MBA in 1936, the committee organised a scheme under which the Association offered a reward of 3/= and the cost of carriage for each seal's head sent to them and the Committee undertook to pay 6/= for proper burial of the remainder of each carcase. This scheme was operative until 1939, but has not been renewed since the war.

When the Committee applied for renewal of consent to expenditure on seal shooting in 1952, the Ministry attached further conditions relating to the recovery of bodies which would have made the cost prohibitive in relation to the results which might have been expected. No shooting was, therefore, done in that year, nor has any been done since.

Following the shooting season of 1936, one year after Steven's final survey work was completed, the Fishery's Officer reported to the CSFC: *Operations this year in connection with the reduction of the number of seals on the North Coast of Cornwall commenced on January 1ˢᵗ and closed on August 29ᵗʰ. Repeated visits were made to the majority of the following places: Portreath, North Cliffs, Godrevy Point, Navax Point, St Agnes, Trevellas Cliffs, Holywell By, Kelsey Head, Porthjoke Cove, Newquay, Trevose Head, Padstow, Trevone Bay, Tintagel, Boscastle, Pentargon Cove, Fire Beacon Point and Beeny Cliffs.*

In the Portreath area which formerly was infested with seals, very poor results were obtained. Apparently, the bulk of seals that were in this area have made their headquarters elsewhere. According to my own observations and from the information of the local residents, comparatively few seals are now seen in this quarter. In the Boscastle district, however, viz: from Pentargon Cove to Beeny Cliffs there are still a considerable number. At Kelsey Head also, especially during the first two visits, there were several seals to be seen. The number killed at the respective places are as follows: Boscastle District 40; Kelsey Head 22; Portreath 16; Godrevy Point 7; Trevose Head 4; making a total of 89 over a period of 8 months. The operations were not confined, however, to the specified areas mentioned as the neighbouring parts of the coast were also taken in. I am rather disappointed at the results obtained as I fully expected to account for at least 150. The unsettled state of the weather, however, frequently hampered the operations and the Portreath area especially failed considerably... In the Land's End district, the fishermen report the presence of a considerable number of seals in the vicinity of the Longships, but the prevailing boisterous weather has prevented any action being taken in this quarter with any likelihood of success… I am, Gentlemen, your obedient servant, W.H. Barron.

Not specified is whether or not, as had been traditional in Cornwall, shooting of seals took place from sea cave shores as well as open beach or island/islet shores.

In 'Notes on Cornish Mammals — An Annual Report, No. 3' — by Dr F.A. Turk, in the Royal Cornwall Polytechnic Society Annual Report, 1961, the adit and seal cave described in Tregarthen's 'Wildlife at the Land's End' (above) were revisited by Ray Fordham and David Lewis.

Fordham and Lewis (1961) related their experience: *Towards the end of the last century a Cornish naturalist, named Tregarthen, visited a 'seal cave' situated about five miles East of St Ives. This year (1961) I was able to visit the same cave on several occasions between September 16ᵗʰ and November 19ᵗʰ.*

Whilst searching for the exact location of the cave Grey Seal cows were occasionally seen swimming in the vicinity. Access to the cave is gained through an old mine adit. This runs horizontally for about 200 yards and penetrates the cave roof in five places. One of these was chosen and the 40-foot descent to the cave floor made on ropes. It is impossible to enter the cave from the sea as there is water covering the entrance at all states of the tide.

During the visits, it was ascertained that five calves were born on the sandy beach at the back of the cave out of the sea's reach. This region of the cave was in almost total darkness and observations were carried out in torchlight: photographs were taken by flashlight.

The noise of our descent usually frightened the adults, who in their anxiety to return to the sea, showed unusual agility in clambering over the huge boulders in the lower reaches of the cave. However, photos were taken of an adult cow that chose to remain with her calf and appeared unconcerned at the observer's presence. A bull was also present on this occasion and neither he or the cow showed any fear in spite of the fact that flashlight photos were being taken. The only aggressive movements were those of the calves who made their characteristic growling and thrusting movements.

The calves generally left the cave when about four weeks old after *their first moult was completed. My final visit was on November 19th* *and on that date all of the seals had left the cave.*

It is hoped that these somewhat scanty observations will pave the way for a more detailed survey in 1962.

In 'Notes on Cornish Mammals — An Annual Report, No. 4' — by Dr F.A. Turk, in the Royal Cornwall Polytechnic Society Annual Report, 1962, the adit and seal cave described above were revisited by **Fordham and Lewis (1962)**. Turk introduces the second article with the following amendment:

It should be noted that, after Mr Fordham had completed the Manuscript of his report printed here (in 1961), *he was able to record yet another young born in the first week of December: it will be seen that this, together with his other records extends the season during which young are produced beyond anything that had previously been suspected for the Cornish populations.*

Fordham related:

This year the seal cave near Navax Point (O.S. SW594432) was revisited and a visit was made to another below Tregea Hill, Portreath (O.S. SW649455). On every occasion I have been assisted greatly by P.J. Evans and D.J. Lewis without whom entry into the caves would have been impossible.

The cave near Navax Point was visited at the end of July but no seals were present. Subsequent visits indicated that seven calves were born, two of which were females. The earliest was born in late August, two in September, two in October and the remaining two in November. One of the calves born in October was found dead: it measured only 2'6" against the usual length of 3' or more. The remaining calves left the cave during the third week when their moult was completed. They were tame when only a day or two old but soon became aggressive with the exception of two which remained tame until quite a late stage.

This year the behaviour of the adults was studied more closely as a result of which coition was witnessed taking place in the sea on the 9th September, presumably with the cow that had given birth to the August calf as by then her lactation was completed. On other occasions the bull approached cows which were with their calves on the beach of the cave: the cows chased the bull and once he was observed to roll away, *but whether this was part of a sexual display or simply a method of quicker retreat is not known.*

Immature seals were frequently seen in a bay about half a mile to the west of the seal cave and a young bull was once found sleeping in a nearby cave. An adult bull was witnessed at sexual play with a young cow but although several attempts were made coition did not take place. On this occasion their play was frequently interrupted by a much younger bull which was chased away by the other. At other times two young bulls were seen playing together.

During August a bull and two cows were seen off Tregea Hill, Portreath. Several attempts were made to enter a large cave in the headland and entry was eventually affected by wading and swimming at low water on the 14th October. The cave was empty but one dead calf was found floating in the long narrow entrance. Although it seems probable the cave is still used it seems unlikely the population here is anything like the 100 – 150 estimated by Steven in 1935. This is difficult to explain as the cave would appear to be more suitable than that near Navax Point, being more inaccessible and having a larger beach.

I would be interested to hear from anyone with knowledge of the present state of other colonies on the North Cornish coast

The efforts by Steven and Fordham were the first to attempt to clarify how seal caves in Cornwall were being used. Steven's identification of seal cave locations, his methods for examining them and the sometimes-rudimentary plan views he produced formed the basis for all the research that followed, remaining so to this day. Fordham was the pioneer of making repeat visits to a seal cave to examine seal behaviour over time — in his case, during consecutive breeding seasons.

The stage was now set for the first well-funded, well-equipped exploration of Cornwall and Scilly grey seal breeding sites by the Seals Research Division, part of the Institute for Marine Environmental Research based at the MAFF laboratory at Lowestoft, Suffolk. It was led by Charles Summers and the eloquently scanty results were published in **Summers, C.F. (1974)**.

The abstract summarises the survey:

Cornwall and the Isles of Scilly were explored for grey seal

(Halichoerus grypus) breeding localities during the 1973 breeding season. The work involved investigating many sea caves on the north coast of Cornwall, in addition to open beach and skerry sites. Pup production was determined by relating the number of pups produced in a sample period to the number produced in the same period (in another year) at Ramsey Island, Pembrokeshire. The all-age population derived from these pup production estimates suggest that the number of grey seals in Cornish waters is about 250 and in Scilly about 120. Haul-outs of several hundred animals seen in Scilly outside the breeding season almost certainly breed elsewhere.

Extracts from the Introduction: *Accounts by Steven (1936) and Davies (1956) of the seals of Cornwall and Scilly* (in Scilly there are no proven seal caves and perhaps just one cave used sometimes by seals), *respectively, have formed the basis for more recent population estimates...Hatch (privately circulated report quoted by Smith, 1966) repeated Steven's survey in 1960 and concluded that shooting had since reduced the stock to about 100. Since both surveys were made during summer, rather than in the breeding season, the estimates of total population were based not on pup production but upon the dubious criteria of cave size (Steven, 1936) and number of adults seen (Hatch in Smith, 1966) ...*

Differences in the timing of the breeding season throughout the country have been mentioned by several authors (including Lockley, R.M. (1966) and Bonner, W.N. (1972). *The dates given by Davies (1956) for the breeding season in Scilly imply an affinity with South Wales, where the peak of pupping occurs about a month earlier than in most Scottish localities. No dates were available at that time for the Cornish season.*

The primary aims of this work were to revisit Steven's cave breeding sites, locate new ones, obtain an up-to-date estimate of the populations, and make observations on the timing of the breeding seasons. A secondary aim was to tag as many pups as possible to investigate through tag returns possible relationships between the seals of Cornwall, Scilly, South Wales and Ireland.

There were two separate programmes of fieldwork. One team worked in Cornwall from 24 September to 5 October, 1973, the other in

Scilly during the first week of October 1973...

In the Methods section, Summers writes: *Reputed breeding localities, and areas searched for new breeding sites, were explored in Zodiac Mk III inflatable boats powered by 20 or 25 HP outboard engines. In Cornwall two such craft worked together while in Scilly a single inflatable worked from the Jane.*

There are so many caves along the Cornish coasts that a complete investigation would take several weeks even in calm weather. Thus, a cave was investigated only if it was a reputed breeding site, or if seals were seen in its vicinity, or if it was large enough to enter safely in the boats.

The most convenient method of exploration was to beach the boats inside the cave. Unless this could be done easily it was quicker to call upon the diving team to swim in ... On days when it was too rough for boating, attempts (largely unsuccessful) were made to enter caves by scrambling down cliffs...

The 'Results from Cornwall' section was based on site visits to localities from Bude south to Land's End, Pedn-men-an-mere (close to the Minack Theatre) to Newlyn and Cudden Point (in Mount's Bay) around Lizard Point to Coverack:

Twenty-four caves were explored including all those which Steven designated as breeding caves. 67 grey seals were seen of which 11 were pups and 3 were juvenile. 8 pups were tagged...

Four localities were confirmed as breeding sites. 3 pups were found on a kelp-covered beach at the back of a cave 110m long in the headland of Buckator. A bull and two cows were seen outside and a third cow came off the beach as the boats entered the cave. Nearby, at the base of the high cliffs, opposite Gull Rock, was an open shingle beach strewn with boulders which effectively camouflaged the four pups found there. Five cows and a bull were seen swimming just offshore. Also, in this area, near Fire Beacon Point, a dead white-coated pup was found floating in the sea. The third breeding locality, between Porthtowan and Portreath, was a cave some 50m long with a large shingle beach. There were two pups on the beach and their mothers were seen in the sea at the mouth of the cave. On the south coast, just north of Vellan Head, a pup was found among boulders at the top of an open, kelp-covered beach. Here too, the beach was protected by sea cliffs and provided effective cover — some time was spent searching for the pup after spotting its mother in the sea.

Other localities, on the basis of such circumstantial evidence as the presence of apparently pregnant females and a patrolling bull, must, almost certainly, be regarded as breeding sites. These are: the more northerly of the two caves opposite the Beeny Sisters which has a small beach, the cave at Gunver Head which has two sandy beaches, the cave at Tregea Hill which has a large shingle beach, a tunnel through the headland at Hell's Mouth and a cave to the west of Navax Point which has a kelp- covered beach (though this last site did not have a patrolling bull). The beaches in all these caves are apparently covered by very high tides, but this is probably also true of the caves where pups were found. However, the fact that some of the pups were wet and readily made for the sea when disturbed suggests that intermittent inundation of the nursery beaches is a routine event in the life of Cornish seals.

It is necessary to consider reputed breeding sites not so far mentioned. The caves at Fire Beacon Point, Pentargon, Trevose Head, Pentire Point East, Kelsey Head and Prussia Cove were all explored. Steven noted that some of these caves have ledges and large boulders uncovered at high tide which might accommodate seals. However, all the pups seen in the present study were found on beaches. None of the caves just mentioned have beaches and only in two of them (Trevose Head and the most northerly of the three Fire Beacon Point caves) were there any seals. It is thought unlikely that pups born in any of these caves would be successfully reared without a beach on which to suckle and rest. Given a beach, pups can probably survive a few hours awash between feeds.

A farmer at St Ives suggested that the grey seals associated with the Carrack Rocks breed in a nearby cave which has an underwater entrance. The divers searched the area and found a cave with a large submarine entrance which narrowed to a fissure above the water line. They discovered that the entrance opened into a large cavern but were unable to determine its dimensions or whether there was a beach, because of the heavy ground swell which prevented them from

54

surfacing safely inside the cave. No seals were seen in the vicinity except the 3 cows in the sea at the Carracks and a large bull which had followed as the boats searching for the cave.

The caves at Rinsey Head, where a Porthleven fisherman claimed to have taken skin divers to photograph seals, did not appear to be likely breeding sites and no seals were seen in the vicinity.

All other sightings of seals, except those seen at the Carrack Rocks and the Brisons are regarded as casual sightings of animals away from breeding sites. Though neither the Carracks nor the Brisons are reputed to be breeding localities it is possible that pups could survive at these places in exceptionally calm seasons.

It is difficult to determine the duration of a breeding season from a short visit. However, something of the timing of the season can be deduced from the ages of the pup present...

Summers conclusions were: *The main grey seal breeding localities in Cornwall are in the Beeny Sisters — Buckator area north of Boscastle, and along the coast from Porthtowan to Godrevy Point. These observations were not always in agreement with those of Steven (1936), e. g. Fire Beacon Point is not thought to be a breeding site, whereas neighbouring Buckator is now known to be one. Breeding in Cornwall is not confined to caves. Beaches are preferred to other terrain. Since cave beaches are inaccessible from the land they are perhaps favoured, though open beaches are also used if sufficiently secure. The proportion of moulted pups in the population indicates that pups are born in Cornwall, like those in Scotland, from mid-September onwards. The season is earlier in Scilly. The total population of grey seals in Cornwall is estimated at about 250. This figure rests on the assumption that the Cornish season has the same characteristics as that at Ramsey Island, Pembrokeshire, and is clearly subject to errors resulting from discrepancies in their maximum mean daily birth rate and spread of the pupping season. Pup counts done throughout the season at the more important pupping localities mentioned above would refine future estimates. The Scillonian breeding localities are the Western Rocks, the Norrard Rocks, and the Eastern Isles. The colony at Scilly is much smaller than is indicated by the size of winter haul-outs...*

In 1973, John H. Prime was a member of Summer's Seal's Research Division (SRD) fieldwork team. In 1982, he returned to Cornwall and Scilly leading his own team. This time the team was representing the Sea Mammal Research Unit (SMRU), into which the SRD had since evolved. His results were published in **Prime (1985)**.

He writes eloquently of the hostile conditions encountered during the expedition, including in the Abstract:

A survey of previously identified grey seal (Halichoerus grypus) breeding sites around the coast of Cornwall, England was carried out during the 1982 pupping season. Adverse weather restricted survey operations and also probably resulted in high, though not necessarily exceptional, pup mortality. There is no evidence of a change in status or distribution of the grey seal in Cornwall since the last survey in 1973, although observations suggest that the timing of the breeding season is earlier than previously calculated. Local information indicates that up to 40 pups are born each year, an estimate that would be refined by regular surveys of all the pupping sites throughout the breeding season, from early September to mid-October.

In the Introduction, he writes:

Cornwall, in the southwest of England, has long been known to hold a small population of grey seals which was estimated to be around 700 animals in 1935 (Steven, 1936). Following a survey in 1973 Summers (1974) estimated pup production in Cornwall at 73 with a total population of about 250 animals. At the time, this represented less than 1% of the total British population. In order to obtain an estimate of the current status of this grey seal stock, a further survey of Cornish breeding sites was conducted in 1982 ...

Usually boat surveys are conducted around the time when the maximum number of pups are likely to be present (Summers, 1978). The results of the 1973 survey indicated that for Cornwall this was about 8– 9 October. However, in order to obtain results that were directly comparable with that survey, and because weather and sea conditions during October were unlikely to be suitable for survey work, the 1982 survey was carried out from 27 September to 8 October.

As described, the Methods would repeat those for the 1973 survey: *The original plan was to use two Zodiac Mk III inflatable boats to* survey the entire coast from Bude to Coverack, on the east side of the Lizard Peninsula. Caves were to be investigated by divers equipped with wetsuits and aqualungs, as in the 1973 survey. Unfortunately, weather conditions in 1982 were so bad that a moderate to large ground swell was always present and it was never possible for the boat or the divers to enter the cave breeding sites identified in 1973 (Summers, 1974). However, in 1973 a number of pups were identified on beaches or swimming in the open sea and it was decided to use boats to survey the coast from Penzance to Coverack in the south, and between the Carracks rocks and Newquay on the north coast. Other known breeding sites were surveyed on foot from the coast footpath, open beaches were visited where there was access from the clifftop.

When seals were observed it was always possible to determine their species and it was usually possible to determine their sex and whether they were adults, juveniles or pups. The approximate age of each pup was determined using the criteria in Radford et al. (1978).

The Results reflect, above all, the destructive effect of the sea state on the survey work:

In Cornwall a total of 45 grey seals was seen, of which 5 were pups... No common seals (Phoca vitulina) were sighted.

The results of the 1982 and 1973 surveys were compared: In the areas surveyed in both years, slightly fewer adults and only half as many pups were seen in 1982. However, almost identical numbers of seals were counted in the areas which were surveyed by boat in both years; also, the localities where seals were sighted were the same in both years, indicating that the distribution of seals had not changed. Boat surveys often provide useful estimates of the number of adult seals in an area because the boat engines disturb seals that are swimming or resting underwater and may attract seals from out of caves. Observations from cliff tops, on the other hand, will locate only seals that are hauled out and some of those in the neighbouring sea.

The largest discrepancy in the number of pups observed was in the Crackington Haven — Tintagel Head area. Summers (1974) recorded 8 pups in this area, many of them in caves which are inaccessible from the land. Only two pups were seen from the cliff tops in 1982.

However, Summers (1974) noted that most of the cave beaches

were probably covered by very high tides. In seasons, like 1982, when those high tides coincide with large, wind-driven swells, these beaches probably become untenable for young pups. It is therefore likely that the number of pups still alive at the time of the 1982 survey was not seriously underestimated. Some additional support for this suggestion is provided by the fact that Summers (1974) found two pups in a cave at Tobban Horse, near Porthtowan, but no pups on any of the adjacent beaches. In 1982 one pup, which had presumably been washed out of the cave, was found on an open boulder beach 200m from the cave entrance.

The concluding paragraph of the Discussion served as a baton held out to anyone in Cornwall, Scilly and Devon with the inclination to fill in the considerable gaps left by the surveys of 1973 and 1982:

The above observations imply that grey seal pup mortality at breeding sites in the Cornwall area can be very high. This is supported by the fact that only three pups were seen in the Isles of Scilly in 1982 following a period of severe weather, whereas 19 pups were found during a survey in 1973. Further, no pups were observed on Lundy in 1982, although on an almost identical date in 1973, four white-coated pups were counted. Clark (1976) reported that of 12 grey seal pups born on Lundy Island 1975, 5 (42%) died as a result of storms and heavy seas. This is considerably higher than the mortality rate, due to storm damage and wash-offs, of 20%, recorded by Anderson et al. (1979) at Ramsey Island, South Wales, where there are cave breeding sites similar to, but generally less exposed than, those in Cornwall.

Summers (1974) converted his counts to an estimate of total pup production by using the estimated age of the oldest pups he found to determine when the breeding season had started. Using figures from Davies (1949) for the distribution of births throughout the breeding season at Ramsey Island, he then calculated what proportion of births should have occurred by the start of his survey and divided his pups count by this figure. If this method is applied to the results of the 1982 survey, the breeding season is estimated to have started six days earlier than in 1973, and approximately 30% of the total pup production should have been born by the start of the survey. This implies that the timing of the breeding season in Cornwall is closer to that at Lundy

Island (Clark, 1976) and Ramsey Island (Davies, 1949) than Anderson et al. (1979) who noted some births occur during the first week of September. However, if the survey had really taken place at this stage of the 1982 Cornwall breeding season, a high proportion of young pups should have been found. In fact, the youngest pup observed was at least 11 days old.

There are two possible explanations for this. Either the breeding season in 1982 had started much earlier than estimated by Summers' method, or all the young pups had been washed away by the prevailing high seas. Some support for the former hypothesis is provided by reports from a local naturalist (K. Jones, pers. comm.) who estimates that between 30 and 40 grey seal pups are born in Cornwall each year with 8 – 10 of these coming from the south coast between Mullion and Kennack Sands on the Lizard Peninsula. He further reports that sick, injured or starveling pups are found on local beaches from the fourth week in August onward. In fact both of the above factors probably affected the results of the 1982 survey and therefore it is not possible to produce a reliable estimate of grey seal pup production in Cornwall for 1982.

The small number of pups recorded on the 1982 survey should not be taken as an indication that the Cornish population is declining, but rather that the grey seal breeding sites in Cornwall are particularly vulnerable in severe weather conditions.

Clearly, as Summer's (1974) recognised, a short survey period during a breeding season which may extend for more than seven weeks cannot provide a precise estimate of total pup production. This is more likely to be obtained by regular surveys throughout the pupping season; these would also provide information on the true duration and timing of the breeding season.

In a summary that is inevitably repetitive, the concluding paragraph stands out both as the epitaph for the 1982 survey and a shining light for the direction and manner in which seal research needed to travel at the sites of the south-west region. For, despite making what were the best-equipped and most expert surveys up to not only that time but also to the present day, understanding of the seal biology at Cornwall sites had been hardly advanced since the inspiring steps in the dark taken by Steven and Blake in 1935:

A more accurate assessment of the size of the Cornwall grey seal population would be obtained by regular surveys of all the pupping sites throughout the breeding season, from the beginning of September to the middle of October.

Having read his paper in 1988, I took his advice and conducted locally-based grey seal research over the next 30+ years.

Stepping Stones to the Seal Caves: Early Insights

South Wales

Mention of seals in Welsh literature appears to begin with the antiquarian, author and naturalist, **George Owen (1603)** of Henllys, although he makes no reference to the sea caves that are so abundant there.

In Chapter 15, he writes: *Lastly, I will end my fish meal with the three strange nature fishes, that is, the seal or sea calf, the porpoise and the thornpole. I call them strange of nature for, whereas all other fish that breed their own kind do spawn, these do engender after the nature of beasts and the females do grow great and bring forth young.*

The seal is covered with hair, like a calf, and has four short legs, and broad pawed like to the mole. This fish comes to land to rest and sleep, and lie together in herds, like swine, one upon another, and at birth time, as Pliny says, comes a-land and is delivered and gives suck to the young till it is able to swim which, he says, will be in twelve days, and never brings above two at a time. The fawn, at the first, is white and is more delicate meat than its ancestor, being strong and wholesome to eat, yet is it accounted a dainty and a rare dish of many men. This fish is very fat, as bacon, and the skin serves to many uses being dressed, especially in times past, for covering of tents, because it receives no hurt by lightning. As says Pliny and Rondelet, the hair of the seal stares at the south wind and goes smooth with the north, but certain it is it does so at the flood and ebb, staring with the one and smoothing with the other...

These... being ravenous by nature, follow the schools of herrings, feeding on them and devouring them, and so, in herring fishing, are taken oftentimes wrapped in the herring nets.

In his book *British Zoology*, **Thomas Pennant (1776)** acknowledges the following correspondence, received from the Reverend Mr Farrington of Dinas in describing the natural history of the grey seal as then understood: *The seals are natives of our coasts; and are found most frequently in Llyn in Caernarvonshire, and the northern parts of Anglesey: they are seen often towards Ynys y moelrhon, to the west of Bardsey, or Ynys Enlli; and the Skerries, commonly called in the British language Ynys y moelrhoniaid, or Seal Island ... they are excellent swimmers, and ready divers, and are very bold when in the sea, swimming carelessly enough about boats: their dens or lodgements are in hollow rocks, or caverns, near the sea; but out of reach of the tide: in the summer they will come out of the water, to bask or sleep in the sun, on the top of large stones, or shivers of rocks; and that is the opportunity our countrymen take of shooting them... they are taken for the sake of their skins, and for the oil their fat yields: the former sell for 4s. or even 4s. 6d. a-piece; which, when dressed, are very useful in covering trunks, making waistcoats, shot-pouches and several other conveniences... The flesh of these animals, and even of porpoises, formerly found a place at the tables of the great, as appears from the bill of fare at that great feast that Archbishop Neville gave in the reign of Edward IV in which is seen that several were provided on that occasion. They couple about April, on large rocks or small islands not remote from the shore; and bring forth in those vast caverns that are frequent on our coasts: they commonly bring two at a time, which in their infant state are covered with a whitish down or woolly substance.*

Browne Willis (1716) includes the following in his '*Survey of St David's Cathedral*' '*Memoirs Relating to the Cathedral-Church of St. David's and the Country adjacent, as it was in the latter End of Queen Elizabeth's Reign*'. Despite his best efforts, these could not be accredited, as he describes: '*I have here copy'd our Author's Words, both to preserve his Witticism, which he seems to have valu'd himself upon; and chiefly to shew the Time when this MS was written, which was about the Spanish Invasion in 1588.*' Therefore, this extract does represent the oldest reference to seal caves discovered while preparing this book: *'In Caves about these Islands (*a reference to Ramsey and nearby islands*), Seals, or Sea Calves, breed, which are taken about Michaelmas (*29 September*) by the Sea- men, who go out for them in Boats, and kill them in their Caves with Clubs. They observe when they strike at these Sea Calves, that if they do not hit them upon the Snout, the Blow goes for nothing; and when they run away, they throw great Stones behind them with their hind Feet, which are very dangerous, if those that hunt them do not take Heed.*

In 1864, published in the Pembrokeshire County Archive, a failed seal hunt is described.

In *'Notes on a visit to Skomer, 1896,'* published in the Proceedings of the Cardiff Naturalists Society, J.J. Neale — who subsequently took up the lease for the Island between 1905 and 1915 — wrote: *'On two or three occasions we saw seals... The so-called gentlemen take a delight in shooting them although they know full well that if shot while in the water the bodies at once sink. They are harmless, interesting creatures but are rapidly diminishing'.*

H. Morrey Salmon (1935) published a paper driven by a long-term interest in seals in a paper entitled *'Seals of the West Coast'*. He was driven by a perception that too much knowledge on the subject derived from anecdotes and too little from scientific examination, beginning with the observation that before 1837, following the examination of a grey seal skull at a meeting of the British Association, the grey seal was not recognised as occurring in British Waters (despite Owens early description of what is, evidently, a grey seal pup).

His earliest source is Thomas Pennant, in the fourth edition of *British Zoology*, published in 1776. In this section, Pennant quotes from a correspondent in Caernarfonshire who states that seals were numerous around the North Wales coast — locations mentioned are Anglesey, the Llyn, Carreg-y-Moelrhon off the west coast of Bardsey, as well as the Skerries. Morrey Salmon comments that grey seals remain common in these localities 'today' — namely in 1935. Concluding his reference to Pennant, he quotes from another unaccredited printing: *'their dens or lodgements are in hollow rocks or caverns, near the sea, but out of reach of the tide'*. While the reference to being 'out of reach of the tide' is inaccurate, this clearly describes grey seal haunts.

He quotes J.C. Millais from volume one of *'The Mammals of Great Britain and Ireland',* published in 1904: *'The coast of Pembrokeshire has long been known as the haunt of the Grey Seal and certain caves in the neighbourhood of Newport and Fishguard are still frequented by it. Some fifteen years ago, Lord David Kennedy shot and recovered seven of these seals in this locality, and in previous years he had killed a few of them but had never seen a male that exceeded 8 feet.'*

He quotes H.E. Forrest who, in 1919, published *'A Handbook to the Vertebrate Fauna of North Wales'.* Forrest states that the grey seal is the sole seal species resident and breeding in the region. He draws on anecdote to state that the grey seal had been numerous 30 years previously and common almost 200 years since. He goes on to write that the harbour seal is an *'occasional winter visitor'.*

Of his own observations, he writes: *It would seem that the breeding animals must retire to caves on the mainland coast, on Skomer, Ramsey, etc.*

In his summary, he believes he has *'shown conclusively that* (grey seals) *have been resident, and breeding, in considerable numbers on the west coast from Land's End to Anglesey for at least 200 years. Today, the position is entirely the same except that numbers have probably increased considerably...*

The scientific study of grey seal breeding seasons in Wales was initiated by J.L. Davies between 27 July and 27 October in 1947 on Ramsey, although he did not enter the seal caves there. Nevertheless, as well as recording 130 pups observed on beaches mainly inaccessible from the land — he viewed them from cliff-tops about 100 feet high, he estimated also pup production in the caves, offering a figure of 60 pups and deriving from these figures an estimated total seal population of 600 for the island. He estimated the total West Wales population at 1000 grey seals.

Davies, J.L. (1949) published his results in the Journal of the Zoological. Society, London.

Additionally, he made detailed observations on seal behaviour prior to and during the breeding season as well as subsequent to it. He observed also the behaviour of immature and other non-breeding seals as well as the inter-actions between certain bird species living adjacent to or upon their haunts. They make this a real treasure among the early papers on this subject.

Another interesting preoccupation of Davies was the cycle of cliff erosion and its effect on sea caves. He notes that what he called sea caves and inlet beaches typically began as a cave, often with a small beach at its head and being longer than it is wide. The cave roof eroded over a variable period of years. Before the process is complete, the cave becomes most shrunken, at which point site classification can be confusing. In my work, I deemed a site — always — to be a cave where it was overhung by rock but a beach for the area out-with the overhang. In retrospect, clearly these should be classified as hybrid sites.

He went on, while making a historical review of grey seal site distribution, to suggest that the grey seals of Wales, Ireland and west England: '*are apparently all cave breeders with the sole recorded exceptions of those at Ramsey and at the Scillies... The fact that breeding has never been known to take place there (Grassholm) may be an indication that the seals that frequent the island are traditionally cave breeders and that such an open situation has no attraction for them except as a lying-out station.*

Third, the majority of calves watched on Ramsey beaches exhibited a tendency to withdraw into small caves or crevices or under overhanging rocks. This may merely be a desire for shelter such as is prevalent in the young of most animals, but it is not unlikely that it is a reappearance of an ancestral urge to find shelter in a cave.

Fourth, whereas caves and inlet beaches are crowded and the breeding season is here long drawn out, breeding on the open beaches is limited both in time and space and there is much room for expansion.'

Subsequently, the same author, **Davies, J.L. (1956)**, published a paper — *'The grey seal at the Isles of Scilly',* based on observations and anecdotal accounts gathered in September/October 1952 and 1953.

Although Scilly has no known seal caves, he drew important conclusions on the place of seals in local culture. *'According to Mothersole (who published 'The Isles of Scilly' in 1910), the seals were hunted in the nineteenth century and their blubber boiled down for candle making... for a long period after (a visit by Millais), a bounty of five shillings was paid for every seal killed in Scilly. The tradition of killing seal calves did not die with the cessation of bounty payments, although the marked diminution in the number of active fishermen has meant the gradual decrease in the significance of this mortality factor.*

During the past twenty years, and particularly since the Second World War, the character of this interference has changed. Scilly is rapidly becoming a favourite holiday resort and boat trips to see the seals are a great attraction... The holiday season extends through September into October and thus covers most of the seals' breeding season. Seals are no longer being killed but they are constantly disturbed and, although it is difficult to estimate the exact effect of this disturbance, it must certainly be an adverse factor in breeding success.

The effect of human interference has been not only direct, as outlined above, but also indirect, in that it has forced the seals to breed on small and exposed islets where mortality from high seas is probably very great. Verbal evidence suggests that the abandonment of more favourable sites is still going on and that breeding in the Eastern Islands has ceased only recently.'

The next stepping stone in understanding the biology of grey seals using Welsh sites was described primarily by **Johnson (1955-1972)** in *'Nature in Wales'*. The project, which began in 1954, included a considerable contribution from Ronald Lockley. This was an adventure in seal 'ring-marking' undertaken under the auspices of the West Wales Field Society (WWFS) in which a sample of grey seal pups at the nursery grounds of Ramsey, Skomer and the mainland Pembrokeshire coast had small, numbered metal tags attached, each to the inner hind digit of a hind flipper. Tags stamped with their address were supplied by the Zoological Society of London and part of the fieldwork costs were defrayed by the Nature Conservancy.

Some earlier marking of seals had occurred in 1946, being undertaken by Lockley and WWFS volunteers. Quantified work by Lockley has been difficult to locate but his considerable experience of seal studies and knowledge of British seals is best displayed in the books *'Grey Seal, Common Seal'*, published in 1966 by Andre Deutsch and *'The Seals and the Curragh'*, published in 1955 by the Scientific

Book Club.

The primary objective, in which the tagging exercises were successful, was to generate recaptures that would yield previously unknown information on pup dispersal routes from nursery sites. 63 pups travelled across sea areas to south and west Eire (from Galway Bay to the Saltee Islands, Brittany, Cornwall, Devon, Scilly, Dorset and even as far as the north coast of Spain (Santona).

Pups also reached North Wales while 44% remained at local sites — within 50 miles of the tagging site.

From 1257 pups tagged in this study, 144 recaptures were achieved.

I believe this is a study that should be repeated, with opportunities to pursue an active interest in charismatic marine animals much increased in the current era compared with the 1954-1975 period (with the exception of two years). For example, there are extremely popular coastal footpaths in Wales and SW England, while seal-watching trips and local as well as county seal groups across SW Britain have never been busier. The likelihood of successful recaptures is, evidently, so much greater than before.

In 1974, one year after sending a fieldwork team to Cornwall and Scilly, the Seals Research Division made another short-term foray, this time to Wales. It covered the period 20 September to 11 October. Although where sea conditions permitted and pups were espied, landings were made on beaches and swimmers investigated seal caves, only one visit was made per site in the 10 coastal areas into which the coast was sub-divided (except at Skomer). The scant results were published by the team leader — **Sheila S. Anderson, 1977**. Seals of all ages were counted and some pups were tagged. It was noted that 180 miles of the 430 miles of coast was not surveyed either because seals 'were known to be absent' or because of rough sea conditions.

A first population size for Wales, heavily reliant upon anecdote, was estimated. Populations north and south of Aberystwyth were estimated separately.

Between 1973 and 1977, Malcolm Cullen (Pembrokeshire National Park warden) identified grey seal pupping sites along the Pembrokeshire coast (Cullen, M.S., 1978, entitled *'The stock of grey seal (Halichoerus grypus) of Pembrokeshire, Dyfed, 1977,* published in Nature of Wales, volume 16). In the same period, Davis and Davis made a detailed behavioural study of seals breeding on Skomer in 1975 (J.E. Davis and H.M. Davis, 1976, unpublished report to West Wales Naturalists Trust entitled *'A study of breeding biology and pup mortality in Grey Seals (Halichoerus grypus) at Skomer Island, Dyfed, 1975, obtained for comparison with data collected after an oiling incident in 1974*). In the same year, a detailed but unpublished pup production count was made on Ramsey that included examination of seal cave sites for the first time.

The systematic Skomer pup production research was continued and developed by the M. and R.J.S. Alexander through the 1980's and published, for example, in a report to the Nature Conservancy Council entitled *'A Study of the Grey Seal (Halichoerus grypus) on Skomer Island, Dyfed, 1983-1985'.* This line of annual studies was continued through the 1990's by J. Poole. An example is submitted in 1999 as an unpublished Dyfed Wildlife Trust report to the Countryside Council for Wales entitled *'Grey Seal Breeding Census, Skomer Island.* In 1996, he submitted additionally an unpublished Dyfed Wildlife Trust report to the Countryside Council for Wales entitled *'Grey Seal Monitoring Handbook, Skomer Island.*

However, the most important and by far the best-funded and best-equipped grey seal study in Wales and the entire region of SW Britain in the twentieth century was directed by Mick Baines for the Dyfed Wildlife Trust (DWT), assisted by Earl, S.J., Pierpoint, C.J.L., and Poole, J. This covered the coast from Aberystwyth to Caldey Island and the funding through, primarily, the DWT was derived from the Countryside Council for Wales (CCW). The study was overseen by a steering group consisting of representatives from CCW, DWT, Pembrokeshire Coast National Park and the National Trust. Throughout, Skomer sites were surveyed separately by J. Poole.

Results were contained in Baines et al (1995).

The study area was divided into 11 sections. An initial report (Baines, 1992) described the results of a comprehensive site survey carried out in 1991, but were partly frustrated by sea conditions that rendered entry to many caves, especially those situated west of

Strumble Head, impossible. In spring and early summer of 1992, a full sweep of the caves between Aberystwyth and Ramsey was made. The intention of the survey was to visit each site every 15 days, or fewer, through the season of pup production — regarded as being between August and December. This resulted in annual total counts of pups per year between 1992 and 1994 of 1298, 1363 and 1332, these being located at up to 225 sites each year. From these figures, a total population of seals of all ages associated with pup production was proposed, being respectively 4578, 4806 and 4722 grey seals. It was suggested that due to a small number of pups possibly not recorded, the population be rounded up to about 5000. Pups were located in 28 site clusters (having no ongoing contact with this study I used the term 'seal locality' for such clusters in SW England). The total number of pups found at mainland sites slightly exceeded the combined total found at Ramsey and Skomer. The mean pupping date was, each year, in the first week of October, with pupping in caves occurring one week earlier than on beaches.

A 6.5m RIB was used throughout, requiring a boat handler who was also qualified to operate a VHF radio. A boat hand assisted the boat handler. A minimum of 2 full-time members of the survey team were required to be on board at each launch. Volunteers also rendered assistance, with mainly 2 being on board. 2 or 4 swimmers were deployed to enter caves or to land on beaches, sometimes via a smaller rubber dinghy. Given a full complement aboard, there would also be a data recorder and a photographer — the latter being required to photograph female seals in the water for identification purposes.

Pups were dye-marked where possible but the durability of the markings was problematic, with dyes becoming either almost or totally indiscernible — something that was also to be a problem in the first major grey seal study in North Wales.

Finally, an INTERREG project, Report No.3 was published by **Kiely, O et al., 2000.** This well-funded, well-organised and excellent study investigated, among other things, the seasonal distribution of grey seals at principal haul- out sites in the central and southern Irish Sea, including pup production. Cave sites were among the sites investigated. The novelty of this study, which ran between 1996 and 1998, was that it was the first year-round grey seal study in SW Britain (and Ireland) published that looked at pup production, moulting and other site use — such as resting between foraging trips.

The results showed seal distribution to be site-specific and seasonal. However, unlike results from west Cornwall, (for example) SE Ireland sites saw significant grey seal numbers year-round but peaked during the season of pup production (September to December) and of the moult (November to March). In general, seal counts were low in May and June, increasing through July to a peak in August before decreasing in September and remaining at that lower plateau through the breeding season until increasing again with the period of the moult. However, looking at SW England by comparison, each seal 'locality' — e.g. Land's End, Boscastle or Lundy — has an annual pattern of seal abundance in relation to the moult, pup production and so on that is consistent with itself rather than belonging to a regional norm. However, it is a comparison of seal use of different sites (mainly Irish islands versus mainly Cornish sea caves) and this may account for any differences.

The Stepping Stones to the Seal Caves: Early Insights

North Wales

A first simple study of grey seals at a North Wales site took place on the Dee Estuary recording seal counts for the West Hoyle Sandbank between 1951 and 1957 at approximately monthly intervals. The work was carried out by J.D. Craggs and N.F. Ellison and published in 1960 in the Proceedings of the Zoological Society of London, volume 135, part 3 and entitled 'Observations of the seals of the (Welsh) Dee Estuary'.

During her visit in 1974, described above in the South Wales section, **Sheila Anderson** (1977) spent three days surveying grey seals in Anglesey, then the Llyn Peninsular and finally the coast from Porthmadog to Aberystwyth — very few seals being sighted along the latter stretch. Despite making only a single visit per site, she identified correctly that the Llyn seals occurred primarily at sites between Porth Cadlan and Ynys Gwylan-fawr, with 11 pups being found. There were also assemblies of seals using the Tudwals. No pups were found, but 2 were reported from Bardsey and only one pup was found on the north coast. No pups were found on Anglesey or its islands, but 2 were reported from the Skerries.

She concluded that the North Wales population was very small, estimating 27–55 pups being born annually. She felt it was unlikely to show any marked increase in the future. She was correct in recognising that pups were born earlier on the Llyn (peak production 22 September) than, for example, on the Skerries (mid-October).

Around 1995, P. Hope Jones and H. Meredydd published a report entitled *'Trends in numbers of grey seals at Bardsey'*. It is based on weekly counts of seals between mid-March and early November under the auspices of the island Bird Observatory, between 1981 and 1993. Observations were restricted to favourite seal haul-out sites at Henllwyn and Porth Solfach (including Carreg yr Honwy, elsewhere named Ynys y Moelrhoniaid in Pennant, 1776).

Maximum seal counts increased from 75 in 1981 to 150 in 1993. It was noted that the pup born on the island in 1954 was *'for the first time in the memory of any of the inhabitants'*. Subsequently, occasional pup births were recorded until an 'unprecedented' 10 were located in 1986. By 1993, up to 5 pups were born annually at island sites, with possibly 3 of these being cave or 'cavelet' (mini caves or deep cliff hollows) sites.

The first substantial and year-round study of grey seals in this region was initiated and funded by the Bangor office of the (then) Countryside Council for Wales (CCW) — now Natural Resources Wales — from 2001. Mandy McMath managed the project and I was engaged to help design and to undertake the fieldwork. Results were presented in **Westcott, 2001.** A partial follow-up study presented in Westcott and Stringell (2002) was undertaken to verify whether the initial pup production results were anomalous.

To determine grey seal (and occasional harbour seal) distribution, as well as carrying out a literature review, the methods used in SW England were emulated by surveying the entire coastline from Aberystwyth in the south to Ynys Enlli/Bardsey in the west and the Dee estuary in the east. All associated islands, including Ynys Mon/Anglesey, were surveyed. Seal sites and potential sites were identified and as a result, six main seal 'localities' were studied. These were the Llyn Peninsular, Ynys Enlli, Ynys Mon West (including Ynysoedd y Moelrhoniaid/The Skerries), Ynys Mon East, the Ormes and the Dee estuary). As in SW England, a very small number of previously undiscovered seal caves (3) were located in the second year of the study. It is also likely that as some sites are used only intermittently (for example due to adverse environmental conditions), it would be sensible to assume a small number of seal caves may yet have escaped detection.

As in SW England, effort was made to visit sites three times every month through the year, or in the event of persistent heavy wave action, as possible. A very few sites were accessible from the land but the great majority were accessed from the sea. Also as in SW England, work was carried out (mainly) alone, making use of a wave ski. The reason for this contrast in methods with similar work carried out in SW Wales by Mick Baines and his team was twofold. Using the ski greatly minimised the potential carbon-footprint and, in any case, funding would not stretch to providing the daily boat support used in SW Wales.

A stronger element of boat support would have allowed more survey work to be undertaken quicker and would have allowed also better use to be made of fair-weather windows — although with tide times varying significantly around the region, in the event usually advantage was taken of working on lee shores; so relatively little potential survey time was lost. I had read and heard reports of seals aggressively cornering researchers for long periods on seal cave beaches. Although I never suffered that fate, the presence of the ski — potentially to be used as a shield — was always comforting in the cave darkness.

Survey work on Ynysoedd y Moelrhoniaid and Ynys Enlli always required boat support — hitching a ride with the lighthouse maintenance men, the supply boats, the RSPB or paying for a ride with one of the local crabbers. Occasionally, the CCW jet-boat *'Pedryn'*, skippered by Paul Turkentine, spent what was always a happy day in support.

A small minority of seal cave sites were used through the year whereas all island and sandbank sites were used the year-round.

In 2001, 102 pups were located of which 20 were stillborn or else had died before the time of weaning. The first pup was born on August 1, the last one on November 19. The onset of pup production occurred earlier in sea caves than on remote or island beaches. The statement in the report that the SW Llyn locality was, by far, the most important breeding locality in the region (50% of all pups located in the region were born here, mainly in quite small seal caves) is incorrect, in that new sites identified in 2002 near Ynys Arw in NW Ynys Cybi had been overlooked in both 1974 and 2001. This led to the misleading conclusion that, where the birth site was known, 63% of pups were born on remote and island beaches compared with 37% of pups born in seal caves. The locality where the onset of pup production was latest was Ynysoedd y Moelrhoniaid, northernmost of the North Wales seal localities. Unweaned pups spent long periods of time in the sea, apparently of their own preference in most observed instances.

Grey seals assembled in their largest numbers at differing times of year at West Hoyle Sandbank near the mouth of the Dee, Ynys Seiriol, Ynys Dulas, Ynysoedd y Moelrhoniaid, Ynys Enlli and at the Tudwals. The moult was observed between mid-November and late April on the three main islands off the Anglesey coast. Spring/summer counts were highest at the outlying sites: West Hoyle Sandbank and Ynys Enlli, as well as at the cluster of sites associated with the Tudwals.

Harbour seals were observed occasionally, most often and in the largest numbers (<4) at Ynys Dulas. They may occur in any month of the year but were not (yet) resident.

In 2002, 110 pups were located between August 18 and November 11. Of these, 9 were either stillborn or otherwise died before weaning. The SW Llyn (predominantly relatively small sea cave sites) remained the most important locality, with 45 pups born. The Ynys Cybi (NW Anglesey) locality saw a steep increase from 9 to 35 pups born, all in sea caves, including several in the 3 newly discovered sites, and none of which died before weaning. The steepness of the rise was due to environmental conditions rendering these caves more easily and more often accessible. In the region overall, 74 (c.67%) pups were born at sea cave sites with 36 (c.33%) born on remote or island beaches. The pattern of pup production resembled that for 2001, with pups born earlier in sea caves than at other sites and the Ynysoedd y Moelrhoniaid sites being the locality where pup production was latest. Most pups were again born in September and October.

In 2004, a slightly different survey of pup production took place between September 29 and November 8. The methods used examined a random sample of nursery sites at intervals of 7–12 days. The use of the CCW jetboat meant that in the end nearly every known site was investigated, with fieldworkers launching from the boat to access sites using wave skis. However, 19 days of potential survey work were lost due to adverse sea conditions.

102 pups were located of which 7 were stillborn or otherwise died before weaning. It is certain that earliest and latest born pups went uncounted. The Llyn Peninsular and Ynys Cybi localities were the most important localities in this survey, with 29 pups born in both. 55 pups were born in sea caves, 47 on remote mainland beaches or islands.

Since then, a major pup production survey was undertaken for the region in 2017, by Clarke, L.J. et al, which showed a massive increase in pup production at Ynys Enlli, as well as very considerable increases in pup production at open beach sites at Ynysoedd y Moelrhoniaid and the adjacent mainland of Anglesey locality of Trwyn y Gader. Additionally, it was found that the Ormes to Angel Bay had developed from a site only occasionally used to become a small but established breeding locality.

The Stepping Stones to the Seal Caves: Early Insights

Isle of Man

Chris Sharpe (2007) carried out the first pup production survey for the Isle of Man Department of the Environment. The small number of pups located were born in sea caves and on remote beaches, with the Calf of Man being their stronghold.

In mid-August 2001, I had made a substantial but incomplete sweep of the Calf of Man as well as SW and NE Man, to discover whether pup production had begun. Sea caves and the remote beaches were explored. Other grey seal sites may exist but time was short. 227 grey seals and 3 harbour seals were counted in a 4-day period. No pups were discovered but it was clear that most of the best-potential grey seal sites were the sea caves and beaches of the Calf of Man. Kitterland, a large skerry situated between the main island and the Calf, was the principal haul-out site at that time of year. Results were included in the 2002 report to CCW described above.

The Stepping Stones to the Seal Caves: Early Insights

Lundy

Lundy occupies an interesting position in the world of SW Britain grey seal distribution. The seal 'capital' for this region has long been Pembrokeshire and its islands (especially Ramsey and Skomer) while Cardiganshire. Cornwall, Scilly and South Devon represent lesser but important strongholds.

Lundy, at its closest point, lies just 11 miles off the coast of North Devon — a coast along which seals are surprisingly rare — and about 40 miles from the nearest neighbouring grey seal colony to the south-west, centred on the North Cornwall coast between Tintagel and Rusey High Cliff. If Lundy could be regarded as the hub of a wheel, other neighbours occur at the Saltee Islands, SE Ireland (c.100 miles), Skomer (45 miles), Ramsey (60 miles) and Cardigan Bay (varies between 45 and 125 miles). This gives Lundy the appearance of a cross-roads between two large, sub-regional grey seal populations as well as serving as the easternmost seal haunt of any size in the region of SW Britain. It also stands at the entrance to the strongly tidal Bristol Channel (known in earlier times as the Severn Sea).

Two early references to seal caves on Lundy refer to the one that has become, by far, the best-known. In his book, Chanter, J.R. (1877), writes:

The line of coast toward the south-west corner is very sinuous and contorted, and the cliffs of granite much broken and hollowed-out by the never-ceasing dash of the Atlantic waves, and many singular caves exist at their base. The most notable one is at the south end, and is called the Seal Cave from being the resort of these animals, at times in considerable numbers. The ordinary means of approach to it is by a boat in calm weather. It can, however, be reached at the low-water of spring tides by a dangerous descent over the cliffs. The cave is very well-known, as it has been the great object of attraction to adventurous sportsmen, whose main purpose in visiting the Island has been a campaign against those interesting but timid animals. The approach to the cave on the land side is by scrambling down a narrow track, just at the junction of the shale and granite, past a spot where a square cavity in the granite forms a seat called Benjamin's Chair, and thence round the face of the cliff by means of slanting ledges and the aid of a ladder, used to pass from one ledge to another, until it is reached. The cave itself is a vault some 60 feet in height and twelve in width, with a sandy bottom at its inner part, gradually rising and getting narrower and darker, until there is scarcely room to pass, and then suddenly opening into a spacious and lofty chamber to which the seals resort, and this again opens into smaller chambers beyond...

Later in the book, he continues:

Seals frequent the Island in considerable numbers. The only species identified is the common spotted seal (Phoca vitulina). (Note that this is an incorrect identification and that the reference should be to the grey seal). *No less than five have been killed at one time in the Seal Cavern* (Note this came to be known as Seal's Hole), *which is their principal place of resort; but they have been much diminished during the last few years, owing to their reckless persecution by the crews of pilot and tug-boats.*

Another early, vaguer, reference to seal caves appears in a book by L.R.W. Loyd (1925) It describes Seal's Cave as where the:

...seals have their headquarters and 'nursery'.

This scanty reference is here considered noteworthy as it may be the first reference to grey seal use of a sea cave in SW England as a site for pup production.

The first of the modern seal studies to take place on Lundy were conducted by Oliver Hook (1964). Working on the island between 1954 and 1957, his study periods were longer than yet attempted at any other SW England site, being between March and November (inclusive).

He appears to have investigated only one (well-known) seal cave site — Seal's Hole — confirming the earlier anecdotal account given by Loyd (1925) as well as occasional observations included since that time in various LFS Reports. He writes:

Lundy has always seemed to me to be essentially a maturing ground for grey seals but occasionally an odd pup or two is born there.

During the four years under review 8 pups have been found, all in Seal's Hole... Of these births, 2 are on the same day in successive years (1956 and 1957), and it would appear that these are pups of the same cow, both born on 6th July, a very early date for this region. It is not unknown for occasional pups to be born on outlying sites, such as Lundy, but it would seem that the Island does produce one or two pups each year, and probably has done so for a long time. In an attempt to discover other breeding sites on the Island the writer organised an inspection of the coastline from a motor-boat on 10th September, 1955, but other than Seal's Hole no caves or small beaches appeared to be likely, as far as could be seen under difficult conditions.

Much shorter visits were made by N.A. Clark and C.C. Baillie (1973). They described a survey conducted between 14th August and 6th September, beginning with an interesting assertion:

There is geographical diversity in the breeding habits of grey seals. Those of Devon, Cornwall and South Wales are 'cave' and cove breeders, rather than 'colony' breeders. It has been established that during the breeding season grey seals tend to 'home' to a specific location, we wonder could this be the case with Lundy?

That part devoted to cave studies was as follows:

As pup birth has been recorded in Seal's Hole, we wished to investigate the cave to explore its potential as a breeding site. It seems that the chamber is flooded by the spring tides but after the late summer springs have passed it is likely that a few square yards of sand beach would remain dry. We made three entries to the cave. On the first we left markers that were swept away by the spring tides. On the second, we again left markers but an aggressive bull seal and an equally aggressive juvenile did not allow us to re-enter the chamber to investigate the tide level.

The following year, the pair returned to conduct survey work for a slightly longer period, 27th August to 24th September, 1974, noting that 'severe gales interrupted observations considerably'. They write:

On 19th September we entered Seal's Hole and found 2 pups (living) aged probably three weeks or less with 3 cows present.

We believe it possible that there were other pups along the East Coast in caves to which we did not gain access ... Harrison Matthews points out that some caves may be used for hauling-out but not for breeding. This could possibly be the case in the large 'Puffin Gully Cave', as, when we entered the cave, no pups were present. However, the entire floor of the cave accessible to seals had been washed by considerable waves during the recent storms and the 2 dead pups seen on the 6th September almost certainly came from this cave...

They add in the Discussion:

It seems that breeding may occur more often on Lundy than has been generally supposed though more observation is needed... However, births have been recorded on Lundy in and between the first week of July and the first week of October. Thus, our observation period of four weeks may not account for all weeks in which pups were born.

In 'Brief visits to the sea-level caves on the east side of Lundy', published in the same report as above, they wrote — mainly accurately - of Puffin Gully Cave:

This is probably one of the largest caves on the Island ... When we penetrated the cave further, we were amazed at its size — it made Seal's Hole look insignificant. It is fairly straight so one can see the whole of the floor of the cave (200–250 feet). It varies from 15–30 feet wide and is widest about 100 feet in. We arrived at a pool about 60 feet in and were just about to go round when we heard shouts from Bob. These aroused some seals who were further in so we returned to the entrance only to find there was a large bull seal swimming a few yards out from the entrance. He was showing great interest in our activities and was not very worried about Bob's attempts to scare him. The swell had also noticeably increased. A seal on land is one thing, but in the water, it is quite another! We did not remain long in the water and scaled the slippery rock in record time. No less than 21 seals came out making a total of 25 in the cave. Again, it made the 4 or 5 occupants of

Nigel Clark (1976) writes alone of work undertaken in 1975. He describes finding more pups than had been located theretofore:

During 1975, 12 pups were found, though I expect a good many more than this were born… It is unlikely that any seals were born, except in caves, before the 14th October and not recorded. Seal's Hole was entered twice, the second occasion being the 22nd September, and only one pup was found. However, it is possible that pups were born after this date. Langham's Cavity was entered only once, on the 8th September, and at least one pup was present. The back of the cave could not be reached since the cow barred our way. Seals were present at the entrance to this cave all through the breeding season and it is possible that it was well enough protected for pups to survive during the severe storms which batter the West Coast in autumn. The swell at the entrance, however, was too great for another visit to be made later in the season.

Puffin Gully Cave was last entered on the 5th October and a total of 3 pups were found, one of which had definitely survived some very heavy seas on spring tides. This leaves only the possibility of pups being born in the unentered caves below Tibbett's Point and the ones not visited on the west coast. Three pups were found dead on the east side which had not been seen previously and I strongly suspect that all three of these pups came from the cave at Tibbett's Point…

I found only 12 pups. However, I would not be at all surprised if there had been 25 pups born on the island…

Lastly, he makes the first published observations of the moulting period published for the region of SW England (although P.Z. Mackenzie, the Isles of Scilly vet, mentioned large winter assemblies that would have been primarily for the purpose of moulting to Summers, which he published in his 1973 paper. Mackenzie's unpublished notes on the seals of Scilly are the foremost lost treasure of SW English grey seal research):

During a brief visit in December, 1975, it was noticed that the seal colony was halfway through moulting as there were a few seals which had not started moulting, a large number in various stages of moult and a few which had almost completed moulting. This seems very much earlier than the dates given for other colonies (Hewer 1974), but many will fall in line with the earlier pupping date observed on Lundy.

Neil Willcox (1986, 1987) took advantage of the 'unusually calm and mild September weather' to expand the effective physical range of exploration of the potential pup production sites, landing there from a boat as well as reaching some sites from the land. He writes that 17 pups were found:

...5 more than in any previous year. This is largely due to the discovery of 2 important new pupping areas which, between them, accounted for more than 50% of the total. Nevertheless, there are 2 reasons for believing that this year's figure is likely to be an under-estimate: Despite the excellent weather it was still impossible to enter a few of the caves, particularly those on the West. Note that the cave known as Langham's Cavity or Double Headed Zawn, in which a pup was found in 1975 was searched, but with no success. A cave South and almost immediately under Pilot's Quay appeared to be promising (a strong seal smell and seal activity outside) and would be worth future investigation. All those pups discovered in the last 10 days of September showed little sign of moulting their natal white coat and were consequently judged to be in the first 2 weeks of their lives. A few appeared to have been only very newly born. This suggests that a later visit might have revealed more pups, though a return to Deep Zawn did not. A live pup on the Diver's Beach on November 19th was a very late date. He concludes that Clark was likely to have been accurate when estimating annual pup production to total about 25, while noting that 'extreme birth dates' were not unusual. He also agreed with Clark's estimate that the main pupping period occurred between mid- and late September.

Stepping Stones to the Seal Caves: Early Insights

Caithness

The eminent eighteenth-century naturalist Thomas Pennant (1771) writes: *The seal-hunters in Caithness say that their growth is so sudden that in nine tides from their birth (108 hours), they will become as active as their parents. On the coast of that country are immense caverns opening into the sea, and running some hundreds of yards beneath the land. These are the resort of seals in the breeding time, where they continue till their young are old enough to go to sea, which is in about six or seven weeks. The first of these caves are near the Ord, the last near Thrumster; their entrance is so narrow as only to admit a boat; their inside very spacious and lofty. In the month of October, or the beginning of November, the seal-hunters enter the mouth of the caverns about midnight, and rowing up as far as they can, they land; each of them being provided with a bludgeon, and properly stationed, they light their torches, and make a great noise, which brings down the seals from the farther end in a confused body with fearful shrieks and cries: at first the men are obliged to give way for fear of being overborne, but when the first crowd is past, they kill as many as straggle behind, chiefly the young, by striking them on the nose; a very slight blow on that part dispatches them. The young seals of six weeks age yield more oil than their emaciated dams: above 8 gallons have been got from a single whelp, which sells from 6d. to 9d. per gallon; the skins from 6d. to 1s. each.*

In the month of November, numbers of Seals (a footnote adds here that 'Sometimes a large species near twelve feet long has been killed on the coast, and I have been informed that the same kind are found on the rock Hyskeir, one of the Western Isles.) *are taken in the vast caverns that open into the sea and run some hundreds of yards underground. Their entrance is narrow, their inside lofty and spacious. The Seal-hunters enter these in small boats with torches, which they light as soon as they land, and then with loud shouts alarm the animals, which they kill with clubs as they attempt to pass. This is a hazardous employ; for should the wind blow hard from sea, then these adventurers are inevitably lost.*

The Seal Caves Today: First Steps

I have no intention here of inflicting upon anyone an autobiography, except insofar as it is necessary to describes my experiences and, somewhere along the way, to relate anecdotes that colour in some of the atmosphere of specific events in the seal caves. I hope what follows can be read as an introduction to how I chanced on the stepping stones that led to the seal caves and to how others might choose to emulate and extend such research.

In 1989, Dieter Klein — then acting as my agent — obtained for me a contract with Century-Hutchinson to write a book about British seals. It yielded me a signing-on fee of £2,000.

I had become interested in seals from 1983 onward while living in Dartmouth where not only did grey seals haul-out on the rocks of the Mewstone archipelago just north of the entrance to the River Dart, but they also frequented the waters of the estuary on a daily basis through the year. That remains unchanged to this day. One of the great pleasures of those lovely days was to take my daughter upstream or out to the Mewstone to enjoy the sights, sounds and the atmosphere of the seals.

This fledgling interest in seals intensified in 1988, the summer of the Great Seal Plague, as the media came to call it. It came to be understood by researchers as the phocine distemper epizootic. Around the North Sea basin, more than 17,000 harbour seals were known to have died from the effects of the phocine (seal) distemper virus. Thousands more died but their bodies were not recovered or counted.

Intense efforts were deployed by organisations and volunteers to recover the seal corpses as well as ailing seals manifesting symptoms of the virus. It is probably fair, with the benefit of hindsight, to characterise these efforts as well-intentioned, but actually unhelpful to the seals, in that they helped to spread a virus as yet unrecognised. Neither is this a detached Olympian view, for I was numbered among the volunteers.

Over the following year, I used my signing-on fee from Century-Hutchinson to travel around the islands of Britain, trying to visit the known seal strongholds, the people who were studying the seals and the people trying to tend injured and ailing seals with a view to returning them to the marine environment and what passes for a normal life. Simultaneously, I was writing my manuscript.

The travelling, exploring, listening, reading and writing took just 6 months, at the end of which I presented my manuscript, receiving in return an additional fee. Quite properly, I was told by Century-Hutchinson that the manuscript would require a considerable amount of editing. However, rather than knuckling down to what, ultimately, could have been a happy and interesting chore, I decided that what I preferred to do was to follow the exceptional inspiration of George Steven and to run with and elaborate the baton John Prime had proffered in his paper of 1985:

A more accurate assessment of the size of the Cornwall grey seal population would be obtained by regular surveys of all the pupping sites throughout the breeding season, from the beginning of September to the middle of October.

Seeing there was work to be done and without a second thought I embarked on that work. With another nod to the benefit of hindsight, the more mature course would have been to continue with both the research and the writing. However, the sun was shining, I was abounding with energy and curiosity and I felt immortal, so I made the choice to abandon that manuscript or, more particularly, the chair and to immerse myself again in the outdoor world.

All I can say in defence of my choice is that, instead of learning and relating seals through others, I have lived them for the past 30 years, learning as much as I have been able through physical exploration and direct observation, and learning the rest through papers published by Professor Paul Thompson, by the seal scientists of the excellent Sea Mammal Research Unit and by all the others. Most inspiring and helpful of all in his advice concerning how to function effectively as a researcher in the absence of funding, as well as the most admirable of all the seal researchers, was Lex Hiby. Although decades have passed now, since last we met, his advice remains luminous, welcome and relevant.

Where to begin? Where to end, and to what end?

I decided I would aim to describe the grey seals of SW England. Here, that means Cornwall, the Isles of Scilly, Devonshire and Lundy, whose borders mark their regular range in the region. Seals may occur anywhere around the coasts of Britain at any time during their travels but their regular haunts in SW England I came to understand are confined to those places named above.

As you have seen from what is written above, investigation of the literature already existing on the subject was not confined to reading scientific journals. Historical references to grey seals — often not yet identified as such, or mis-identified as 'common' or 'brown' seals — were particularly interesting in a region where I could confirm almost immediately the discoveries of those who went before me: that their sea cave haunts are an important element in their lives.

Whether in the West Country, Wales or Caithness, historical references going back at least to the late sixteenth century describe seal use of sea caverns or holes of the cliff. The particular importance of these non-scientific anecdotes is that they provide evidence that seal use of caves has been well-known, locally, for centuries. It is reasonable to assume this behaviour goes back millennia and that it is absolutely not a modern reflex. It is not a retreat to the last secret places, made in response to the phenomenon of increasing leisure use of the coastal zone exerting pressure on sites previously used by seals. While that is an element in the wide picture, clearly some grey seals have always chosen to make use of sea caves.

The Seal Caves Today: Finding Them

Coming mainly from the sea, I surveyed the full length of the coasts of Cornwall, Scilly, Devonshire and Lundy between 1989 and 1993, aiming to identify every seal site. Some of these sites have been destroyed since by cliff collapses and cave erosion. Other new sites will have been founded as a result — something of which I have sought to keep apace in my site-based seal database.

Many of the initial results were formalised in a thesis for which I was awarded an MSc by the University of Greenwich in 1993. I had been encouraged in this by my tutor, Mark Simmonds, who had invited me to conduct this work under the auspices of the University from 1991.

Coming from the sea. It sounds simple enough, compressed into a short sentence.

At the very outset, I had to seek a water craft that would be fit to help me do sea cave research on shores renowned for being surf-bound and along coasts offering relatively few safe havens. It had to carry me into the gloom and the dark of sea caves. It had to be sufficiently robust to withstand collision with rocks in the cave confines without shipping water. I needed to be able to disembark on to whatever shore I found within to complete my site survey with least prospect of damaging misadventure to myself or to the craft. It had to carry me safely back into the ever-welcome light. Furthermore, it had to carry me safely through any surf and over any incoming waves in the vicinity of the sea caves and remote beaches all the sea miles back along the coast to the point from which I had launched.

At the launching and landing site — usually a beach, sometimes a harbour — it had to be something I could carry without assistance back to my vehicle, often up steep cliff paths, as well as being something I could carry either inside my van or upon its roof.

There at the end of the 1980s, I was tempted to buy a sea kayak, but was concerned at the risk of capsizing in the cave surf in darkness and running the risk of damaging my head or face or being unable to slither to safety from the cockpit if I found myself in difficulty in a maze of rocks and surf. Additionally, I was concerned at its unwieldy length. I was soon to discover that many sea caves have narrow fairways and that these would have made turning about extremely awkward or impossible.

Therefore, I chose to use a wave ski, known as a surf ski to some. The one I have used is white and the construction is of polypropylene. It measures approximately 2.8 metres in length and 85 centimetres maximum width. On the underside near the stern — what I knew initially as a skeg, but have since learned to call a fin — exists to assist steerage and also balance. On the top surface, the paddler settles into an indented sitting place. Forward of this are two long furrows, into which the legs can be settled, culminating in two toe- loops under and against which the toes can be braced while paddling is under way.

In appearance, the wave ski closely resembles a thick-bodied surfboard except that the polypropylene is a hard rind around a hollow interior. It varied in height between the top and bottom surfaces to up to 15 centimetres. It has no in-built storage space. It was a close relative of the rescue boards then being used by lifeguards on Cornish beaches – something that I qualified to be.

One final and crucial characteristic of the wave ski is that so long as the mid- stem of the paddle is tied to the forward part of the ski and so long as the paddler remains attached to the ski via an ankle leash, everything essential to recovery in the event of a capsize remains available throughout. Furthermore, being buoyant and tough, the ski could function to some extent as a shield in the event that the paddler was in the sea (but attached by the ankle leash) being driven on to rocks.

Any health and safety plan would incorporate such a requirement. Additionally, it would specify the need for a helmet and a lifejacket to be worn. Indeed, I was advised to wear a helmet in the caves and did experiment with one. However, I found it disrupted my ability to hear clearly — something I found to be of particular importance in the caves: regularly, I would switch off my lamp and listen for the unseen things in the dark, as the sense of hearing seemed enhanced in such places — and so for head protection a woollen hat, a bandana or a peaked cap served. Others, of course, would be best-advised to wear a helmet.

I did learn the hard way to attach the paddle and myself via the ankle leash to the ski. There was an early September day during the 1990s when I had been checking seal sites under North Cliffs, between Bassett's Island and somewhere west of Godrevy Point. There had been no menace promised by the weather forecast. Indeed, it was a lovely sunny day with the sea being all but calm because the wind was south-easterly, force 2: perfect there and then for visiting these particular seal sites without risk of misadventure.

There was no need of haste and thus I came by leisurely stops and starts under the blue skies in sunshine around Navax Point, in and out of the lovely enormity of Kynance Cave to Kynance Cove and then to Mutton Cove. It was while visiting those sites that the weather became transformed. Whipped out of reach was the kindly south-easterly and, in its place, swaggered a south- westerly that in half an hour cranked up to what I estimated to be a force seven. Gone was the tranquil sea. Now, white horses and a short, steep swell were abroad.

I had different options. I chose the wrong one and then wrong again. I chose to make the shortest paddle against the wind to attempt a landing on the rock shelf below nearby Godrevy Point — something I had achieved several times previously in similar conditions. The first part I achieved after something of a struggle but then I had to achieve landfall without smashing my skeg. Consequently, I decided rather than surf ashore I would catch the back of a breaking wave and be tugged ashore thereby at a less headlong speed. This, I managed; however, it was still a landfall of sufficient violence to smash the skeg.

Immediately, there in the white water, I was stripped of my ability to steer. Like handling a car on black ice, I could not prevent the ski shearing sideways at speed towards a nearby inlet that looked conical as the hat of a dwarf, but a hat that was a total commotion of boiling white water. I was swept over the edge into this commotion. Ski, paddle and myself parted, although I had no space to give it thought at the time because — immediately — I was being swept at madcap pace toward the innermost point of the inlet, or to the tip of the dwarf's hat. All I gave thought to in the moment was that something of me was about to be broken, so violently was I bound to be smashed against the rocks. The thought developed into a question simply answered: would I prefer to break an arm rather than my skull? And so I folded one arm about my head, ready to take the impact.

In the event, I think what happened was that the very force of the incoming surf rebounded from the innermost rocks of the inlet, rebounding with me caught at its heart but in a way wonderfully miraculous. Somehow it had pillowed me and thus preserved me against making least contact with the rocks. Almost as fast as I had been swept in, now I was swept seaward, but not so fast that I was unable to retrieve my ski and haul myself aboard. Thus mounted, there was a second, less fearsome, run with the surf into the inlet before I was flushed out for a second time and this time able to retrieve my paddle. Thereafter, I paddled seaward as powerfully as I could and although the steerage was squiffy; I began to make slow headway around the Point — probably another wrong choice but not, this time, one for which I was punished.

It took me at least 45 minutes to paddle about a quarter of a mile against the wind and the messy swell to reach safety on the nearest sandy shore, just to the west of the headland.

Funnily enough, although there were rivals, my principal memory of that drama while at risk in the churning surf was of the people staring down at my vicissitudes from the cliff-tops, just as though they were watching someone on television. It seemed that no-one thought to call for help from the rescue services. Maybe they had more faith in my ability to survive the misadventure than I had felt for that brief, memorable span of time. Or else, maybe they recognised the rescue services couldn't have arrived in time to save me.

Here, then, despite the folly — entirely my failure — described above, is a notably stable craft well-suited to the inshore zone of water that I was using. It would be fair to describe it as a sea donkey when set beside the much speedier racehorse thoroughbred that was the sea kayak. It is true that the kayak would have made much lighter work of the coastal passages I was to make between launch points and sea caves, but the donkey has proved to be a trusty steed, has never let me down and I would trade her for no other.

Furthermore, the ski has proved to be the most portable of all the craft I could have chosen. Carriage is facilitated by looping one blade of the paddle under the lower of the two toe loops while the ski is standing upright and wedging the blade at right angles to the stern end of the ski. Carriage is achieved by standing the ski upright, bows down, leaning the stem of the paddle against your shoulder and then taking there the full weight of the ski on the central stem of the paddle. The ski is swung up so that it rests approximately parallel to the ground while being almost horizontal on the (for example) right shoulder. When settled thus, the left hand grasps the loop through which the front paddle blade has been thrust. Thereby, this hand holds the ski steady against whichever way the wind might seek to blow it. Or, in the event of a strong wind blowing and an allowing substrate, the ski can be dragged along behind while reversed, using one of the two hand-straps situated behind the seat.

The wave ski is as light as can be — lighter than a sea kayak — but grows wearisome during portage. Nevertheless, it can be carried for a kilometre without distress, further still — with increasing discomfort — so long as the wind does not blow too fiercely.

I have used several paddles. Since the stem of one broke in my hands while I was paddling shoreward from the Tudwals off the North Wales coast, I have always used a carbon fibre stem because I was advised it is less likely to break than any other. The paddle doubled as my crude measuring stick for determining the cave dimensions and the extent of different sub-stratum types. Including the blades, usually it measured about 2.03 metres in length, while blade-length varied but currently measures 47cms. I ringed the paddle stem with electrician's tape at intervals of 30 centimetres from the left-hand paddle to assist in the making of lesser or more detailed measurements.

Once I had decided upon the choice of water craft, the next imperative was to identify what would become the tools of my trade.

If I was to facilitate work in dark places, obviously, I needed to carry a waterproof lamp. I learned immediately that small torches such as a head torch or a simple water-resistant torch in a rubber casing were useless. In the comparatively vast space of all sea caves, their beams were totally consumed and rendered useless by the greedy darkness. Following an expensive period of experimentation, I went on to misuse two and a half decades-worth of Kowalski 1250 diving lamps that always provided superb illumination. The problem with this lamp — mine, not theirs — was that it was designed to be used exclusively underwater by divers and not above the surface, as I was mainly using them. This continual misuse caused them, eventually, to malfunction. Most recently, I have been using a Finn Light, which I have found to be as effective a light source as the Kowalski's, if less easy to carry.

To avoid becoming parted from the lamp, I have used unbreakable twine, so that it would remain at all times attached thereby to a carabiner on my belt. While I was working on cave beaches or in their shallows, the torch was hand-held and the precaution was hardly necessary (except that it might have been dropped and lodged in some inaccessible place between the more massive boulders or in a murky pool).

At many other times the attachment was essential, for example, while paddling on waters of unknown depth in total darkness one hundred metres or more in from the cave entrance. Then, I had to hold the light between my bent knees, being glad of the attachment when I bumped into or over rocks. I might also be being bumped — inadvertently rather than deliberately — by the seals that, oftentimes, were around or languidly submerging under the ski in the otherwise encompassing darkness.

There were alarming times when an assembly of seals would stampede down off cave beaches with the single desire to reach the security of the water. Such events should always be expected around high water, when some cave beaches are crowded with seals. It was why I made the huge majority of seal cave visits in the low half of the tidal cycle, aiming to avoid or at least to minimise the inevitable disturbance and pandemonium. At such times, they behaved as if blind to the ski, battering it in passing and occasionally carrying me backwards clear of the water on their undulating backs. This happened mainly by surprise in confined channels and was probably equally alarming to both parties. Definitely it was a time for having the torch securely attached to my belt via the carabiner.

Also attached to my body — to a leg — was a small, sheathed diver's knife, the principal purpose of which was to cut myself free of occasionally entangling derelict monofilament fish netting drifting or snagged in cave-beach approaches and interiors.

The final essential items of equipment were a pair of dry-bags, one having a 60-litre capacity, the other 40 – 50 litres, so that the smaller one could be stowed inside the other. The smaller bag carried the essential recording gear used on the expeditions. I carried notebooks, pencils, a penknife, a spare torch, a camera with a lens-wiping cloth, the sound-recording unit, a mobile phone and a towel — the latter to be worn around the shoulders while I was working so that before using my other tools, the damp or grit could be wiped from my hands.

Why use two dry-bags rather than just one?

Initially, courtesy of always trying to keep costs to a minimum, I used only a solitary dry bag. This worked for a while but eventually a day arrived when I had crossed a boulder beach and swum on around a small headland to reach just inside the entrance to a very large and remote sea cave. The sea had been quite rough — marginal in terms of whether I was going to reach it or turn back — so I was feeling elated on the first cave beach while I knelt, unclipped the fastening and then unrolled the top of the bag.

That elation ceased the moment the sea-water began pouring out of the innards of the no longer dry-bag. Inside, my camera, an external flash-gun, a sound recording unit and my mobile phone were all destroyed.

Evidently, the skin of the dry-bag had been punctured.

Along the way I had needed to rest the dry-bag on the rocks at different times. I had also been knocked by the sea swell against cliff walls and brushed against them while walking along ledges between different swimming points, sometimes allowing the dry-bag to fend me off. Not everywhere but in some places, barnacles covered these sea walls. Barnacles must have pierced the quite tough but not indestructible skin of the dry-bag. Between-times, the swims were sufficiently extended that even though the dry-bag in effect mainly floated on the surface; it was time enough to fill it with water. It took many months to replace the equipment which, thenceforward, would always include two dry-bags — the outer one of which could be punctured and admit water as long as it protected the inner bag against the same.

Preferring to travel as light as possible at all times, I have preferred also to use the ski as little physically encumbered as possible. Therefore, I have never worn a full-length wet-suit because I have found it always to be oppressively restrictive. A dry-suit, although I own one, made me far too hot. Most often, I have worn only surfer's baggies (in effect, swimming trunks that reach the knee) and always I wore ankle-length wet-suit boots, for essential foot protection against abrasive cave floor rocks. During the coldest months, I wore a 'shortie' wet suit, the arms of which reached midway down over my upper arms while the legs reached midway down my thighs. In addition, I wore — occasionally — a woollen hat or a bandana. More often, I wore a peaked cap — in strong sunlight but also in rain and hail or when much spray was being blown off the crests of waves, making my eyes sting in the absence of the useful peak. Only in hail or snow did I ever wear wet-suit gloves.

These, then, were my little-changing accoutrements that served through 30 years of seal studies. You may wonder why I did not emulate Summer's and Prime's surveys by using inflatable rubber boats powered by outboard motors.

Aside from the carbon footprint and the noise issues, from beginning to end, I was never able to afford such luxurious tools.

For a very long time, from 1989 until 2001, I received none but the most minor grants to aid the seal research — a trend that seems likely to continue in the foreseeable future. However, Cornwall Wildlife Trust was particularly supportive through that period, notably in the form of Paul Horak and Mark Nicholson, who publicised my efforts and results and also introduced me to the public as 'Cornwall's Seal Man'. Subsequently, they put out an appeal to raise money to support the seal studies which ultimately furnished me with £10,000. This precious windfall helped me to fully equip myself for the first time as well as to get around the West Country to the remoter launch-points during the succeeding years that allowed me to continue my explorations of the entire coast. I will always be grateful to Paul and Mark, as well as to the Cornwall Wildlife Trust, both for that and for helping me feel less lonely in my work.

In the period 1989 to 2001, I tried a variety of ways to earn money to support both my family and the research. Most enjoyable of these was leading wildlife cruises out of the Dart River and north along the coast to Berry Head. The advertised highlight, but also my personal highlight, was to pause by the Mewstone to observe the grey seals at their easternmost rocky haul-out site, regularly used, on the north coast of the English Channel. A grey seal outpost. During these trips, I sold a series of seal postcards based on photographs I had taken and, from 1997, as well as copies of a book I had written entitled 'Grey Seals of the West Country and their Neighbours'. During the same period, and while working on the wildlife cruises; in addition, I offered evening badger watches on Dartmoor. I took groups of up to 12 people initially to look at badger-shaped tunnels through the bracken and badger latrines, culminating in a walk around the excavated spoil heaped by the badgers outside their sett entrances. Here was always the outside possibility of finding a badger skull or interesting fragments of pottery. Later, I took the groups deeper into the moor to watch a sett from which often the badgers emerged in full daylight. As the look-out station was beside a lane, subsequent retreat in darkness to the cars could be achieved with minimal risk of misadventure.

These were very happy times, very happy ways to earn a summer living. Otherwise I was poor as a church-mouse. Even so, I never envied the lavishly-funded expeditions into Cornwall by Summers or Prime, partly because they did so little to advance the initial insights into the where and when of seal cave/seal site use achieved by Steven. If anything, their disappointments were my incentives.

I did regret that I failed to achieve a closer working relationship with Mick Baines and his team doing their partly similar work looking at pup production including at sea cave sites in W and SW Wales between 1992 and 1994. Although there was a contrast in the methods we employed — namely in that they used mainly RIB's to reach the vicinity of the caves before deploying swimmers to undertake the survey work whereas I used the wave ski both to approach and survey the candidate sites — there were similarities in our output. Had we collaborated, I think I would have been the principal beneficiary because they were a team whereas I was a lone and often very lonely wolf; but the Welsh team was advised to focus strictly on the work they had been funded to do and so the opportunity never evolved.

Nevertheless, if I could proffer another potential research baton in the spirit of Prime, I would like to see the political borders erased from the research and have attention paid to the seal haunts from Devonshire to Scilly northward up the Welsh coasts to the Isles of Man and Rathlin, west to Ireland, in a three-year, year-round study of seals using the sea caves, beaches, islands, islets, estuaries and at sea. Beyond seal research, the objective would be to install an integrated research and management system for sites and sea areas used by the seals similar to the tri-partite collaboration practiced by the Netherlands, Germany and Denmark in managing the seal populations of the Wadden Sea.

Seal Cave Research: The Early Days

In the early years, I was earning a living working mainly in Devonshire while living mainly at Poljigga, near Land's End, less than 2 miles from what was to be my principal research locality throughout all the years of this adventure. For the sake of a probably inadequate fig-leaf of privacy, as well as reference, here it shall be called Seal Bay.

I began the research with a double objective, the first of which was to identify every site used by grey seals in the coastal zone of Cornwall, Scilly, Devonshire and Lundy. This began with some trawling through literature on the subject, not only scientific records but also historical references in books, as described earlier. It was especially pleasing to rediscover seal haunts first mentioned hundreds of years ago and this helped, entirely properly, to stifle any sense I might have had that I was the first person ever to visit, for example, some of the more remote seal caves. Another comment supporting that view I heard in those early days, with reference to caves in the vicinity of St Agnes. It told of how, a generation or two before the present day (then, in the early 1990's), when they were boys, the man telling the tale and his friends had swum in and out of the sea caves there, some of which were also being used by seals.

One of these caves is mentioned also by Winston Graham in his second series of Poldark books, subsequently further popularised as a television series. The Great Seal Hole he mentioned proved to be one of the most dramatic of the SW England seal caves; but more of that later. The moral of the tale, happily to my way of thinking, is that not all accurate and interesting references to seals and their haunts are confined to scientific papers.

Neither was library and internet research confined to anecdotal treasures or to papers in scientific journals. Some references to seals are found marked on Ordnance Survey maps among which most interesting of these were the 6" to the mile maps held in libraries. As well as containing the exceptionally precious references to 'seal holes', here was the best chance of finding the names of sites not included on the lesser scale Ordnance Survey maps available in shops. Always, it mattered to me to call a place by its true name. In a way, recovering the names of sites all but lost to general usage was one of the great pleasures of this part of the adventure, being one of the only ways to retrieve the little we can of the history of specific but unconsidered places.

Another source of guidance to the seal places emerged following illustrated talks I had given about seals in localities around the south-west. In their aftermaths, people would share their own sightings. Of these, probably none were as well-informed and helpful as the inshore potters and netters working small boats from local harbours — the people who I feel have more to do with seals, either as neighbours or as business rivals, than anyone but the seal naturalists and scientists themselves.

However, the first and by far the largest, most challenging of all the adventures alluded to here was the survey of the entire coast. For example, it did not occur to me until experience and discovery dictated otherwise that a minimum of several visits is required, in the different seasons, before the status of any site used by the seals could be fully described. Moreover, the farther the sites were from my Land's End home, generally, the more daunting and less likely to be complete was each local exploration — except where I took up residence in such a locality for a prolonged period, as when fulfilling a contract for Natural England or what was to become Natural Resources Wales.

The problems were, primarily, the accessibility of sites during the low water half of the tidal cycle, to which — nearly always — I sought to confine my work. Always, this was determined by wind speed, wind direction and their influence on sea state, further complicated by oceanic weather systems far offshore. With a background as a surfer, I never thought I would feel such a thing, but wave action — offshore or onshore — was the bane of my research effort, as it had been for all those who one way or another preceded me into the seal caves. Aside from bigger swells making access even to the localities of the caves impossible for sometimes prolonged periods of time, there were lesser but equally thwarting challenges. Being squeezed into the seal caves, waves actually grew in height.

An example is that on a day of mainly quite small waves, they could become twice as high inside a cave, smashing down with force to become surf somewhere in the interior. There, the surf might rebound off walls or eruptive rocks, or suck back strongly off the shore, creating highly confused and unstable conditions. Many times, I have sat astride my ski wondering whether or not to proceed and enter the cave. Many times, I have found what felt initially like marginal conditions proved not to be so, close to my destination and so I turned away from exploring the cave that day. Being in the midst of such an event, cave acoustics amplified the sounds of the surf. I hope I have not been alone in sometimes finding those thundery, thumping sounds daunting.

In localities such as the Boscastle coast — even as I write 'such as', I am acutely aware that nowhere is 'such as' that coast — the potentially perfect weather conditions prevailing inshore can be complicated by storms raging out in the Western Approaches, sending their heavy pulses shoreward to render cave entry impossible. Local knowledge, therefore, is always essential.

The reality of the first four years of exploration was that, as indicated above, I chased weather windows or, more correctly, quiet sea state windows. Given allowing conditions, and recognising that the great majority of my fieldwork was conducted alone and during the 6 to 7-hour window around the time of low tide, I made mainly there-and-back passages along the sections of coast where seals might have been. This meant I excluded beaches that were easily accessible to people — because seals mainly shun these, unless exhausted or sick — although if such sites were flanked by cliffs, then those cliffs were explored for their sea caves or lack of them. In reality, I was exploring the coast in approximately 5-mile sections. Every 'hole in the cliff' was investigated, as were all the skerries, islands and islets along the way.

Plan views, drawn approximately to scale and noting substrate types, were drawn for many potential seal caves so as to make future access less problematic, and in the event of any seal-signs, notes were made. These might have referred to tracks, seal-shaped hollows in soft substrates, the fishy 'scent' of seals, faecal remains, seal corpses and live seals. Wherever I found tracks or hollows, I erased them before departing the cave to ensure there was no prospect of double-counting them. Anecdotes from local people relating to seal use of sites were also recorded.

Subsequently many but not all of these records were entered into a Microsoft Access database, designed at the Bangor office of the Countryside Council for Wales (now renamed Natural Resources Wales) initially for the years of seal monitoring I was to carry out in North Wales.

In this database, the first page of every site was given a name with a site number. The Ordnance Survey reference was included. The largest amount of space was set aside for a site description, including measurements where possible.

The second page describes access to the site, including best launch points, landing places and all the potential navigation hazards between the two.

The third page reviews current site use and impacts bearing upon them, from fishing to extraction, collection to leisure use, sewage outfalls to military use, etc.

The fourth page is used to display a plan view for the site and its vicinity.

The final 'chapter' is dedicated to each survey event for that site exclusively. Page one gives the date, sea state, the start and finish time of the survey, the tide height at low water, the times of high tide and low tide plus wind direction and speed. Page two records every pup found at the site during that visit. Page three records separately males, females, immatures as well as unidentified seals present on site during that visit. A box is here available to record the number and sex of seals in the sea adjacent to the site, as well as any comments. Page four relates to disturbance observed or known to have occurred recently at this site.

Working Inside the Caves: The Survey-Proper

All across SW Britain, waves spend themselves on great spreads of shell-sand beaches. Some burst into final glorious expression against the base of renowned cliffs, shaking the very foundations of the world as they explode whitely up vertical faces of rock. Still others run into the black-entranced sea caves. Have you ever winced, hearing the repeated dull, elemental booming as the surf rebounds from the back of those confined, mysterious spaces? Have you wondered, as I have, how any life might survive such percussion, knowing only too well that we could not? Have you watched spent waves recoiling into the daylight only to collide and make more commotion with the following wave?

How impossible it would be to swim and survive in such waters. For us. Yet, can that be a head you see, that small black buoy-like mark holding position as if at anchor amid the acres of white water crowding in upon the cave entrance, surging back and forth? What manner of mythic, colandered creature can remain at ease, so still, in so much tugging, swirling, surging and elemental violence?

Perhaps it is as the very essence of life that it does indeed survive and even flourish in wild places such as these black sea mouse-holes appear to be when seen from the tops of the high cliffs. Within these mouse-holes, seals take their rest, produce and care for their deceptively helpless-seeming young. Here, also, in entrance waters or low tide pools, they mate, often concluding these encounters with prolonged episodes of extraordinary tenderness. Here, in these seemingly inhospitable refuges, they go about their commonplace, round-the-year cycle of simple being.

If you are very lucky, you will have heard these caves singing, for there is much more here than the monstrous percussion of the surf to be heard. If threads of the wind bring it your way, you might hear a weird wailing of natural choral song. If you have that much luck, then you will be hearing one of the most evocative natural sounds produced anywhere in the British Isles, amplified by the marvellous acoustic chambers that the seal caves are: the crying of the grey seals. More precisely, the singing of the female seal; for it is not, in fact, song but an eloquent oral rebuff to male seals who have been pestering her. They have interrupted her rest where she lays, in the oval hollow that her great body has made in the sand; sometimes the rebuff is snarled, open-mouthed. Sometimes it finds expression as a prolonged, ululating wailing.

Deep inside the caves, there are seals — in wintertime, at a very small number of sites, scores of seals — resting on beaches, often in total darkness. In autumn, they use these places for their nurseries. Here, they raise their young until they are weaned. At times of need, when the wilder seas run, no-one sees the seal mothers insert their bodies between their fragile pups and the race of the surf, acting as temporary maternal breakwaters. At this time too, in deep-water cave entrances or in tide pools remaining at low water, they mate. In winter, great and overwhelmingly single-sex assemblies gather now that the pups are gone. They emanate a fine, fishy perfume as they go through the physical discomforts of the annual moult. In the equable micro-climate of these caves, steam rises from bodies resting close together. For they are warm, being lavishly blubbered against the cold of the sea where more than 85% of their lives are lived.

At any point through the year in all weathers, some caves are occupied by varying numbers of seals, using them for their own reasons. Young seals, making their first odysseys away from the sea cave nursery site, often find refuge at other sea cave sites during their first year of life. The great majority use them simply as places of rest between fishing trips or while on journeys to visit the neighbours. As for the caves themselves, many are used exclusively as nursery sites.

As remarked previously, I have found that my sense of hearing is almost as important to me as my sight in the sea caves. How it works, I do not know, but I believe it helps me sense, for example, head-high projections or other obstructions. It often locates the presence or the location of any seal before sight comes into play, mainly because I try to work as deep into the caves as possible without switching on my lamp which is certain then to alert or possibly disturb any seals within.

Therefore, disliking having my ears covered, I wear either a woollen hat or else a scarf tied around my head like a bandana. This absorbs the worst of any knocks when you are moving with great caution. Also, it gives a fraction of a second warning of a collision, often in just enough time to take avoiding action. In these situations, it is best to use your wall-side arm as an 'antenna'. Keep it stretched out before and slightly above you. This, also, will help protect your head. At the same time, because you may slip or fall with the next step, it remains essential to give continuous background awareness to how/which way you might so do to avoid injury.

Additionally, it is essential to scan up, down and around all the time. As well as physical hazards, you have to remain aware that a seal might not only be resting on the main fairway or in cubby-holes but, occasionally, will be resting on a ledge above your head.

Where a tide pool obstructs your progress, allow 12 minutes for any seal resting therein to emerge. This should be sufficient time for any seal sleeping submerged to surface to breathe. I have never recorded a seal remaining submerged even when asleep for longer than that. The danger here, as Ronald Lockley discovered in Pembrokeshire, is that seals resting there may bite.

Of the small number of tools used in caves during survey-work, the one most likely to be subject to malfunction is the camera and its lens. The first imperative is to make sure the camera is switched on at the time it is prepared for use, following the opening of the dry-bags after achieving cave entry. The second is to be sure that attached to the camera is a lens cloth (in a mini dry-bag), because condensation forms on both lens and viewfinder in the sea cave environment.

Apart from photographing the cave interior, the most important targets are the head-and-neck patterns of the female seals (differing on left and right profiles and serving as seal 'fingerprints', as every pattern of markings is unique as a human fingerprint) and the snout shape and any neck markings of the male seals.

The camera must be used in conjunction with the torch, in order to achieve sharp focus, but it is vital to avoid shining the torch directly into the eyes of the seals. It is recommended you shine it just to left or right of the target side of the head/neck, if focussing on one, and either just above or below the heads of an assembly. Direct light irradiates seal markings and so renders captured images unusable.

If working alone and you are in a position to take shots, it is sensible to get into the habit of holding the torch between your lower thighs — just above your knees — leaving your hands free to keep the camera steady.

Remember that compact digital (CD) cameras may have a delay between achieving good focus and capturing the image. If seals are moving, follow them with the camera in this interval or your specific target will move out of frame. Remember also that CD cameras require an interval of 'recovery' between shots, especially where the flash has been used. Repeat shots need to be taken at camera speed, not your speed.

Regards what images you need to catch, I suggest that normally you take first a shot of the cave environment, including all the seals in the image. Not only does this 'set the scene' but it gives you a chance to re-count the seals when looking at the enlarged image on your laptop screen and also to double-check that you were correct in how you assigned sexual and age identity. You may also then notice details that you missed at the time, such as an incidence of netted or tagged seals. It may also serve to capture seal identification images. Ideally, this will be a 2-person operation. In that case, and if it can be done without disturbing the seals, one person should walk alongside one of the cave walls and the other should walk on the opposite side of the cave fairway, keeping apace. Then, if a seal exits the cave, it can be photographed from both sides.

It is important to remain inside the cave — intruding —for the least possible span of time, always.

When the survey is complete, the time the survey began and ended as well as the site name, date, times of high and low tide, the height of the tide, the sea state, wind direction and speed can be recorded having departed the cave. So far as time, tide and the conditions allowed, I found it essential to make revisits to every site in different seasons. Initially, I made a random visit, assessing from the presence of seals and their signs whether it was definitely a seal cave. From identifying the features of caves that were definitely used by seals, I listed also those caves that contained neither seals nor their signs, but which resembled that range of sites already known to be used by them.

By the end of the second year of exploration, based on my discoveries of seals and, especially, their pups, it was evident that pups were being born between May and December — apparently, mainly between August and the end of October. This perception would change over time, as I discovered that rather than there being a neat 'regional' pup production season, as offered for other regions of the country, the timings varied significantly between seal localities around the region.

Nevertheless, the great majority of pups were and continue to be born between late-summer and mid-autumn. Interestingly, in many cases, I was to discover these were the only times in the year that seals made any use of these sites that always I have called nursery caves.

Aside from the late-summer to mid-autumn nursery visits, I identified two other 'seal-seasons' for making visits: winter (roughly speaking, the period of the gathering ashore of the large moulting assemblies) and spring through to mid-summer, when sites are used mainly as what Steven would have called 'seal lodges' or resting places used between foraging or travelling trips. Seal caves appear to be least-used between April and the end of July although, as ever with seals, there are exceptions.

Although this appears straightforward, there were always local exceptions to the general regional results. For example, the season of the annual moult can extend for longer than usual, into mid-spring, albeit with smaller seal assemblies than those occurring at the height of the season. For another example, a small number of pups are born out-of-season every year although not at predictable times or sites. For another example, the number of pregnant seals in a particular locality can crash — did crash — due to an exceptional event of (fatal) seal by-catch in bottom-set tangle and trammel nets. As a result, pup production can be distorted in numbers and in timing for not only the year of the catastrophic event but for a number of years thereafter. It will either settle at the new, lower level or slowly recover until a typical level of potentially breeding females for the locality is restored or recruited, coinciding with the continuing presence of sexually active males.

There was only one way to iron out the wrinkles mentioned above — to locate and describe what appeared to be anomalies but proved to be variations between localities. This, also, was conducted from the outset.

I needed to identify one seal locality whose sites I could monitor not only during the breeding season but through the entire year. The locality was that one closest to home, Seal Bay in the vicinity of Land's End. Apart from being a locality not previously identified by Steven, Summers or Prime, all the sites could be monitored via a short, interesting walk over the cliffs. Furthermore, the seal cave sites were all accessible from shores reached with only a small degree of difficulty, or after swims of not more than 100m., while the remaining sites were either on small, cliff-backed (accessible with difficulty) beaches, on rocks close to the shore or in waters close to shore. In short, observations could be made at every site that allowed seals to be identified either by sex, if adults, or by age, if they were pups or appeared to be in the first up to three years of life.

In that period, seals were monitored as often as opportunity permitted, all through the years and their seasons. The results of this monitoring informed the regional survey work. However, because these sites are used through the year and because two of the sea caves were, and remain, regionally important, they gave an initially misleading impression of how most cave site clusters in the region are used. Being so heavily used through the year, they failed to flag up the considerable extent to which seal caves are used exclusively in the season of pup production across the region.

However, they did give a very clear impression of the variability of the cave substrate types, revealed at low tide through each year, as well as the variations in extent and depth of any low water pools. Another important feature proved to be the (variable) angle of any sand or gravel slopes rising to the back of the cave. This has an influence, in turn, on the breaking of waves and the extent of reach of the runs of surf inside the cave: the steeper the slope, the shorter the reach of the surf and, therefore, the seals using especially the top of the slope would be subject to significantly less disturbance than in the event of the slope being shallower.

Furthermore, when the tidal cycle moves from springs to neaps, given heavy wave action in a sand-substrate seal cave, sands above the reach of the turbulent sea can be left untouched while the sands below can be eroded dramatically. During such conditions, the untouched sands above the reach of high tide surf form a plateau that becomes increasingly exaggerated in height as the sands around its base are eroded. Successive eroding tides can form a steep hill to the foot of the plateau, thereby ever-shortening the run of the high tide surf and thereby protecting the plateau.

The most memorable such event occurred in early October one year while four white-coated pups were stranded on a plateau that measured more than 3m in height. They were entirely safe from the ravages of the surf, but the mainly vertical wall of sand proved difficult for the seal mothers to surmount. Two mothers elected to remain with their pups throughout the remainder of the period of lactation while the other two mothers managed to delve a steep track through one edge of the plateau wall to reach their pups daily.

I was proud of having managed to survey such a stretch of coast, once that had been accomplished. There were periods when I was accompanied by good friends. Kai Abt, Ian Rappel, Martin Hunt, Nick Tregenza and Neil Goodchild come immediately to mind - and those were the best of times. The fears encountered during periods of solitude shrank in good company and in its place, there was lots of laughter even when a particular cave in marginal sea conditions daunted the pair of us to the point that we dared not enter it, or when one of us experienced a misadventure. It is difficult to look graceful when teetering across weed or mucous-covered boulders, or making a false step in a deep pool.

In the seal caves, misadventure is always hovering above your very next step. My personal motto was and still is 'expect the unexpected'. It is entirely possible to do so but far less possible to expect the particular feature of the unexpected that lies in wait. For example, whether crossing a boulder beach under the sky or in the shadows and torchlight under a cave roof, always one part of my imagination is given to how I am going to land if I slip or fall as a result of my next step. Or: how can I keep injury to a minimum or avoid it altogether.

I haven't made many mistakes across the 30 years, not because I am so good but because I haven't dared to make them, so very far from help and potential rescue as I have been. And yet, very early on in my work, while being accompanied by Ian, a near-catastrophe befell me while on a monitoring expedition to a seal cave that here I shall call the Lightning Cave.

It is best entered by one of those vast sea doors that many Cornish sea caves can boast. However, because the sea was rough that day, we clambered down a cliff on to a mainly rocky shore that is dangerously slippery — excellent preparation, then, for anything the cave might hold. Without misadventure, we took the side gate into the cave and followed a partly narrow rocky corridor to the interior, in one section having to wade chest-deep through a pool of water. Beyond the pool, the much wider main fairway of the cave lay broadside-on to our path while the high, rough-hewn wall beyond flickered with dark-blue light as if lightning was playing along it. The accompanying thunder was provided by the surf breaking on the main cave shore. Somewhere just above the reach of the surf, two seals were wailing, making their ever-lovely cries that forever evoke for me the atmosphere that is there at the edge of the world.

Massive boulders were spread before us. Maybe 3m below them lay a shingle beach. We approached the edge with the caution that accompanies every sensible movement inside a seal cave, scanning what lay ahead by torchlight. The trouble was that our torch beams were weak — my fault. I remember this adventure had been unplanned, occurring simply because we chanced to be in the vicinity and happened to have time enough to explore a little more that day. The torches had seen much use in the earlier hours and so the most part of their energy was spent. Consequently, we were only using one torch, keeping the other as a reserve.

Today, I would never visit the caves without carrying a fully-charged torch and if I had company, every companion would be carrying a torch likewise fully-charged. Indeed, ideally, we would all carry a spare torch in our field packs; however, I have never had the money available to enjoy that luxury for myself or for my companions.

In the Lightning Cave, we were scanning for the lesser rocks that would help us clamber down to the main fairway. I never worked out how I came to slip. One moment I was scanning, the next I was falling through the air. Worse, I was falling in such a way that I knew I could not avoid landing on my back. Simply, it happened so suddenly that I had no time to adjust my position — not that I could have known how because I had no idea on to what substrate-type I was falling.

In the event, I did not land on the substrate. I landed on a seal with a dry pelage. My memory, which may not be accurate, was that it felt soft and velvety.

It must have been asleep because, for a few seconds, it made no reaction at all; and neither did I. Recovering from the main shock, both of us then spent a few more seconds scrabbling ineffectively to make any movement at all for there was no 'getting a grip' in the deep gravel the seal had been resting on. I suspect we must have been of one mind, wanting nothing more than to get away from one another. That followed. Our efforts displaced me into the deep gravel where both of us struggled to achieve sufficient purchase to complete our getaway from one another. In due course, however, the seal made best speed in the direction of the sea while I ran several paces in the opposite direction. I was hugely relieved, hugely fortunate, to be unhurt; hugely relieved, too, that the seal had not bitten me. By the way, the seal undulated seaward, neither had it suffered injury.

That was the only occasion inside a cave when I fell.

Working in the Sea Caves:
Drawing up Plan Views

Every seal cave needs to be mapped – the shape being measured and sketched, hazards and other features being identified. They need to be mapped at high water spring tide (HWST), high water neap tide (HWNT) and at low water spring tide (LWST). On each plan view, the current extent of the sub-stratum types (for example sand, gravel, boulders and low water tide pools) is measured – bearing in mind that the extent of sub-strata can vary enormously, even daily, according to wind direction, wind speed and sea state.

Nine examples of seal caves showing HWST, HWNT and LWST plan views are set out on the following pages. These seal caves were mapped in Ynys Mon (Anglesey), Cornwall and Devon

Yellow indicates sand, pale brown indicates gravel, pale grey indicates boulders, ledges and bedrock, bright blue indicates tidal pools and green-blue indicates seawater.

HWST

HWNT

LWST

Cave Length: 250m
Entrance Faces: NW

HWST

HWNT

LWST

Cave Length: 50m
Entrance Faces: SE

HWST

HWNT

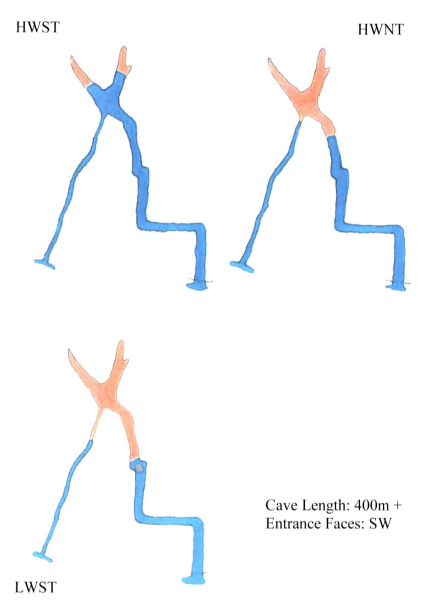

LWST

Cave Length: 400m +
Entrance Faces: SW

HWST

HWNT

Cave Length: 85m
Entrance Faces: W

LWST

HWST

HWNT

Cave Length: 175m
Entrance Faces: SSW

LWST

HWST

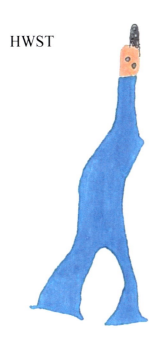

HWNT

LWST

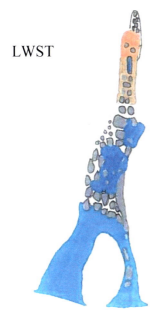

Cave Length: 140m
Entrance Faces: NE

HWST

HWNT

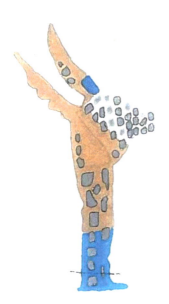

Cave Length: 85m
Entrance Faces: W

LWST

HWST

HWNT

Cave Length: 185m
Entrance Faces: NE

LWST

HWST

HWNT

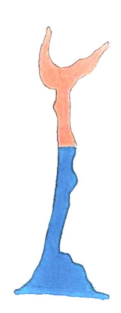

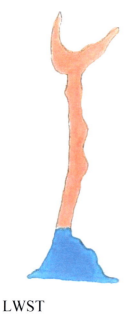

Cave Length: 125m
Entrance Faces: SW

LWST

Seal Marks on Sandy Sea Cave Beaches

An adult seal moving over sand will leave a broad — perhaps 30 centimetres wide — substantial churned up 'wake' that runs in what may be a long line from wherever it had been resting to wherever it reached the sea (according to wherever the tide-line was at that point). On other substrates, it leaves no mark (bedrock or boulders). On either side of the wake, separate from it, there are chevrons of fore-flipper marks. As their movement entails making a vaguely 'breast-stroke' movement through the sand, a miniature dune will be on the hind edge of these flipper marks. It will indicate whether the seal was moving to or from the cave — a detail that is always helpful to know.

Young seals vary quite substantially in their early development, so precision in estimating age from a simple sighting is impossible except where the undersides are visible. However, as evident in the photographic key I have compiled, young seals — likely, but not certain, to be in the first three years of life — leave a more light-weight track. The marks are as for the adult seal but that the central 'wake' does not exist. Instead, there is a continuous line that might have been traced quite deeply in the sand by a stick. It is as if the smaller seal, being less 'blubbery' than an adult, has a keel on its underside that it drags through the sand.

Whatever age the seal, such tracks often begin obscurely in dry sand above the reach of the sea and conclude in wet sand.

In the event that there are many tracks, I mistrust my ability to count separately more than up to seven tracks, especially where the seals are not moving in a straight line and most especially where the cave fairway is narrow. In the latter instance, tracks tend to criss-cross. Therefore, in my record for that visit, where it is clear that at least seven tracks can be distinguished, I note 'a minimum of seven seal tracks made since the last high tide' even though very many more seals may have been present. In all record-keeping, in the absence of certainty, I have always tried to ensure that nothing is ever over-estimated.

It can be extremely difficult, is always more difficult, to make sense of tracks in soft, dry sand.

Where seals have spent a long time asleep, they leave either quite deep torpedo-shaped or comma-shaped hollows in the sand. Most commonly, such hollows are situated at the base of, or close to the base of, the cave walls near the far reach of the surf at high water (which smooths the surrounding sand). Less well-defined hollows may be located above the high-water mark, not necessarily at the base of the walls. Less commonly, hollows occur away from the walls, usually above the high-water mark.

Whatever information examination of the seal tracks suggests, they should be erased before departing the cave so they can play no complicating part in the information you glean from your next visit.

Different Uses of Seal Caves

How is it possible to distinguish one type of seal cave from the others?

At the outset, you may be in doubt as to whether the cave is used by seals or not. In the greater span of the study, as familiarity grows, it helps to have some sense of the variety of behaviour displayed by grey seals over the course of the year as well as considerable variations in what might be called personality. However, what you learn at one site may resemble hardly at all what you might learn from another.

Experience has made evident that grey seals make three principal uses of sea caves:

Fishing Lodges

Grey seals have long been known to use sea caves as natal and nursery chambers as well as what G.A. Steven referred to as 'lodges' — in effect, resting places used either between daily or periodic fishing excursions or during longer passages along coasts or across seas.

In addition to normal assemblies, moulted pups may often be found alone in a cave that may not be much used otherwise or even not at all by seals. In effect, these are young seals that have left the nursery site and are now feeling their way, by trial and error, through the most perilous first year of life. They are struggling to find enough food to eat because their hunting skills are initially rudimentary and their lungs are not fully developed, so they are limited in the span of time and the depths to which they can forage underwater. At the same time, they are learning, usually tentatively, to co-exist with other older seals. Also, at the same time, they are also using their senses to con out, day by day, a map of each their own water-worlds, finding welcome rest on fragmentary margins of land — sand or stone, outside or within a sea cave — here and there at the margins of their personal odysseys into life.

On the other hand, especially cave-born seal pups often become familiar with the life-aquatic during the first days of life, preferring often to rest in cave pools while sleeping rather than on the sandy fairway or to spend long periods submerged outside the cave entrance when the sea is sunlit and quiet. Even so young, they are possessed of an extraordinary hardihood that is one of the essential basic building blocks they need if they are to survive the first year of life. Nevertheless, daily it must be an exhausting experience, especially being at the base of the pecking order in any community of seals in whose company they find themselves. This must be even more so for those pups born in the latter half of the breeding season when sea conditions are usually becoming more hostile, causing more commotion in the seal caves and presumably ensuring that early lessons essential to their survival are harder learned.

Where a lone seal is encountered in a cave, most often that seal is either a young seal in the first year of life or a mature male.

Natal and Nursery Sites

I have always differentiated between natal and nursery sites because that is what the seals do.

A natal site is where a seal pup is born. If you are lucky, your survey visit will coincide with the birth itself or, more commonly, the discovery of a placenta still present on the substrate. If you are luckier still, it will be warm (although be warned: advice from the government is that there is a small risk of catching brucellosis from handling it). A warm placenta confirms the pup was born since the last time of high water.

Nearly always, such a site naturally develops into a nursery site. Here, the pup will be fed on demand or up to 7 times a day at the outset. Here a normal development will see it grow plump on a diet of fat-rich milk that turns the pup from a white scrap of hair and bone to a great barrel of lard.

It may share the site with other pups that have been born there or have sought refuge there, co-existing at first and later playing together, especially if there are cave pools to be entered and explored at low water.

However, some (not all) seal mothers are greatly stressed by the proximity of other seals, in particular of other seal mothers. They express their anxiety by attacking and often wounding the other seal mother when she attempts to pass by en route to visit her own pup in the deeper interior of the cave. There can be substantial loss of blood during these conflicts and sometimes one female will have part of a fore-flipper bitten off. Flippering — the waving or vibrating of the uppermost fore-flipper — from one adult seal to another signifies a wish to be left alone, to have the other seal back farther off — but can also result in bloody consequences.

Also, just as some seal mothers will feed a pup who is not their own, the stressed mothers will respond to attempts by a stranger-pup to solicit a feed, initially by snarling in blood-curdling fashion. If this fails to deter the pup, she will then nip it. Often, this draws blood, usually on the lower central part of their dorsal surface (back). The bite is administered to an accompaniment of fearsome-sounding snarling.

Consequently, while some mothers will respond by settling into a pattern of fighting her way to the side of her pup perhaps several times daily, others elect — on the high tide — to swim past her rival and to lead her pup through the waters of the cave and out into the light. Thereafter, the pair will keep company, sometimes swimming considerable distances (possibly for several miles) along the coast to find a beach, whether inside a cave or not, where the remainder of the period of lactation can be lived out peacefully.

Other seal mothers and their pups are swept out of natal caves by the force of storm surf. In that event, so long as they stay together, they should come to no harm. In time, they may find refuge on a sheltered shore and there, continue the nursery period — the period of lactation.

It is important to be aware when making the initial site surveys that the existence of a beach at the time of high tide is not essential for a seal cave nursery site, despite thoughts to the contrary in some early scientific papers on the subject. Even new-born pups will swim, at need, for more than four hours at high water while the cave beach remains yet covered by the sea or by the repeated runs of the surf. This I have observed on many occasions wherever seals use sea caves. However, evidently seals prefer to have a beach available at high water inside the sea caves.

Grey seal pups in Cornwall, Lundy and Devonshire may be born in any month of the year, depending partly on which stretch of coast they are using. Nearly all pups are born between May and December, but the great majority are born between August and October, usually (varying from year to year and from locality to locality) with births peaking in September. There is no predictable sequence — say beginning at Land's End in May and concluding in Devon in November. The timing of pup production appears haphazard (but predictable in its timing) from locality to locality. I am not entirely certain of this, but my impression is that the timing of pup production influences the timing of moulting by erstwhile seal mothers but not the males.

Moulting Sites

Moulting may sound like an event of lesser interest than the season of births. Far from it. The greatest grey seal assemblies in the sea caves I have explored in SW Britain occur between late November and March. Then, as many as one hundred seals may be found using any of the very few moulting sites they frequent — possibly sites that have been so-used for centuries.

At present, I believe that the principal grey seal moulting assemblies in south-west England occur among the Western Rocks and on Annet in the Isles of Scilly between December and April. These uninhabited islands offer necessary privacy against wave action except when the heaviest seas inundate them. It may be that they are joined during this (primarily) winter period by seals from Brittany, Wales and Ireland, forming some of the largest assemblies that occur during the course of any year in south-west Britain.

Almost as important — it varies from year to year — are three beach sites on the mainland coast of north Cornwall — Beeny, Mutton Cove and River Cove.

Numbers are less in the seal caves but not less impressive as a spectacle. To me, it is the greatest spectacle of the seal year: the sight, sounds and scent of these great hulks of sand-dusted animals all together in the one great sea cave gathering, leaving unused a great deal of surrounding space on the sand-hill. A pall of steam raised from their blubbery bodies hangs over the assembly in the deep gloom.

During this period, they can be tetchy with one another but they are content to remain hauled out deep inside the moulting caves of Cornwall, Devon, Lundy and Wales over periods of several tides. At such times, they seem to emerge from the caves only with reluctance.

It is a time in the seals year when it is possible, if making the quietest possible entry to the caves, if remaining close as possible to one of the cave walls and if remembering to offer no profile for them to recognise against any light behind you, to enjoy observing the very best sights of grey seals in their most private moments.

I crawl into such theatres on all fours or even slither, where the terrain permits. Familiar with viewpoints that will conceal me, it is possible at some sites where they rest on sand-hills to make approximate counts of the seals while also identifying their sex without recourse to the lamplight that will inevitably lead to a disturbance event.

In the event that they do stampede or are absent at the time of your visit, check the sand for a matting of shed hairs to confirm that they are moulting.

The most interesting seal behaviour I have observed in a sea cave at moulting time happened one December. This cave is situated close to home but reaching it in the winter months, and then returning without misadventure, is always a challenge.

To reach it entails a clamber down to a boulder beach, more of a dance than a walk or a trot across the boulders, a wading through sea-worried, waist or chest-deep shallows, a clamber across a small field of massive boulders, a short swim to a minor promontory, a trot along narrow ledges between periodic runs of breaking waves and a final leap into the sea followed by a short swim to reach a rocky slope up which, often, the helpful surf has carried me. There is a final contest with the swell or the surf along a faint and mainly diagonal cliff-base track before I reach the welcome safety of one of the cathedral-high caves.

Within are two great sand-hills, the first of which is usually at least half-covered with great boulders. Only rarely do I find a seal in this entrance hall and then it is always a young one in the first year or two of life.

No; the seals prefer the innermost reaches of this cave. To reach the interior, always I creep, bent over, or else I crawl, close as I can be to the left-hand wall and seeking, despite the betraying gradient, to offer no obviously human profile to any seal watchful in the deeper dark ahead of me. If they catch sight of my approach, they would stampede down their slope and into the sea.

There is, dependant on the tide, one final obstacle. Because this cave has a second entrance, on a neap tide there is always water barring my way at the bottom of the sand-hill, even at low tide. On a spring tide, at low tide there would be no water, only a spread of sand interrupted intermittently with boulders of a moderate size. During neap tides, I would have to wade chest-deep across the water, which enters the cave in pulses of swell.

On this occasion, it was the time of spring tides so that there was a risk of being seen as I crossed the part of the fairway leading out to the lighted entrance of the cave that I have always called the Seals Entrance. I continued to crawl forward, settling behind a modestly-sized boulder. Ahead, in the deep gloom to which my eyes had become partly accustomed, I could see a large number of what I was sure would be adult male grey seals — for this is a site where the males always gather to moult before the females.

At first sight, winter assemblies here always resemble a rugby scrum and the larger assemblies always appear, at first sight, to consist of fewer seals than proves to be the case. A pall of steam hangs like a cloud above the assembly for these seals are very warm, each adult being wrapped in a duvet of blubber that may be 5 centimetres thick or more. That is useful to seals in the cold sea, but is otherwise in a cave where only scant breezes ever blow and where the temperature feels much the same, the year round. Here, the pall of steam shows they are ridding themselves of excess heat.

They appear, at first sight, to be packed together in the one dense group, but for a few outliers. They seem to be almost on top of one another but this, also, is a trick of the eye. Peering up the pale hill, my excellent Leica binoculars reveal that most of the seals are maintaining a small distance from their neighbours — that, in effect, they have created an extensive maze through which run cramped pale veins of sand. It makes sense, for if they were resting against one another that could only serve to crank up even further their body temperature.

From my place in the shadows and prone behind a smooth granite boulder, I began my few normal tasks. I noted the substrate type: sand, as usual, with a very few knobs of granite protruding through. Indeed, only on one occasion — it was late winter — has this unexpectedly sheltered and therefore stable slope been anything but a sand-hill. Then, three months of heavy storms had eroded all the sand from the entire cave. In its place was an unbroken spread of middle-sized boulders. It was like chancing upon a very familiar cave now reduced to the bare bones of itself — to its under-clothing. Perhaps those boulders had been there all the time, are still there, under the sand. Certainly, it altered the atmosphere of the cave, making it much starker, just as the brown granite boulders served to make it a darker, more forbidding place.

The mobility of the substrate, especially the finer substrate types — primarily sand but also gravel and up to middle-sized boulders — is a key feature of seal caves. They are moved a lot at more exposed sites by surf action. They are not only moved in and out of the cave but also 'rearranged' within the cave. This has the effect of altering the angles of slopes. It can have the effect of altering the length and depth of any low water pools or of any entrance waters the cave has.

It is the same in the bays outside the sea caves. Here there are seabed sandbanks that are constantly being rearranged as to height, extent and location. In turn, this affects the nature of where and how steeply the waves do break. This goes on to influence the degree of exposure of the beaches in and out of the caves. Once the sea state reaches Beaufort scale 4, especially when such conditions endure for extended periods, it helps, also, to make access to sea caves either easier or more difficult by altering the place where the waves break.

Attempting to count shadows on the sand is a thankless task, for the gradient appears to make 'clumps' of seals merge into super-seals, making them uncountable. However, on this day, unexpectedly, I received the help of two talented young assistants.

The steaming assembly was mainly quiet. Now and then, a large adult male — they seem always to be large, especially in the caves — would stir and snarl half-heartedly, through a partly open mouth, at an equally large neighbour who might have rolled over while yet asleep and unwittingly intruded into debateable space. This mild bickering never developed into more bloodthirsty aggression. A code of tolerance appears to prevail at these secret cave-bound moulting assemblies where every seal is likely to be feeling physically itchy or otherwise uncomfortable.

Among the thronged great seals, there are always a few young seals. Very few of these may have been born in the last pupping season but most are a little larger. These are in their second or third year of life, growing in confidence having survived the first, most perilous year of life, but not yet being sexually mature.

On this day, two yearlings elected to play a game of tag in the maze between the much greater bodies. As they chased one another, they must have been less than careful in their movements for the great beasts began to stir, uttering the half-hearted snarls and sometimes waving a desultory fore-flipper in the general direction of the nuisance. When the two delinquents disappeared briefly, the movements of the disgruntled adults gave them away.

The game continued without further developments for a long time — at least ten minutes. The grand finale came when the two yearlings emerged just below the seal resting closest to the Seals Entrance — but still about 30 metres up the hill. Here, as if of one mind, they paused, looking at one another for at least five seconds. And then, surely for no reason other than mischief, they began to bolt downhill toward the entrance tunnel.

It was as though they had rung an alarm bell. The entire assembly of seals became alert. Heads were raised; necks extended or turned over a shoulder. A few began to follow the youngsters half-heartedly but this only alerted more seals. The trickle became an avalanche into which were sucked even the few isolated seals that had been sleeping at the top of the hill. Across the full breadth of the cave fairway, down they came, galumphing. But, as they never failed to do, near the bottom of the slope they veered toward the lighted corridor that opened to the sea. As they veered, the line thinned so that they passed me in a formation not more than three seals broad. It made the counting so much easier.

Since the beginning, in all situations, I have been in the habit of distinguishing males from females from immature seals, keeping a running tally on all three throughout. If there are seals in the sea in addition to those on the shore, I run a double tally. It works, I suppose, because I am so used to doing it. So it was now, with just the seals ashore to be counted. It turned out to be a big count for the 1990's — 44 males, 2 females and 6 immatures. Between then and now, assembly sizes have increased in number — peak counts now sometimes slightly exceed 100.

Outside the cave, the seals paused in the greenish swell just to seaward of the breaking waves, to stare back into the glooms of the cave corridor. They did not see me. With the passing of the last undulating seal, I had stood up, hastening up the sand-hill to scan for any lingering seal — sometimes I happen upon one that is deeply asleep, deeply unaware of the drama. Not this time. Other than seal tracks, seal-shaped hollows and very few substantial faecal deposits, there was nothing of note but moulted hair.

All that remained that day was to visit two more (less challenging) caves via the medley of clambering, trotting and swimming described earlier. At the end of the working day, before the joy of showering or taking a bath, there would be an hour of entering up my notes and sometimes adding a precis of the events that made the day memorable.

Different Uses of Seal Caves

The presence of a number of vigilant mature female seals, possibly attended by one or two mature males, in cave entrance waters (or their approaches) between May and December in SW England waters (varying in time between localities) is indicative of the highest likelihood that grey seals are using the cave and that it is almost certain to be a nursery site.

Many papers and books suggest that the presence of a mature male seal in the cave entrance waters or their approaches signifies the cave is used by seals. This is true, as females are often (not always) intolerant of any male seals sharing their nursery beach.

However, they do tolerate them sometimes. This is particularly so with males that learn to be very slow, discreet and verbally non-aggressive with the seal mother(s) in a cave. By appearing heedful of every admonishment from a female, he seems to win her trust. She reciprocates by allowing him to rest, firstly, in the shallows then on the edge of the beach before edging progressively closer. This theatre occurs in periods of several days, serving ultimately to be in prime position to mate with her during her oestrus window that lasts for just a few days. In the event of such behaviour, no seal holds station in the entrance waters.

The persistent hunger cries of the unseen white-coated pups are another of the surest indications that a sea cave is being used as a nursery site by seals. Higher pitched than those of the adults, briefer and much 'breathier', their cries convey great distress. Just like human children, they are quite capable of crying themselves to sleep. By the time that sleep claims them, their cries have become shorter, quieter and now have come to convey a sense of exhaustion.

All seals when at rest have strikingly irregular breathing patterns. It is as if they forget to breathe for prolonged periods. Perhaps they dream of swimming in the watery deeps, unbreathing while so doing? Remain alert to the possibility of hearing such quiet sounds.

Outside the season of pup production, the presence of a solitary seal or a very small number of them in the entrance waters or approaches — most probably travelling immatures or resident males — may indicate the cave is being used as a lodge.

Assemblies of mature seals, probably all or nearly all of the same sex, may be seen outside cave entrances or in a nearby neighbouring bay, especially between late November and the end of March. They are indicative that the cave is being used as a moulting site. Such a cave will be substantial in size, fit to accommodate more than fifty seals at a time at high water and will be remote from easy access by people.

The nature of the cave visible from the entrance can also be indicative of likely use by seals. The presence of a beach accessible to seals between high water and low water is desirable from a seal viewpoint so long as it is inaccessible to people. A deep-water entrance yielding within the cave on to the beach plus pools in which they can submerge would be a particularly attractive combination to a seal. Their preference for such a site would be enhanced further if there were either cubby-holes (tunnels of varying length) leading off the main cave fairway or a 'kennel' — an annex, at the very back of the cave, beyond the main fairway.

Neighbours of The Seals in The Seal Caves

Exploring also seal haunts outside the sea caves was always a happy, interesting adventure, especially when the islands they used for resting places were shared with nesting cormorants and shags, guillemots, razorbills and puffins, kittiwakes and fulmars as well as the ever-scavenging gulls. For more than half of every year, on the islands, I worked with the sweetly-foetid smell of seabird excrement in my nostrils and trod among the often partly-feathered skeletons of the young birds that failed to survive or among the partly consumed fish the young birds had regurgitated in or beside their nests and subsequently ignored.

I came to be surprised, come the end of the breeding season, when shag nests did not contain upholstery of what looked like two-dimensional trees — by then, usually white and apparently encrusted with coral, or else blackish if stripped of the coralline encrustation. Pink sea fans *(Eunicella verrucosa)*, they were the colour of smoked salmon when freshly brought from the sea by the shags.

Pondering on nesting shags is not down to chance for, over time, I came to find a connection between nesting shags and seal caves. Often, I discovered shags nesting in seal caves, usually but not always at least 6m above the high- water mark close to the entrance. In that event, usually one shag made use of a perching ledge just outside the cave entrance. Below this ledge, over the weeks, the shag excrement accumulated, becoming rather like the white chalk base to a plate bearing the name of a house. The words 'seal cave' might as well have been written there.

Another incidental discovery that I made about shags was to do with nest construction. It became apparent that on nesting islands that lacked much vegetation, much use — even up to 100% — was made of derelict fishing gear, in contrast with nests built on sites that were well-vegetated. This mainly took the form of fishing line rather than net fragments, but often there were hooks and weights attached. Clearly, this meant there was a risk of entanglement of the young birds that over a season tend to trample the exterior rim of the nest, thereby coming into contact with the potentially entangling material. However, there was a surprising second effect that I found to be more lethal.

The Brisons are two largely bare islands situated in the far west about one kilometre off Cape Cornwall. Locally, the site is known as 'General de Gaulle in his bath' on account of the resemblance. Shags there were using huge amounts of derelict fishing line — more, perhaps, than at any other site in their SW England range. This was something I would monitor from January because, in some years (it varied) the first elongate, pale blue eggs were being laid that early. Shag nesting seasons are 'staggered': they do not lay their clutches (nearly always consisting of 3 eggs) all at the same time but over as many as three months. Given a month for incubation and 2 more months before full independence for the surviving hatchlings is achieved, as well as the weeks of nest construction, overlap occurs on the Brisons (as elsewhere) with other species nesting there.

Razorbills and guillemots do not make nests, but lay their eggs on the Brisons ledges and shallow slopes. Inevitably, they lay their eggs near the shag nests. The problem I discovered was that when the auk hatchlings began to roam the local area in May and especially June, their wanderings took them to and over abandoned shag nests. Here, a small number of them became inextricably entangled, with their legs always the entangled part. Of the young birds found there during every auk breeding season visit, between one and four were always dead while I was able to release a tiny (always lesser) number of casualties that were yet alive.

Obviously, there is no nesting material available to shags in the seal caves except for any seaweed to be scavenged from the tideline — something I have never observed them to do, having never seen them to alight on any cave floor. In effect, then, the shag nest sites resemble those at the Brisons. That may explain why the very first shag nest I examined in a seal cave was constructed exclusively of fishing line. I really only properly recognised this construction after finding two hatchlings dead on the cave floor below the nest. Having clambered up a cave entrance wall for about 8m, seeing the nest from above I found the use of fishing line was exclusive. Despite the two dead birds, a third youngster yet remained alive in the nest cup.

I cannot suggest why the two young birds died — certainly not on this occasion from entanglement. However, the nest construction material had been disturbing — the first such nest I had ever seen. It triggered my subsequent interest in the use of derelict fishing gear in nest construction, plus its consequences — if they proved identifiable.

As well as shags — which were the most common seal neighbours — I found the nests of feral pigeons, kestrels, rocks pipits, choughs, swallows and house martins in seal caves. Very rarely, notably in the wake of storms, I found a live but exhausted guillemot resting above the tide's reach in a seal cave. More often, almost always in the winter months during the rare spells of severely cold weather — usually with large clusters of icicles hanging from the cliff walls outside — I happened upon a robin or wren foraging along the high-tide seaweed dunes. I did search for bat roosts but found none. I was told, possibly correctly, that the humidity was too variable.

Seal caves with low water pools usually had the most interesting mix of inter- tidal and sub-littoral life. Quite often, I watched shoals of sand eels sharing a low water pool with white-coated seal pups taking the first few swims of their lives. The pups were interested in much that they found but seemingly not the sand eels, who seemed to know they had nothing to fear; yet. The same held true for the shannies, gobies, father-lashers and the other small, well-camouflaged fish left confined by the ebbing tide.

The walls of the pools, as well as the walls above the surface, carried a variable amount of decoration. Many of the most exposed caves, and most of them were exposed, contained raspberry spreads of the common sea squirt, *Dendrodoa grossularia.* Inevitably, beadlet anemones were common. Nearly always, they would be the usual colours: maroon or, more rarely, green. Exceptionally, I found in the darkest, wrinkled recess of a cave a yellow beadlet and once — as can be confirmed by Nick Tregenza, who happened to be sharing that adventure — we chanced on a beadlet that was cobalt blue. However, although it was not the most common cave anemone, the ones I came to associate most with the seal caves were strawberry anemones. Always they seemed to be at least twice as large as any other but the daisy anemones. Furthermore, I came to know some as individuals because they never seemed to move, grow or shrink, even over a period as long as a decade.

Different algae grew on the cave walls. Those growing near the cave entrance as a maroon baize looked beautiful against the rising sun, as did *Chondrus crispus*, growing in the entrance pools of certain caves. This grows not as a baize but somewhat resembling a maroon (sometimes, maroon and green) tree in leaf, but it has one enchanting feature which is to manifest near the tip of a frond a blue or violet iridescence that disappears as soon as it is removed from the water. Other handsome algae growing in cave entrance pools include the (sometimes) yellowish-brown sea oak *(Halidrys siliquosa)*, the blue-green *Cystoseira tamariscifolia,* and the dark-green and velvety *Codium tomentosum.*

However, overwhelmingly, the signature alga for sea caves across SW England is to be seen to best effect at low tide. These are the mauve-coloured encrusting *Lithophyllum* species, growing between mid-tide and below the low-water marks. They look like a colourful skirting-board at the base of the cave walls as well covering many cave floor rocks and, especially, coating cave floor rock pools. They appear ubiquitous on rocky SW shores, probably the most common of the algae growing in the inter-tidal zone.

The cement-like calcareous squiggles of *Spirorbis* curled like repetitive white graffiti everywhere on, especially, the tops of rocks and stones, providing secure homes for never-seen worms.

The amount of deposition of algae in the caves could be quite stupendous at times, but was generally patchy — primarily a feature of the period from mid-autumn to early spring, that period when the roughest seas ran. Where the sea state was less than 4, only minimal traces of deposition occurred. However, wherever it accumulated, there too would be found large numbers of those most agile and scavenging amphipods, sand-hoppers of the *Talitrus spp.* Flies and beetles also occur in great numbers along the strandline.

From late summer to mid-autumn, some years there are the most uncountable and gorgeous strandings of By-the-wind Sailors — dark turquoise in life bleaching over the season to transparency in death — along seal cave and other tidelines.

Spiders occurred at the very back of some of the longer caves near ground level and probably on the roofs and other high places beyond the reach of the surf. These I sometimes met, most often by blundering into their gossamer strands, although usually I avoided them as they gleamed entirely clearly in the torchlight.

What Happens When Old Seal Caves Die?

Grey seals in SW Britain make considerable use of a large number of sea cave beaches as nursery sites during the season of pup production (e.g. Baines et al, 1995), especially — but not exclusively — during the period August to October. A very small number of sea cave beaches are also used as moulting assembly sites, most heavily between late November and March but continuing in some years as late as May.

The surveys of large seal breeding assemblies estimate grey seal pup production usually from aerial counts made by photography and thermal imaging above open beaches. Such an approach is entirely appropriate in locations where breeding occurs on open aspect habitats. However, in SW Britain, grey seals use sea caves for breeding, moulting and other key life stages. For example, 28% of pup production in south-west Wales occurred in caves between 1992-1995 (Baines, et al). In north Wales, 36% and 67% of pup production occurred in caves in 2001 and 2002 respectively. In north Cornwall (Boscastle district), 63% of pup production occurred in caves. In south Devon, 90% of pup production occurred in caves in 2007 In Lundy, 60.5% of pup production occurred in caves in 2009. With such a high prevalence of cave use by seals in this region, a focussed study on the importance of sea cave habitat is required, and therefore also to what happens when old seal caves die and are no longer available to the seals.

Typically, few seals are present on nursery beaches at any one seal cave site. Narrow fairways predominate in seal nursery caves. This lack of space causes seal mothers to come into aggressive conflict with one another while moving to and from the sea and their pups — due to infringement of essential personal space required by seal neighbours.

Additionally, beach-crowding occurs over the period of high water, when wave action exacerbates the risk of conflict between the seal mothers or between mothers and pups other than their own. At such times, additionally, it clearly becomes more important to interpose their bodies between the run of the surf and their pups to protect them against wave action, from being rolled into the surf, as well as engaging in the contest for the diminished space available.

On the other hand, they are helped by the fact that — usually — only essential seals are present during the nursery period: mothers, un-weaned pups, weaned pups and at least one male seal, awaiting the imminent onset of oestrus in the lactating females. Non-breeding seals wishing to haul out to rest only rarely attempt to use these sites. By contrast, moulting seals assemble in close-knit, predominantly single sex groups numbering over 100 at the handful of seal moulting caves. It should be noted that all seal moulting caves are used as nursery sites in the preceding season. Nearly always, moulting does not begin until the last pup has weaned and presumably its mother has ceased the few days of being in oestrus.

Previous studies had shown that several localities (clusters of geographically separate sites) along the Cornish coast were used by grey seals (Steven, 1935; Summers, 1974; Prime, 1985 and Westcott, 1997 and 2010) for pup production, nearly all of which consisted predominantly of sea caves. The same papers emphasise that achieving access to these sites was extremely difficult as they are both remote and, more crucially, subject to often heavy, sometimes prolonged, wave action.

Between 1991 and 2017, while concentrating research on the two westernmost grey seal localities, additional occasional explorations were made along the entire north coast of west Cornwall between St Ives Bay in the west and Perranporth in the east, as well as the coast between Tintagel and The Strangles in north Cornwall, in effect to keep a finger on the pulse of what was going on in the seal world beyond the primary research area: in case something of significance was being missed.

It was evident from these explorations that several major cliff-collapses had occurred, with the impression being that the rate of erosion was quickening if compared with the previous decades. Dramatic cliff-collapses were recorded on social media, notably one of the North Cliffs headlands, which actually fell geographically in one of the primary research localities. Some of these collapses destroyed completely caves that had been used previously as nursery or moulting sites. Others partly destroyed sites or otherwise altered their physical character. Increasingly, stretches of cliff edge were being fenced off in the interest of public safety. Signs proliferated, warning people against using certain footpaths down to beaches lest misadventure befall them.

At the same time, other invisible cliff falls were occurring, entirely out of sight, inside the sea caves.

There were four events that caused particular concern in the context of pup production, four events that destroyed or mainly destroyed seal nursery sites. One of these events also rendered unusable by seals a major moulting site.

Before and After: Before Great Seal Hole

In 2010, there was what appeared to be a relatively minor cliff-collapse at Newdowns Head, a kilometre west of Trevaunance Cove. However, an enormous boulder now blocked entirely the entrance to the long (c.60 metres) narrow tunnel that previously had made a serpentine passage before yielding within on to the wide (c.10 metres) main chamber. This cave was well-known locally, as it had been for hundreds of years, as Great Seal Hole.

The complex conformation of the cave meant that the impact of wave action was greatly dissipated upon emerging from the narrows of the deep-water entrance tunnel into the wide space of the main chamber. This made the site, especially the small beaches situated around its rim, particularly attractive to seals seeking refuge from wave action and most of all to the combinations of female seals and their pups. Here, at least 18 and 16 seal pups were born and nursed respectively in the 1999 and 2000 breeding seasons — the counts are likely to have missed some pups due to them being opportunistic. The major research effort was focussed elsewhere during that period.

Great Seal Hole had the distinction of being one of six

exceptionally important Cornish sea caves used the year-round by often large assemblies of seals. It was the only such sea cave site between Boscastle and Land's End. In the winter months, assemblies of up to 50 seals gathered within where they kept close physical contact. Here, always, seals could access the sea easily without running the risk of coming into conflict with more nervous seals.

North Cliffs

In 2010, there was a second major headland-tip collapse, this time along the North Cliffs. Prior to the collapse, there were eight caves and one substantial cleft around the rim of the cove, all being subject to wave action over the high-water period.

The collapse, along with wave action, has transformed the cove itself by considerably raising the level of the beach by comparison with what existed previously. Now, it slopes much more steeply than before. Together, these features have the effect of preventing the sea, in the form of high tide or as wave action, from reaching the four sea caves that remain — except during spring tides and when stormy seas are running.

The cliff-collapse totally destroyed the cleft as well as four of the eight caves. A fifth cave, now resembling a large, steep-sided burrow more than a cave, has not been used since by seals. The two outermost sea caves on the south side of the bay, farthest from the collapsed headland, were never previously used as nursery sites.

Between 4 and 6 pups had been born annually at the destroyed sites.

The most important cave in terms of pup production, P-Cave, yet remains although in much altered form. It had been transformed from a cave that in the entrance half consisted of an exclusively rocky substrate of mainly middle-sized boulders but for a wall of massive boulders in the entrance itself. The rocky substrate sloped down to a pool of varying depth, with a length of about 15 metres and a width of about 6 metres at low tide. Beyond the pool was a steep hill of shingle leading up to the back of the cave; and upon this slope the pups were born and nursed, when they were not swimming in the pool.

During the first two years following the collapse, seals made no use of this cave.

Numbers of pups known to have been born here between 1994 and 2010 varied between 2 and 8, with 5 to 7 being the norm. As such, it was one of the three most important seal nursery sites in the locality.

+ Cave

As important as Pool Cave, situated about 400 metres north of the North Cliffs caves described above lies + Cave.

It is a cave entered via a rock-cluttered deep-water channel that yields to a beach of medium and large boulders. Beyond these boulders the cave divides into two tunnels that have a substrate of, primarily, shingle, pebbles and cobbles. It is in these tunnels that the nearly all pups are born and nursed, with always between 5 and 10 being counted per season.

More than 25 years ago, just before the cave was first entered in search of seals, a 'window' had appeared in the north wall of the cave, by way of a middle-sized wall-collapse. The slope of great boulders thus created stabilised within the cave, reaching up to the window.

Following the 2011 season, there was a second wall-collapse which served to crowd the cave floor with more boulders than before. This made it more difficult for seals to reach the two tunnels in the low water half of the tidal cycle except by means of great exertion which caused them to cut and otherwise damage the claws of their fore-flippers.

Adit Cave

In Navax headland, there is a very well-known seal cave, here called Adit Cave. Historically, especially in the 18th and 19th centuries, seal battues took place here, when parties of men entered the cave and, by torchlight over the low tide period, slaughtered the seals within by clubbing or shooting them to death. This is described by Tregarthen and others.

Adit Cave has two deep-water entrances which merge within to form a pool. The cave fairway is exceptionally long, running more than 150m into the cliff. The substrate is a mixture of large boulders, bedrock and low water pools. The part used as a nursery by the seals lies about 110m in. Here, there has long been a sandy beach with a few rocky outcrops, sloping up quite steeply to the back of the cave, where there is another chamber with a floor of cobbles and small boulders. This deepest recess of the cave was never, apparently, used by the seals during my many explorations.

Midway into the cave, an adit running parallel to and above the roof opens into the cave and from it, a knotted rope dangles to the cave floor

Between 1994 and 2014, the number of pups recorded each season varied between 5 and 7. In that time, three rock-fall events were recorded. The first, in 1997, and the second, in 2002, were both relatively minor in scale, apparently small ceiling falls that simply left behind small piles of broken rock where previously there had been none. The third, in October 2014, was major. This time, between two visits to monitor pup production and development that were separated by 10 days, a massive rock-fall occurred at the back of the cave, almost entirely obliterating the nursery beach and creating in its place a mountain of rubble about 40m in length.

During the pre-collapse visit, there had been three young white-coated pups, three seal mothers and one male present on the beach.

Before and After: After Great Seal Hole

Four site visits have been made since low water access was rendered impossible by the massive obstructing boulder. No seals were found in the cave on any of these visits, in contrast with them being ever-present before during survey visits.

Seal deficit: 16-18 (maybe <25) pups no longer being born annually at this site. Moulting assemblies of <50 seals were no longer known to be using this site.

Where have the seals gone: Unknown. Best guess: Tregea Hill Seal Hole has been used in times past, but has only been very little used since major culls took place there in the late 1930s. It is another spacious cave with a narrow, deep-water entrance and is the best seal cave anywhere in the region not known now to be used by seals.

North Cliffs Cove

20-plus season of pup production visits have been made since the headland- collapse.

Four caves, one cleft: obliterated.

One cave greatly altered in character: no longer used by seals.

Two caves (south shore) altered: not used historically by seals except as overflow sites: 1993–2011. 2012: no pups born. Three pups were born in 2014.

P-Cave: greatly altered in character, including pool being much diminished in size, although interior shingle hill remains unchanged. The floor of cave initially (2011–2012) had the consistency of thick, wet cement and was not used by seals. By 2013, the substrate was firmer and two pups were born. Four pups were born in 2014.

Seal increase: 2014: 2 pups at altered (improved) sites Seal deficit: 4–6 pups at obliterated sites.

3–5 pups at P-Cave. Net deficit: 7–11 pups. Where have the seals gone: 2011–2012: Unknown

2013–2014: HM: beach, cave and cavelets (see below) was used, a new site c.400m S of North Cliffs Cove.

2014: + Cave was used.

+ Cave

Three seasons of 20-plus visits per season of pup production have been made since the further collapse of the cave window.

Seal deficit: 2012–2013: no seals born here.

2014: 10 pups born here — the highest recorded figure to date for this site. Possibly, a fraction of these seal mothers originated at the North Cliffs sites.

Where have the seals gone: 2012–2013: Unknown.

2014: Full pup production resumed.

Adit Cave

No change occurred until the late part of 2014 season, when no more pups were born after the major ceiling collapse.

Seal deficit: Unknown: erosion event too recent. No results possible yet.

Conclusion

In total, sites that used to produce more than 30 pups annually have disappeared along this stretch of coast in just four years — a significant percentage of seals born annually at Cornish sites.

The majority of grey seals appear to have responded to the loss of habitat by using other local seal sites — not always previously used for pup production — much more intensively than before, as at HM. A minority appear to have returned to sites of origin, as at + Cave and those caves on the north shore of North Cliffs Cove (much less affected by the cliff collapse).

This remains an evolving story. + Cave requires currently that seals expend more energy than previously in moving between the nursery site and the sea. On the other hand, the extra rocks cluttering the fairway of the cave also confer a greater degree of protection to pups against wave and surf action when using the wider tunnel.

P-Cave is more susceptible to human intrusion than previously primarily due to the great reduction in size of the cave pool but also because it is very much easier for people to enter the cave now. Previously, there was much more of an uncertain scramble over jagged and slippery boulders.

The two 'new' North Cliffs cave sites are very exposed to wave action. Here, pups have to swim during the hours of high water on spring tides.

The haven of HM may yet prove to be less of a haven than it seems. Although it is inaccessible from the land, it is vulnerable to access from the sea. Disturbance at this site during the season of pup production could cause the seals to abandon a site that has not yet, perhaps, acquired the 'familiarity' of traditional sites that have been used over decades and even centuries.

Although no single survey has yet achieved a reliable figure for pup production at Cornish sites, studies at individual localities suggest currently (2020) it is not more than 200. The potential loss of 30 pups from this number represents a considerable fraction of this edge of range grouping of SW England grey seals It should also be noted that accidental by-catch of seals in local fisheries (especially bottom-set nets), with 70–75% being sexually immature, may cause as many seals to die in Cornish waters annually as are born at Cornish sites (Glain, 1998; Westcott, 1999).

Lastly, Cornwall is a premier tourist destination. Disturbance of seals from low water haul-out sites resulting from visits by commercial as well as private craft is commonplace, despite efforts to ensure best ethical practices at such sites.

This shows that this regional group of seals, the southernmost breeding group of grey seals in the NE Atlantic (but for c.10–20 pups born every year off the coasts of Brittany (Vincent, 2002), is under exceptional pressure.

Future coastal erosion studies must take account of the full range of actual and potential impacts on seal caves as well as other seal sites.

Where Seals Go When the Old Caves Die?

In this survey, three of the sites examined fell in a locality where long-term observations were current. Only Great Seal Hole fell outside the long-term survey area. There, initial visits suggest seals have abandoned the site but it should be noted that this perception is based on four visits subsequent to the rock-fall, all made around the hours of high tide. Site visits previously had always been made around the hours of low water. Therefore, seals may still be using this site.

At the North Cliffs Cove sites, initially all seal sites were abandoned in 2011 and 2012 after the headland collapse. Low level pup production resumed in the 2013 season. It doubled to four in the 2014 season, when two new cave sites were also used.

The 'missing' seals appear to have moved about 400m south along the coast to HM, where there is an extensive beach of sand and shingle at low water spring tides in addition to a single and a double cavelet as well as a substantial sea cave. In previous years, these sites have been used only intermittently during the period of pup production and then mainly in the form of resting places to which locally-born weaned pups made their first coastwise swim away from the nursery site.

However, ten pups were born at these sites in 2013 with eight pups being born in 2014.

The threat to this site may be from further erosion (a middling such event occurred in 2018) but also from the fact that this is a very popular viewpoint. There is also a café set back c.100 metres from the cliff edge. The 'secret' seal pups of the previous time are now highly visible and are clearly widely known to be there.

It may be that a lesser number of seals went north, not south, as far as + Cave, where normal pup production appears to have resumed. As the internal cliff fall at Adit Cave was similar in size to the + Cave fall, and as a fraction of the breeding beach remains, it may be that there will be either no interruption to 'normal' breeding or an interruption of just one or two seasons. It may also be relevant that this cave has a prolonged period (August to October) of regular use compared with all other local cave sites except + Cave. It remains to be seen whether the internal cave collapse at Adit Cave will affect the use of the site as a seal nursery in 2015.

Table 1: Pup production at all monitored sites along North Cliffs coast since cliff collapse: 2012 – 2014.

Year	August	September	October	Total
2012	1	7	1	9
2013	2	14	5	21
2014	2	25	4	31
Total	5	46	10	61

Table 2: Pup production at individual sites subject to cliff falls: 2012 – 2014.

2012	Cave 1	Cave 2	Beach 1	Cave 3	Cave 4
August	0	0	0	0	2
September	0	0	0	0	1
October	0	0	0	0	1
Total	0	0	0	0	4

2013	Cave 1	Cave 2	Beach 1	Cave 3	Cave 4
August	0	0	0	0	2
September	0	2	4	3	2
October	0	0	2	1	1
Total	0	2	6	4	5

2014	Cave 1	Cave 2	Beach 1	Cave 3	Cave 4
August	1	1	0	0	0
September	6	3	2	5	4
October	2	0	1	0	1
Total	9	4	3	5	5

This tells of one locality I was able to monitor in passing as well as the affected elements of a locality that was subject to long-term monitoring.

Other and even more dramatic cliff collapses have occurred over the 30 years of these seal studies.

The three hearts of grey seal distribution in SW England are centred on the Boscastle coast, the Godrevy coast and in the Isles of Scilly. The greatest collapse of which I saw evidence occurred at Beeny, which is the major cliff-backed beach — as against seal caves — component of the Boscastle coast seal locality.

For monitoring purposes, I divided the broad bay beach tucked under Beeny Cliff into three. Most southerly of these is a long, quite wide and remote beach more difficult to observe from the coastal footpath than the other two because blind-spots remain. This south end of the bay under Beeny Cliffs is of primary interest as a winter-into-spring moulting assembly beach. In the 2000's assemblies there numbered in excess of 200 grey seals. Similar counts were made there in the late 1980s/early 1990s by someone for whom I feel nothing but the highest regard and affection. It was an observation point, before ever I knew of the place, for that unique pathfinding student of peregrine falcons, Dick Treleavan.

The south end of the bay under Beeny Cliffs is of primary interest as a winter-into-spring moulting assembly beach but some pups are also born there while still more take refuge there when flushed from sea cave nurseries in the locality by the particularly heavy wave action that beats upon this part of the coast. It is a site easy to recognise, being separated from the other beaches by a big stack with a wide corridor running through it at the top of the beach and by massive boulders lower down to the low water mark.

Largely sheltered by Gull Rock, the north end of the bay is used mainly as a nursery beach. Pups are born there in numbers that vary between the years but as at the south end, pups born in caves just to the north of the bay take refuge here if storm seas flush them from their vulnerable natal sites. For a resting-place, sometimes they use smooth, flat boulders speckled with a golden dust of copper pyrites.

Largest and least-used by seals of these beaches is what I call midway beach. Here was the broadest beach, hedged on both sides by fences of boulders. Very steep cliffs used to rise from the back of the beach with surprisingly small caves nibbled into its base. These I scoured, as everywhere else in my searches for seals and their young and there I might find just one or two, always in the season of pup production. Most often, I found none. As well, then, it was here that the breadth of the cliff collapsed, totally consuming the small, nibbled caves on one thunderous occasion. Totally consuming the beach places where seal mothers had lain with their pups on sunny days of August and September. Totally consuming the memory of my own footprints.

My strongest abiding memory of the beach that was lost was of another sunny September morning. I was squatting, watching from a place of concealment. A seal mother was tilted over on one side and seemingly relaxed, exposing her lovely speckled belly. A fat pup, maybe 13 days old, was suckling, seemingly oblivious to the world. Farther away, a second pup was asleep. It had been recently born, maybe 2 days since. Some distance beyond lay the placenta while the seal mother watched attentively from a place grounded in the shallows.

I was not the only one to notice the placenta. From a grassy slope just above the beach, a fox paused to scan, yet again, the locality. I watched it trot down to the beach while wondering whether or not the young and helpless-seeming pup was at risk. Apparently not. The fox came by a circuitous track across the beach not to the pup, which was ignored, but to the placenta. This, the fox proceeded to eat. Afterwards, it returned to the grassy slope.

The other great rockfall is a hazier memory. There was another great cliff-collapse at or near Hanover Cove (quite near to Cligga Point). Consumed here was also a cave I had explored with my friend, Martin Hunt. He had taken me to the back of the cave, to examine a pile of clusters of iron pyrites crystals — also known as fool's gold. Well, we were happy fools that day and happier still not to be there when the cliff came tumbling down.

In review, there seems to have been acceleration in the rate of cliff collapses and of smaller erosion events inside sea caves since the late 1990s. I am not, with regret, a geologist or a seismologist and I am uncertain whether this is being studied. I assume it must be but have been unable to locate where.

Tentatively, I can report that my daily and three decades-worth of observations of the weather of the seal coasts — especially wind speed and direction, as well as of sea state — suggest what is generally recognised and now forecast. Summers appear to have become hotter and drier. Winters have become stormier and wetter. The tendency toward these extremes may make the cliff rocks more friable or more likely to collapse. It seems highly likely to me that it would have such an (erosive) influence of the mudstones and siltstones that clad so many Cornish cliffs. While I will bow to expert opinion, whatever the cause, it seems certain to continue for the foreseeable future.

Questions We Might Begin to Answer After the First Years of Monitoring the Seal Caves

One year of study of seal behaviour at any site is insufficient to learn how, when and why the seal caves are used, as should become apparent below. Sea conditions, driven by weather conditions, forever exert their great and variable influence. Consequently, once I had identified the grey seal localities in SW England and located what I hoped were all the sites in each locality, I selected the locality closest to my home and made a detailed, years-round study of seal distribution and behaviour there.

This locality consisted of 5 seal cave sites, 2 remote beach sites, 3 skerries, an islet and 2 inshore resting places. There was one additional, seasonally important islet site situated well offshore where accurate counts could not then be made: Longships.

After two full years examining these sites, well-imagining that results obtained might be anomalous, I decided to additionally examine another seal locality. This consisted, initially of 12 seal caves, one cleft with a beach, four beaches and one islet — but proved to be subject to rock-falls and erosion events inside caves and so concluded as 11 seal caves, five beaches and an islet.

The original locality was subject to 5 years of initial study (1994 to 1998), the other locality was subject to 3 years of initial study (1996 to 1998). Three visits per month were made to each site, always on the same day but varying due to time constraints between the two localities. No pattern of visits was imposed. They were governed by sea state: whether it was possible to reach every site or not, in order to count, sex and — in the case of the immatures — differentiate them from adult seals. Sex was not ascribed to the immatures due to the potential for error. Results at the original site showed that seals used the sea cave site through the year at two of them, only in the seasons of pup production and moulting at the third and rarely only at the remaining two.

Usually, seals used the caves in greatest numbers over the hours of high tide — substantial sandy beaches being available during that period in three of them. This was apparent from seal tracks and sleeping-place hollows. Usually at high tide (due to bickering over resting places plus invasions of space) or between two and three hours of the ebb-tide, some or all seals abandoned the caves. However, usually, also a number of seals remained on cave beaches, resting during the entire tidal cycle.

The bickering over the high tide period did not lead to major acts of aggression between mature seals outside the season of pup production. Nevertheless, this would be, mainly, a time of restlessness oftentimes attended by much seal vocalisation.

The evidence also showed that rather than abandon the caves when storm seas were running, seals remained in the caves — either on the beaches or beyond the wave-break inside the caves.

While the seal caves nurseries were in use, numbers were pared down, almost always, to 'essential' seals only — namely mothers, un-weaned and weaned pups plus either a solitary mature male or also a challenger male.

Although there were more caves in the second locality, these were used very much more lightly through the year. In fact, they were used mainly only during the season of pup production. Small assemblies of seals did occur at two cave sites during the moulting period but the likelihood is that this was only a sporadic event as large assemblies of moulting seals were using two nearby sites on cliff-backed beaches. Evidently, more space was available to them there, unlike at the original locality.

In conclusion, seal cave use appears much heavier and occurs year-round in this region especially wherever remote, cliff-backed beaches or islands offering resting-places free from wave action on-site are unavailable. This was not studied in so much detail at the important

Boscastle coast sites but appears to apply there. Caves are used through the year but during stormy interludes, outdoor beaches exist where they may take refuge without risk of human disturbance. The physical nature of the cave indicates the likely use made of it by seals. The first element of importance is the location of the cave in its locality: which way is the local coast orientated? How exposed to which winds is the stretch of coast orientated?

The second element relates to the existence close enough to the cave entrance of helpful physical features. These might include rocks, stacks, reefs, sandbanks and islets. Any of these features may reduce the potential exposure of the site to the predominant winds driving wave action, ensuring the sea consistently impacts upon the cave interior with lesser force than would have been the case: a crucial element in making a sea cave useful to a seal

Arriving at the sea cave entrance, the compass orientation of the entrance can be a crucial factor. It will be preferable to seals if it opens in a direction sheltered from the predominant winds, which mainly blow from the south-west to north-west quarter in south-western Britain.

Another feature concerning the cave entrance is whether boulders have been piled at some level between the high and low-water marks by wave action; perhaps, occasionally, by internal cave erosion events. This offers a degree of protection to the cave interior by functioning as a dune or breakwater of boulders. Such breakwaters staunch the power of the incoming waters by creating a buffer or by causing a 'premature' wave-break. Where wave plunge power is premature, the impact of surf action on the interior sites used by seals is reduced. The erosive potential of the wave is also reduced where it breaks upon massive entrance boulders and because the rocky dune serves to prevent sand being sucked from the cave.

Often in partnership with a low-water breakwater, many seal caves have deep-water entrances at low-water. The length to which such deep-water entrances penetrate the cave interior, and the depth, is variable — very rarely exceeding 200 metres. Evidence shows that grey seals exercise a strong preference for being able to enter the sea or haul-out from it within the cave, in the lesser light of the cave, rather than out beyond its entrance.

In the event that a deep-water entrance yields on to a cave beach inside the cave, the relationship between the dimensions of the entrance and the main cave chamber within is important. Some (usually) narrow, deep-water sea cave entrance tunnels curve or snake for what may be a considerable distance (in my experience, up to 200 metres) before eventually opening into the great chamber that is likely to be the main resort of the seals. This is, most often, high-ceilinged and may be filled with water during some part of the tidal cycle. The great power of even large incoming swells is here immediately dissipated by being absorbed into the sudden and great widening of the main cave chamber.

Usually, on the far interior of what is, in effect, a great cave lake, a beach or beaches of sand or boulders rise steeply to the back of the cave, often with a curving aspect. However, from the research point of view, you need to be ready for the degree to which natural light varies in such a cave. Where the incoming swells rise almost to the ceiling of the entrance tunnel, they can block out the light almost entirely. In the gaps between them, a more generous quality of light prevails.

Another adaptation is also required. In the interludes of darkness, it can be hard to imagine ever escaping from the cave — back to the ever-welcome light. However, the suck of the sea to seaward contributes to the ease of escape.

The ideal combination would have a narrow entrance tunnel (it might be straight, curving or serpentine) opening into a much wider main chamber, with both elements being high-walled. In that case, the power of the sea would immediately be substantially dissipated where the chamber widened. That being so, its impact on the site would be minimal.

Where the entrance tunnel is wide, a boulder beach will serve to reduce the power of the incoming waves far better than do finer substrates, but in the absence of a beach remaining in the deep interior beyond the reach of wave action at high tide, this is likely to be sub-optimal as seen from the seal perspective.

For the shape of their entrances and the great chambers beyond, I call these most favoured seal caves Mateus Rosé caves.

A second positive scenario from the seal viewpoint would find the force of the sea greatly reduced where it meets the steepest possible beach within, more particularly where it is a beach of large boulders below the high-water mark. A steeper fairway is subject to a shorter run of surf than one more shallow, given the same surf conditions. Shallow beaches are susceptible to a potentially very erosive beach-break by the waves and their longer runs of surf.

Finally, there is the element of the width of cave fairways. A few are little wider than the width of a normal human body. Some may be barely wide enough to admit a paddled ski into the cave, given the manipulation of a steeply-angled paddle. These are narrow caves where it makes better sense to propel the ski by using your arms as levers against the cave walls. More typical, middling caves can be categorised as being between 1.5 and 4 metres wide while the wide caves have fairways of 4 metres width and more.

In theory, the wider the fairway, the better — especially where caves are used as nursery sites. Wider fairways allow seal mothers stressed by what might be akin to some form of social claustrophobia to be given a wide berth by other seal mothers and pups, thereby avoiding the risk of bloody engagements that would occur where the fairway was less wide.

The presence of a sand or gravel beach upon which grey seals can rest without being disturbed at high water on a spring tide is a very attractive feature to grey seals. A deep-water entrance yielding within the cave on to the beach ensures them more immediate access to the sea than if they had to galumph over a varied terrain to the entrance of the cave. Pools at least the depth of a seal's body over the low tide period appear to be consistently attractive to a seal. Their preference for such a site appears further enhanced where there are either cubby-holes (tunnels of varying length) leading off the main cave fairway or a 'kennel' (an annex) at the very back of the cave, beyond the main fairway.

Where the cave has a high roof, has a main fairway of greater rather than lesser breadth, and if there are islets or emergent reefs outside the cave entrance that serve to protect it against the impact of wave action, these also contribute to the 'seal value' of a cave. Lastly, where there is a particularly long deep-water passage leading to the beach following a zigzagging course, the presence of a substantial emergent skerry along its course serves as a reef creating a premature wave break, ensuring that incoming waves lose their main power at that point, before reaching the beach itself and any seals thereon.

The shape (including the height) of the sea cave has much to do with the behaviour of swells, wave action, type and potential mobility of substrates within the caves. This is substantially determined by the geology of each site. Examples include the not-uncommon Y-shaped caves where the sea enters via two entrances and meets in cross-waves that may be violent and confused. Thereafter, its power already partly quelled, the swell runs more quietly into the deeps of the cave. Its progress is even less destructive when the substrate consists of middling or large boulders, which absorb considerably the power of the surf. Deep pools spanning the fairway also reduce the impact and reach of surf whereas it runs swiftest over shallow-sloping sand.

A variation on the cave shapes described above — and there are variations to every shape described here — is the hammer-head cave, where the two entrances face one another broadside on to the main fairway of the cave. Such a cave can be expected to have a beach that escapes the worst of the conditions that might be raging out-with.

Straight and wedge-shaped sea cave fairways appear to offer little protection to seals where there is an incoming swell or surf. Where seals make considerable use of them, almost always it will be in small numbers and it is likely to be because the entrance is sheltered by its orientation from the prevailing swells and/or because the substrate is steeply angled upwards toward the interior.

Some relatively straight cave fairways fork dramatically and early, at the far reach of the sea at low tide, which serves to inhibit the power of the sea in at least one of the tunnels. Other caves run relatively straight until in the deep interior they fork dramatically to twin ends. Although its beaches must be subject to heavy wave action and surf-race, one such site in Wales is the principal nursery cave for the entire region. Following the lesser storms, seal pups survive there, so long as their mothers remain in faithful attendance (which they do, usually). This holds true whether or not they are forced to swim over the period of high water, when violently turbulent conditions must be commonplace. Only the great storms see the mother-pup pairings flushed from the cave on the backwash and forced to peregrinate a short distance along the coast to a very nearby safer haven.

Newborn pup, mother and placenta in a nursery cave

There are randomly complex-shaped caves such as the h-cave described among the anecdotes (below). I know of one complex cave that, in effect, goes off in all four directions from a point near its heart with additional chambers leading off two of the tunnels. This ensures there is always potential rest somewhere within for seals, no matter how fiercely the sea might be raging outside.

Shape allied to the extent of shelter from the prevailing wind and wave action along with the extent of penetration by the sea and the availability of a beach beyond the reach of the tide at high water are the primary features of the most heavily used seal caves. There are several important secondary features.

The substrate type or variety influences the use of a cave site by seals. They appear to shun caves in which there are none but huge boulders piled, presumably because they offer no potential for movement across them and there is the risk of falling between them.

They do use caves where the boulders are huge so long as they can move between them.

Being wrapped in considerable duvets of blubber, seals experience no discomfort while resting on bedrock (including ledges), middling-sized or small boulders, cobbles or pebbles — although they do show a preference for resting on long-settled rocky substrates. However, they show the strongest preference for resting on sands and gravels, where available.

Sands and gravels are the substrate types most prone to mobility during the cycle of the year and its varied sea conditions. Periods of quiet seas with small, gentle waves tend to have no effect on sea cave beaches whereas storm waves very soon either reduce them, especially with their erosive suck, or cause accretion by driving sand into the cave.

The existence of tide pools at low water seems especially important during the season of pup production. During that period, far more than any other, these pools which may be as much as 2 metres in depth and wide as the cave fairway seem to take on particular importance. They may be sandy-bottomed or have bases of bedrock or boulders. When the pups are born, very often they sleep in these pools. This may be for physical comfort: in the earliest days of life, while they look like little more than skin and bone, they take their first swims and dives in these pools. It may be water is a more comfortable medium in which to rest than upon sand, pebbles or rock. Often, these swims may be sociable, made in the company of other pups.

Alternatively, seal mothers may prefer to rest — at the surface or submerged — in these pools rather than ashore. Again, this may be a sociable behaviour as they tolerate other females sharing the same pool at close quarters. Or, it may demonstrate that some seals are more sea-centric than others. Certainly, conflict between them in this situation has not been observed.

Finally, these pools function as mating sites. Usually, the male pursues the female (in her late lactation-period oestrus) down the cave fairway. In the pool shallows, while they are yet moving, he takes her nape firmly — but without biting — in his mouth. Where the water is sufficiently deep, he forces her below the surface and manoeuvres into position to mate, his ventral surface (underside) to her dorsal surface (back). The manoeuvring may take a prolonged period of time, particularly where the female appears undecided as to whether she wishes to admit him or not.

Following mating, they remain entirely quiescent in the water, at or just below the surface. Her back remains turned to his front. His fore-flippers rest upon her flanks. They can remain so for as long as 90 minutes. Then, typically, it is the hunger cries of her large pup, close to weaning now, that causes the female to break off the engagement, swim to shore, haul out and make her way to one of the final suckling sessions.

Where there are no pools available at low tide, mating takes place in the sea cave entrance waters or in the sea just outside the cave entrance. It appears that they prefer to mate in shallow, often weedy, water

Typically, use is made of clusters of seal caves in every locality as 'safety-valves'. This applies through the year and not only during the season of pup production. Where stormy conditions impact on the main site, another site on the far side of the bay, its entrance facing in a different direction, will be used as a site of refuge by adult seals (particularly during the moulting period) as well as by pups.

Pups look incapable of swimming any distance but while on a tagging expedition with Dr. Duguy (La Rochelle) and Bernie McConnell (SMRU) in the early 1990s, we found that overnight a pup aged about 10 days and tagged last thing one evening was, the following morning, resting on an island more than a kilometre distant.

The pup-tagging expedition, on which I served as the 'native guide', was an attempt to learn whether the seal pups found starving on the French coast might have originated at the Isles of Scilly. However, as no recaptures of tagged seals were identified subsequently, the question remained open. The very interesting results of the Welsh pup-tagging work conducted by A.L. Johnston were possibly unknown to Dr. Duguy, as they were to me at that time.

In several localities through the sea cave breeding range of grey seals I have seen mothers giving their pups 'piggy-back' rides in the inshore waters as well as in cave pools. The pup appears to dig its long claws into the neck hair of the mother and either to cling on or to half haul-out there. Even while submerged, always only during shallow dives by the mother, the pup remains attached. This is a variant — a useful support to have available — in the event of the pup needing to make a long-distance passage. However, the white-coated seal pup swims independently most of the time it is in the sea.

The final feature evidently attractive to grey seals is the company of other seals, even though oftentimes seals may be found alone in sea caves. Most often, these are moulted pups (that may not yet have abandoned their nursery site) and yearlings that appear to be feeling their way around a world in which the remainder of their lives will be lived. Less often, the individual will be a mature male. Females are least likely to be found alone, except when the birth of a pup is imminent.

The most favoured caves, including cave-clusters in the same bay, are used by seals — often in considerable numbers — on most days of the year.

These caves are put to multi-purpose use by the seals: as lodges, natal and nursery sites and as moulting sites. However, seals use the largest number and variety of sea cave sites in the season of pup production. Some of these are not otherwise used, except perhaps very occasionally for a lodge, in the remainder of a year. This is partly due to an evident need of privacy or at least the absence of conflict between seal mothers at this time so that full attention can be given to the pup. It should also be remembered that the timing of the breeding season varies considerably over a period of 5 to 9 months from locality to locality and year to year in south-west England and to a much lesser extent in north Wales.

There have been autumns when episodes of severe storm sea conditions (not necessarily prolonged) have caused the swift and massive disappearance of sand from the nursery caves. Where this happened on a neap tide, there have been repeated occasions when not only was there huge deposition of kelp to depths of two metres, but much or all of the sand accumulated below the neap tide high water mark was removed from the caves. The sand above the neap tide high water mark remained as before except that now it remained as a plateau up to three metres above a mainly vertical drop to the remnant of the lower part of the beach. Pups remained on the interior plateau so seal mothers remained with them through the tide cycle or came ashore only at high tide to clamber up ramps of soft sand to feed them.

Another (temporary) physical feature that bears upon survivorship of un-weaned seal pups results from secondary storms lacking extreme erosive power. These seas can also deposit masses of kelp on to nursery beaches. Wave action sweeps most of the kelp to the daily varying high-water mark and there it gathers in a dune that grows slowly ever higher. It is not uncommon after such storms to find a kelp-dune measuring up to one metre in height.

That this is enormously helpful to the seal pups may seem surprising but in fact now the kelp-dune functions perfectly as a soft-engineering structure. I have watched such dunes yielding, always ever so slightly, creaking back just a few centimetres at a time, as wave after wave breaks against them or the surf races over the substrate into them. While the kelp-dune gently yields and then returns to the original place, the white-coated seal pup at the base of the cave wall immediately behind it sleeps. Resting on its back, its fore-flippers folded across its chest, it snores and snuffles, twitching now and then, following the strange interrupted breathing pattern of its kind. The seal mother quite often will be resting broadside-on, facing the cave entrance at the apex of the kelp-dune, maintaining her vigilance.

There is a sinister side to kelp accumulations in sea caves that becomes especially apparent only during the season of pup production. Some kelp is torn by the huge power of the surf from holdfast anchorages. The remainder is carried through the water column from seabed resting places. On passage, often it picks up oil — whether freshly dumped or churned up having been long since dumped — that adheres to fronds or stipes. When deposited on the cave beach, the first sign of it in the deep gloom, if you are walking there barefoot, is that your feet and ankles turn black. More concerning, the white coats of the suckling seal pups are blotched with oil. Because they scratch or wipe their faces a lot, much oil ends on their faces, around mouth and eyes.

Once, I happened upon a draggled seal pup 100% covered with oil. It looked most woebegone, but a few days later it moulted. Perhaps there remained oil on its pelage, but the adult pelage is blotched black anyway so it was no longer clearly apparent whether it remained fouled by the oil. On another occasion, in another year, I watched a moulted pup pushing its enquiring face into a clump of heavily oil-fouled rope and netting in the cave entrance waters. I shouted from close quarters, but the seal ignored me being more intent on its exploration. I was able to do nothing helpful.

In the West Country sea caves, moulting assemblies are dominated mainly by males, although not exclusively.

At this time, especially females appear to have an 'eclipse' pelage, where they appear — misleadingly — to have only a fine pale dun-coloured pelage, as if they have no blotches, when dry. However, when they enter the sea, it becomes evident that they are well-marked with the black blotches typical of the species. In this, they resemble white-coated pups during the latter part of the period of lactation. Ashore, with a dry pelage, they appear to have moulted, to be wearing their first adult pelage. When they enter the sea or a pool, it becomes immediately apparent that they still have white coats. However, it is equally evident that the white hair has become sparse. While wet, the first adult coat remains apparent through the inadequate screen of white hairs. At this stage, the white hair resembles the efforts made by men almost lacking in hair to comb too-thin hair across an otherwise bald pate.

It is a sign that the first moult is nearing completion.

At an earlier stage, the first sign that the pup-moult is under weigh is when the white-coated pups acquire a 'grubby' appearance. In effect, not only is their white hair becoming shorter, but also it is becoming thinner — something that is a continuous process for lactating pups.

Moulting adults appear to undergo a similar process except that their loss of hair tends to be patchier, especially in the case of the males.

The last aspect of the seal caves to be mentioned is human impacts. Their reaction to human entry into the sea cave is nearly always to stampede from the cave less carefully and sooner than they would have done at a time of their own choosing. In so doing, in a rocky habitat they may cause minor injuries to their claws. In the panic to reach the sea, there may be snapping or biting (although biting is extremely rare).

There is a risk that pups or yearlings might be trampled, although I have not observed this.

Under no circumstances should a powered vessel enter a cave. Aside from this being a dangerous manoeuvre, it is certain to disturb any seals resting within. Seals in the water — at the surface or submerged — may be injured by their tendency to explore propellers.

Historically, kayakers have proven more likely than any other people on the water to cause disturbance to seals resulting in a stampede into the sea. This may seem incredible to them but I could substitute 'wave ski' for kayak and it would hold equally true. This has been observed repeatedly during seal behaviour monitoring exercises.

I was paddling more than 125 metres distant from a seal haul-out site on ledges of a lighthouse island in north Wales when the assembled seals began to crane their necks and the first of them began to slide into the sea. As per the advice written into the many protocols for minimising or avoiding disturbance, not only did I cease paddling tangentially toward them. Also, I began to ease my way backwards away from them. However, the flow of seals continued until all of them had entered the sea.

The essence of what happened was that I should have stopped or diverted when the first seal raised her head, staring fixedly at me. That was the tripwire moment — the point when the scales were perfectly balanced. In such instances, the amending manoeuvre can result in just one or a handful of seals being spooked into the sea. This site was not usually so sensitive. Surmise suggests there had been a spate of disturbance events in recent days, leaving the seals on edge.

To make matters worse from my point of view, at the same site in another year, I was resting on my belly in the cliff slope grasses carrying out behavioural monitoring. There were about thirty seals resting on the rocky ledges below. A jet ski carrying the driver and one passenger came by at full speed. The man driving was shouting over his shoulder to the lady sitting behind him as they passed the seals at a distance of about 10 metres. A few seals lifted their heads. Then they settled again. There was no other reaction.

Contrasting the two reactions by the seals, it is evident that seals do not share the same prejudices against jet skis shown by many people.

As for their reaction to the wave ski (and to kayaks), this may indicate they associate humans and harmlessness with noise. The paddlers often sit approximately amidships or a little farther back on craft sitting low in the sea. I have wondered if then we bear some disturbing resemblance to a killer whale, our upper bodies resembling the upright dorsal fin of the males. I cannot think how else a paddler might threaten danger in their minds.

On any particular day, when might seals be using a cave? Strangely, they seem to prefer to use caves around the hours of high-water, as can be seen by examining their tracks and hollows or by observing the seal cave entrance over the full tidal cycle monitoring comings and goings.

Once ashore and, especially, once dry, seals evidence a dislike of being splashed or otherwise wet. Consequently, they are driven even deeper into the cave, ever higher up the beach, by the rising tide and its probing runs of surf. Where the seal assembly is numerous, this leads to much bumping, leading to changing position trying to escape the reach of the water. It can be an uncomfortable, unrestful time.

After the tide has turned, the seals have no goad causing them to continue jockeying for position. They settle and, mainly, sleep.

In the sites I have studied, seals tend to depart the cave during the uncomfortable high-tide melee or else from two to three hours after high-tide. This can be read from the seal marks on the between-tides sands, from the place where, abruptly, they cease.

Lastly, more important than any other consideration — even the imperative to seek to avoid disturbing any seals within — everyone should be punctilious while inside a seal cave, to check repeatedly that a safe exit remains open.

A Grey Seal year in and out of the seal caves of SW Britain: Introduction

Grey seals spend up to 85% of their lives in the sea (or estuary waters). When out on foraging expeditions, tagged seals of all ages tracked by the SMRU have revealed that to travel up to 50 kilometres to foraging grounds and 50 back again is commonplace. Neither is a passage of 100 kilometres on the outward leg outside the norm. Much longer passages have also been recorded.

Their work also indicated that grey seals, in effect, visit their neighbours. They travel to sites that might be 25, 100, 200 miles or more from what might be regarded as their home area and there they may remain for up to several months.

Translated into the Cornish context, that means there is no reason to be surprised if a seal using the sea cave beaches of West Penwith, the North Cliffs or the Lizard is sighted in the Isles of Scilly or off the south Devon coast. There should be no surprise discovering seals of the Boscastle cave beaches being sighted near Lundy, Padstow or Ramsey in SW Wales. There is no surprise if seals using the Lundy sea caves are sighted on the coast and islands of SW Wales. There is no surprise if seals of the Land's End turn up on the Saltee Islands off SE Ireland, on Skomer or Ramsey islands off the tip of SW Wales, on the shores of Anglesey, Man or Rathlin or among the islands of l'archipel Molène off the west coast of Brittany.

Grey seals, it seems, belong primarily to sea areas while associating with certain inshore localities where they need to haul-out and rest. While they seem to prefer hauling out in the company of other seals, it is not uncommon to chance on lone seals resting ashore.

The earliest clues as to how far seals may travel along the coasts and across the seas of SW Britain came from the pup-tagging work led by A.L. Johnston in SW Wales between 1949 and 1972. This wonderful piece of work, so long before its time, showed pups tagged at Welsh nursery sites appeared not only on the Welsh coasts but on the west coast of Ireland, the coasts of Lundy, Devonshire, Cornwall and the Isles of Scilly, the coasts of Brittany and even farther afield. These were the passages made by moulted pups as they first ventured out into the world, learning to forage as they went (or dying in the attempt, as was commonplace) while also — as I fancy, anyway — making their own map of the world. It is a study I believe that could bear to be repeated on a wider scale, now that people are more alert to the need to report sighting tagged animals. Also, the tags themselves are now more diverse and potentially visible.

In the paper on grey seals at Cornwall and Isles of Scilly sites produced in 1973 by the Seal's Research Division (led by C.F. Summers), there was a reference to anecdotal comments by P.Z. Mackenzie, vet and early seal naturalist on the Isles of Scilly. He spoke of large winter influxes of several hundred grey seals to sites on the Western Rocks that were 'from Wales'. That is a presumption, for example, that could be tested.

There has been some plastic hat-tagged and satellite relayed data logger tracking of grey seals released from Brittany sites which has shown seals moving NE toward south Devonshire and N towards the west Cornwall localities of Land's End and Godrevy. Indeed, there were memorable clusters of sightings of hat-tagged Brittany seals off Godrevy in the last decade of the twentieth century, notably by Terry Hocking. While there with him one day, I sighted seven hatted seals, five being from Brittany with one from Wales and the other being from Norfolk. It may be making far too much of a lone clue (although other sightings of lesser numbers of hatted seals were made there and at Land's End during that period) to imagine the tip of the great south-western peninsula of England, is a major cross-road for seals in passage.

From 2000, photo-identification research, initially by Oliver O'Cadhla and Mick Baines, later satellite relayed data logger tracking by CCW supported by the SMRU, showed seals taking just one day to cross the Celtic Sea from Ireland to Wales or vice versa.

In 2002, in her PhD thesis, Cécile Vincent related SMRU-supported tracking studies of seals travelling to the coasts of Devonshire, Cornwall and West Wales from release sites in Brittany. Of these, the story of the visit to SW Devon was most entertaining, in that the seal spent just two hours on the Devon coast before returning immediately to the Breton coast.

The Inshore Year of the Grey Seals

At the outset, it is important to recognise that grey seal use of inshore waters varies from year to year as well as from day to day. This variety is their response to the environmental variables to which they are subject. Of particular importance among these are wind direction and speed, sea state (which may not relate to current local weather conditions but to oceanic storms and hurricanes maybe thousands of miles away sending bigger seas pulsing toward the land) and wave action. Wave action causes mobility of substrates and changes shapes of sandbanks as well as the angles and substance of sand-hills inside the sea caves. For example, the heavy, plunging seas of winter can cause huge erosion of material from sea caves, depositing it elsewhere in such a way that it forms a new reef or sandbank outside the cave entrance which will serve either to make the interior more or less exposed.

There are also the 'seal variables'. The company of seals changes daily as some depart on foraging expeditions while others return. Some may be travelling along the coast or from across the sea. A few may be resident. Some may be out of sight, utilising the seaward quarter of offshore haul-out sites; or poor light quality may inhibit accurate identification of individuals. There is so much still to learn.

Where to begin the year is a poser. As noted earlier, every seal locality in the West Country has its own season of pup production that may or may not overlap with that of the neighbouring seal localities. There is no simple pattern that tells, for example, it begins earliest in the west and progresses to the latest in the east. In fact, it is a hotchpotch. It is safe to say that the season of pup production influences the time of the annual moult and therefore the key events in the year of the grey seal.

April To July In and Beyond Seal Bay

April is as good a month as any in which to begin the story of their year.

By April, the winter assemblies have largely — but not always — dispersed from Seal Hole and Marshfrit Cave. There have been exceptional years when occasional moulting assemblies were still to be found in May in Seal Hole. However, from April onward, the seals usually occur in only small numbers in the caves, apparently using them exclusively as lodges. Typically, there might be seven — mostly males — in Seal Hole, resting some distance below the high-water mark. This suggests that at a certain stage, the group thought of departure, perhaps because of the run of the surf into their dry bodies. This would have caused them to 'do the banana', where they curl up hugely at both ends. At such times, they are trying to keep their extremities out of the reach of the shock of wet and cold.

Healthy grey seals have bodies in effect wrapped in duvets of blubber some 5 centimetres thick. However, they have little fat on their flippers and head. Then, if we were looking at them through infra-red eyes, we would see that because they are capable of thermo-regulation, they have pushed much of the heat in their bodies to the places covered by least blubber so they can get rid of it. Thus, head and flippers are very warm when they are at rest. If a wave then runs up against their bodies, despite their adaptations to the marine environment, they feel the cold — can even be seen to shiver. It is a reflex action that causes them to lift fore and hind-flippers and head as far out of reach of the water as they can. This is what I call 'doing the banana'.

There might be a lone yearling or a juvenile sleeping deeply off the main fairway in a cubby-hole in Sunlight Cave. More often, there is a solitary set of tracks signifying a seal had either explored the cave on the middle two hours of the tide and departed or else had rested there over the hours of high water only, departing on the middle of the tide.

Marshfrit Cave is most often empty.

The same holds true for the two outlying caves, Smoothie's and Elephant's Hide, which are only exceptionally used by the seals — usually yearlings or juveniles — and then they remain in the entrance waters sleeping or else resting upright and awake. These caves, with their massive boulder substrates, are never used for hauling out.

There is another cave belonging to this series situated in the neighbouring bay which has a long deep-water entrance yielding on to a beach of large, rough-edged boulders. Cinnabar Cave is an unpromising haul-out site but seals do rest in the entrance waters, bottling while they sleep — dry snouts pointed to the cave roof. Despite the unattractive resting place, sometimes lone males do haul-out there.

Not far along the cliffs from Cinnabar Cave is the narrow Zawn Cinnabar, a long, narrow, oblong inlet of the sea under high, sheer walls. The sea yields here on to a beach of middle-sized, sea-smoothed boulders. Seals rarely haul out here — it appears to serve mainly as an autumn refuge for up to three moulted pups at a time, departing their natal sites in the caves of the neighbouring bay beginning their independent lives. Adults occasionally haul out here but more often sleep in the waters outside the wave break.

On the far side of this bay is the shallow belly of Sharkfin Cove where, usually, clear waters offer water sleeping places for males or juvenile seals above a sea-floor of smoothed boulders or, at high water, shell sands. The cove seems to attract passing birds in need of shelter and offers good perching places for peregrines, kestrels and even short-eared owls. I have seen ravens perched there but they were hunched up and miserable at the time as two peregrines were repeatedly buzzing them. It was as if the falcons were going up and down on a pulley. Peregrines and ravens are said to be fairly evenly matched but hereabouts I have only ever seen life being made difficult for the ravens. Two were brought to ground by a pair of peregrines one spring morning and there they remained cowed until the peregrines tired of swooping low over their cowering heads.

Over the years, the Mermaid's Pool has been as interesting to study as the seal caves.

Beyond Sharkfin Cove, the cliffs are sheltered by low-lying skerries to seaward. So often I have watched seals emerging from the caves in the seal headquarters of Seal Bay. Some linger, playing in the turbulent white waters swirling around the emergent rocks below the headland that offers some shelter to Seal Hole. Others simply swim by and then on across the bay behind the turning wheel of the wave-break over the shifting sandbanks. They come alone, in pairs, in groups of up to five. Later, the others follow. All of them rendezvous at Mermaid's Pool.

To seaward there may be a considerable swell but there is usually a period around the hours of low tide when the waters inside the skerries are calm, perhaps the surface being scuffed by whatever there is of breeze. Often, these turquoise waters are entirely clear. It is possible to watch the impressions of seals drifting upward toward the surface where they become wet-headed and substantial again.

Most often, males and juveniles frequent this place although females occasionally dominate the water assembly. Again, as in the caves, the principal behaviour is rest or sleep but there are variations.

Prolonged water dances will often be taking place there. This is where two seals — most commonly immatures, less commonly immatures with mature females and never involving mature males — play in the water together. They appear to seek to maintain a point of contact throughout, although that is occasionally broken, resulting in a water chase before the play is resumed.

Their behaviour consists of much rolling of their bodies on the longitudinal axis while at the surface. Indeed, that is where they are likely to remain throughout, rarely submerging. In that time, they may several times fleetingly 'haul-out' one on the other, as part of the 'dance'. The pace of their activity varies, too.

Other pairs of dancers may be close by. Mature seals using the same waters as a resting place, usually sleeping or cat-napping, show little interest in the dancers. Other lone immatures or lone mature females may watch intently from the side-lines but the dancers remain exclusive of the other seals.

To date, dances observed have lasted for up to six hours.

At no other time are grey seals as unaware or heedless of their surroundings as when engaged in water dances — except, presumably, when they are hunting.

The final striking feature of the seals use of Mermaid's Pool is how they react to stormy seas, to huge piles of white water successively surging across the skerries and destroying the relative tranquillity of the water resting place inshore of them.

The seals appear not to alter their intentions at all. They remain at the same water sites they use whether conditions are calm or seething white surf. Although they are subject to some tugging here and there in so powerful a commotion of waters, for the most part while at the surface, it is as if the waters pass through them. They seem to have minimal effect. It is like watching darkly-bobbing storm colanders. The seals appear to stand mainly upright in the water while at the surface although occasionally they will be logging. The spume sometimes gathers on their heads but otherwise they seem little affected by the conditions.

Another feature of this season is male-male pre-season aggression.

The onset of the breeding season may yet be four months away. The very lack of any particular focus for intensity in the seals is misleading for this is the season of conflict among the mature males. This is the period when they test their strength and when hierarchies are established. Typically, this happens at haul-out sites. Size has much but not everything to do with the outcome, more massive seals being older seals. Their confrontations have a six-fold scale of intensity that appears designed to avoid violence and bloodshed unless absolutely necessary.

Least violent among these is where a mature male, stares fixedly at a younger, often much younger, male with the result that the younger, smaller male abandons the site.

Where staring fails to have the desired effect, the larger male will vocalise, snarling in his throat or in open-mouthed threat at the other seal until it departs the site.

The next level of belligerence is where the larger male starts moving directly toward where the target male is resting. The less confident male turns about and flees the site.

If the first three levels of threat fail to achieve their objective, engagement ensues. At the fourth level, where a male has begun to move aggressively toward a target male, the second male may not immediately yield ground. Often, this (literally) gives pause to the aggressor, allowing for a brief stand- off and reconsideration on both sides. However, especially where there is a size difference, the aggressor usually sees off the target seal by resuming his deliberate advance — although this may be a staged result, may require a series of advance-partial retreat, advance-partial retreat, until the less confident male finally turns and flees into the sea toward which he has been retreating.

By the fifth level, the contenders are likely to seem very evenly-matched. Their treatment of one another is aggressive but more circumspect than when expecting the easy victories described above. There will be vocalisations by both parties. One will approach the other but in this case the target male will either yield ground at first, almost as a reflex, before coming to a determined halt or will yield no ground at all. An exchange of aggressive vocalisations will ensue until it becomes apparent that they have reached an impasse.

Although immediate violence is a possibility, they are more likely now to engage in what might be regarded as a seal version of arm-wrestling. Jockeying for position, trying to seek whatever advantage is offered by the terrain, they lean against one another, massive neck straining against massive neck. By this means, it seems they gauge their respective strength. Upon that basis, they decide whether or not the huge expenditure entailed in combat is justifiable.

If it becomes evident to them that one has the advantage, the other seal must extricate himself and seek to reach the sea without sustaining injury, for as he wheels about, signalling his surrender, the other seal will pursue him, snarling and seeking to bite him. In effect, having won a cheap but narrow victory, his interest is now to engender fear in his opponent. He will harry and bully him all the way to the edge of the site to achieve that objective.

The sixth level of intensity follows where the 'arm-wrestling' proves inconclusive. While still leaning into one another, they will open their mouths wide and attempt to get a hold on the neck-flesh of each other, striking repeatedly with mouths agape. It is as if they are trying to puncture each the hide of the other in order to create thereby the opportunity to take a more secure grip, twisting and tearing until they have bitten off what may be a cooking-apple-sized chunk of skin, blubber and flesh.

Both are likely to succeed in that endeavour. Their necks and mouths will likely become dark-red with blood flowing from lesser and greater wounds. The conflict may be prolonged, lasting as much as a half-hour or more until one eventually breaks off the engagement, wheeling away to seek the refuge of the sea or, as sometimes happens, a deep pool somewhere on site. Here, the vanquished and bloodied seal may well appear dead but feigning death is a defensive smoke-screen, a part of what they do at need.

When two mature males are contesting on a site for dominance, the smaller males and all of the females are likely to retreat hurriedly to the sea. The battle is not a seal-spectator sport. The females show no interest in the outcome — for, indeed, a male may become dominant for the season but that does not guarantee him a welcome from a female when she has come into her brief season of oestrus.

It appears that females have the final choice as to whom they mate with. Again, their choices represent that feature of the species: wondrous variety. Some show fidelity to a particular male over several years; others mate with several males in one season while others mate only with the dominant male or perhaps with none at all.

What is not visible inshore except occasionally is the foraging for fish. All accounts of seals suggest that this season is spent putting on weight, gaining condition in preparation for the harsh demands put on the bodies of the main participants in the season of pup production: the pregnant females, the dominant males and what might most properly be called the attendant males.

The effect is most apparent in the females. Look at the shape and condition of them as they haul themselves, fresh and gleaming, from the sea in May-time and then look at the jaded, emaciated females hauled out in October and November.

The behaviour of the males of all ages is particularly interesting. It is commonplace where a haul-out site is used by both sexes or solely by females for the males to remain in the sea, cruising by those rocks where the females are resting. As they pass the hind end of the female, the males sniff at them in passing, presumably to check whether or not they are close to oestrus. This happens up to four months before the females are likely to have come into that condition. Later in the same tidal cycle, the males often try to haul-out close to the female, to share her site. Usually, the female resists strongly, using extended vocalising (moaning or open-mouthed snarling) and strongly waving a fore-flipper at him (flippering). Usually, her resistance is effective but the most persistent males may eventually achieve an inferior haul-out position adjacent to her.

I have not seen it described in the literature on the subject but it seems that familiarity between individual males and females may be of significance. Where apparently successful it appears to serve, in effect, as a dogged form of seal-wooing (see next section).

Occasionally, an early-born pup appears on the sandy beach in Seal Hole, in any month but most likely between April and June. This is an occasional happening possible in any seal locality. The reason for these 'out-of-time' births is uncertain but may be connected with the timing of the first oestrus experienced by a young female or it may be that the suspended development feature of seal pregnancy did not occur.

August to Late-November in and Around Seal Bay

Continue to bear in mind that the months used in these sub-titles vary from locality to locality.

In Seal Bay, Marshfrit and Sunlight caves tend to be used only very lightly, often not at all, once the season of the winter assemblies ended.

In Seal Hole, it has been otherwise. This most remote of the caves is used almost daily through the year. Many of the seals using it can be seen around the hours of low tide in the Mermaids Pool but when the seas are running quiet, the same seals venture a considerable distance offshore to Two Tides Rocks, a major haul-out site almost entirely inaccessible to people. This is one of the least disturbed non-sea cave seal sites in England or Wales and has been since at least the fifteenth century. From here, in springtime, they may return with the tide to the cave beach, continue on to visit one of the neighbouring seal localities for a few days or weeks or else venture on to the fishing grounds — taking their chances with the widespread web of seabed set-nets: horizontal (tangle nets) or vertical and horizontal (trammel nets).

In mid-summer, what they do will be related to whether or not they have a part to play in the imminent season of pup production, unless the seal arm-wrestling contests have persuaded them otherwise.

Until late July or early August, the trend for the number of seals using both inshore and offshore haul-out sites is increasing while the caves are used less than at any other part of the year (for the most part). This does not imply that haul-out numbers increase in a smooth curve.

As ever, weather and wave action as well as the number of seals then out hunting for food can render the offshore sites uninhabitable or lesser used. For example, forty may be hauled out one day, just five on the following day with twenty-three on the third. Four days of heavy seas may then intervene so that the site is rendered inaccessible to the seals through that period and perhaps for a day or two more thereafter. Whereas the seas off the North Wales coast can quieten in a few hours, especially on the oceanic coasts of the West Country, they are more likely to take two days or more.

Generally, however, the largest assemblies of the year are hauled out on the offshore sites during this period (although these are smaller than the cave assemblies gathered for the moulting period) while the lowest counts tend to be higher than lowest counts made during other parts of the year. Thereafter, however, numbers begin to fall away quite steeply although there are occasional days when an unexpectedly large assembly may gather on the rocks, bucking the trend. What this indicates is a matter for conjecture in the absence of seal tracking (using tracking telemetry). However, it should be borne in mind that many seals only play a belated part in the breeding season while many — those too old or too young to produce young or to compete with other males for dominance — are not at all involved.

It is likely that through the first half of this period, pregnant females are dispersing to the natal sites they have probably known since birth — they return at least to the vicinity of their birth-places, if not to the precise site. They are preceded, usually, by the locally dominant males. The males are the first to take up position in the watery approaches to the natal / nursery cave which — in effect — they defend against most other males.

He has what appears to be a rough way of greeting the prospecting, pregnant female to the site that, presumably, she intends to use. He challenges her, rearing up in the sea and forcing her under water with his overbearing chest. It is as if he has to demonstrate his fitness to guard the approaches to what, very soon, will become her site.

After their encounter, if she has not been deterred by her rough wooing, she hauls out on to the sandy natal cave beach.

At the outset of a small minority of seasons of pup production, the first female coming ashore to give birth is accompanied by another female who appears not to be pregnant. Why this should be — or whether it is simply a matter of happenstance — is impossible to determine. It is difficult to avoid imagining the second female is playing a tacitly supportive role. She has never been observed to remain present for longer than two days after the birth of the first pup.

In Seal Bay, all three caves are used for pup production. If a pup is born 'out of season' — perhaps between April and June — it is most likely to be born in Seal Hole which, in the earlier years but not recently, has been the least used for a nursery place. The highest number of pups born in a season in Sunlight Cave was 11, in Marshfrit Cave was 8 and in Seal Hole was 4 in the initial 5-year study. Between 5 and 22 seals per season have been born in Seal Bay in every surveyed season since 1994. In terms of numbers born, the locality is of middling importance in a regional context.

The main island breeding localities in south-west England are the Western Rocks (including Annet) and the Norrard Rocks of the Isles of Scilly. The main breeding locality in the sea caves is the Tintagel to Rusey High Cliff coast, despite the fact that it is susceptible to occasional spectacular cliff-falls and the heaviest wave action.

The breeding season-proper in Seal Bay begins in August (after which in some years there may be as many as up to six weeks before the next pup is born — in effect, making it another 'out of season' pup) but more often in September and early October. Total numbers born vary dramatically. In one 5-year sequence, there were 18, 15, 12, 5 and 10 born. Most subsequent surveyed seasons have recorded numbers between those extremes but in recent years there has been an upward trend. When large numbers were born, the main pupping cave in the early part of the season was Sunlight Cave while later in the season it was Marshfrit Cave. When numbers born were few, the main caves used were Sunlight Cave and Seal Hole.

The reason for the variation was found to be connected with the number of seals taken by the local set-net fishery. There is also the possibility, not established, of predation by killer whales — small numbers of which occur sporadically off the Cornish and Isles of Scilly coasts every year — and large sharks. For example, a Greenland shark was landed by a boat fishing out of Newlyn. The shark was hoisted up by a winch on deck and while suspended in that position regurgitated its stomach contents. The account given said that these included the vertebrae of either a seal or porpoise. The shark was identified from a combination of body shape, length and because it had green eyes.

This incident is included because although the account contains uncertainties, it happened in the first decade of the twenty-first century. As such, it is a clue rather than a fact.

Over the past 30 years, I have seen five seals with diamond-shaped scars on their dorsal surfaces. I am not sure whether these were made by sharks but believe it is more likely than not.

Deaths in the sea caves of white-coated seal pups while under observation have been surprisingly few. Each of the three caves — as well as peripheral sites — offer haul-out space to pups above the high-water mark and each of the three is sheltered at least in part against direct wave action. The primary cause of mortality has been where pups were stillborn. Pups have never been abandoned at these sites and to date there has been just one instance of female upon female aggression leading to bloodshed.

Zawn Cinnabar is used only occasionally as a natal/nursery site by a single female seal who may use the boulder beach for only as many as three consecutive breeding seasons. Never more than one pup has been born here in a single season. This site is also used by moulted pups as a first station of call en route away their nursery period at the Seal Bay sites. Dead moulted pups are more likely to be washed into this narrow beach than anywhere else in the locality.

It seems probable that many births take place around the period of high tide, judging by the number of warm placentas (afterbirth material) discovered during site visits. If the placenta had been washed on to the cave beach after spending time in the sea, it would not have retained its warmth. Remember that the Ministry of Agriculture has a warning posted not to handle any seal placenta due to a very small risk of contracting brucellosis.

Environmental conditions in the sea caves in August and September are usually particularly benign. In most years, there is usually little deposition of marine debris by the tides, although all of them will retain long-standing deposits at the back of the cave, sometimes for longer than a year. Daylight hours, though beginning to dwindle, are long. For a period of every day, if there is no cloud cover, the sun shines fully into Seal Hole and Sunlight Cave; both enjoy lengthy periods of good illumination. Winds tend to be mainly light during most years. In that instance, wave action presents no threat to the nursery.

Grey seals appear only ever to produce one pup, presumably because the huge transfer of energy that takes place from mother to pup precludes the possibility of a second pup surviving. Seal mothers may lose up to 40% of their body-weight during the period of birth and lactation. They are left emaciated by the effort.

The new-born pup has usually suckled during the first hour despite showing little ability in locating one of the two projecting nipples (which are normally kept retracted within slits on the ventral surface near the tail flippers). It may be dripping milk. The milk is fat-rich and thick, having the consistency of runny mayonnaise.

While still unborn, the pup is white-coated although the coat may become stained yellow or orange by the amniotic fluid in which it is nestling. After birth, it may remain stained to the fourth day of life, by which time it has been washed off by the sea. The hair is quite long initially, looking particularly fine on the crown of the head. The red umbilical may be quite long on the first day of life, shortening as it is worn away by the pup moving over the substrate. By the seventh day at the latest, it will have been reduced to a small black disk. On the first day, the coat looks baggy and ruckled: the pup looks like skin and bone. The claws are long, the eyes are huge.

Around the mouth, the pup has many mystachial whiskers. There are four or five superciliary whiskers over both eyes as well as two on the top-side in the middle of the snout.

When it cries, the pup utters a breathy, mournful 'waaah!' When hungry, it cries incessantly; the cries growing hoarser the longer it is denied a feed. It can sound not unlike a human baby. Like a human baby, it can cry itself to sleep.

For the pup, feeding can be a noisy, lip-smacking affair. Usually, a feed is followed by a small amount of movement preceding a sleeping session.

For the mother, helping the pup to the nipple can be a frustrating affair. Often, she spends many minutes attempting patiently to usher the pup toward it by gently flippering, as if gesturing to where it is, or even just by resting a flipper lightly on the pup's head. Nevertheless, often, the pup remains confused, sometimes giving up the search without having fed and just wandering off, as if it has forgotten its hunger.

On the other hand, some mother and pup combinations are extremely successful from the outset. Some pups fall asleep at the nipple — again, resembling human babies. At such times, milk may continue to flow from the nipple of the relaxed mother. It continues to pour into the mouth of the pup and out at the sides, running as a rivulet across a rocky substrate or pouring into the sand. It is just one more example of the great variety of behaviours exemplified by grey seals.

The same is true of the seal mothers. Some feed on demand. At the opposite extreme, some hardly come ashore on the high tide to offer a feed. Many mothers, whether particularly solicitous or highly anxious at feeding time feed their pups while resting on their sides in the shallows of the sea. Then, their bodies usually — not always — rest to seaward of the pup, offering some shelter against any wave action.

This may explain why some pups, while still crying with hunger, will enter the sea to swim in search of their mothers, where both parties are entirely happy to feed.

Either mother or pup may interrupt an apparently unfinished feeding session at any time and wander away.

Between feeding bouts, many mothers — especially during the first week of life — will remain ashore for all or most of the time with their pups. In this period, if there is wave action on to the nursery beach, especially around the time of high water, the mother will insert her body between the pup and the run of the surf, serving as a breakwater and thereby keeping the pup from being rolled in the surf or sucked into the turbulence of it.

From the second week of life onward, the mother often but certainly not always spends more time in the sea.

A minority of mothers spend the entire 15 to 19 days period of lactation ashore with their pup, feeding on demand. It is among the mothers remaining ashore that aggression sometimes occurs. As sea cave fairways are often less than four metres wide — rather more than two seal lengths - but as seal mothers tend often to occupy the mid-fairway while awake and watchful, it appears that some seal mothers require an exclusion space around themselves and their pup. This amounts to a body-length at least. They fight to protect this exclusive area. This may suggest that the prime site is that situated closest to the cave entrance but above the reach of high tide.

Consequently, less aggressive seal mothers may abandon the site and lead their pups to other less troubled nursery sites. More share the same cave bearing bloody wounds. There are then prolonged exchanges of blood-curdling, snarling vocalisations

Female against female aggression may be a factor causing some mothers to remain throughout in the sea and to be nervous of coming to shore — but probably this only applies in a minority of instances. For others it is a choice from the outset.

While in the sea, the seal mothers remain keenly vigilant. Typically, they keep line-of-sight contact with their pup. At this time, when the male approaches them he is seen off, usually following an underwater encounter. Here, there is no aggression between the females.

The pups spend much time sleeping and quite a lot of time soliciting the next feed — especially where the mother remains between feeding bouts in the sea — while some time is given to exploration. Some pups seek to solicit feeds from other seal mothers present on the fairway. A few succeed but most are driven off. Snarling seems to have little effect on the pups, rarely daunting them. Often, they suffer small, painful wounds, usually on the dorsal surface, where they have been nipped even as the snarling reached a crescendo and following a short chase.

Where there is a low water pool in the cave, they swim, dive and are more likely to play there with another pup than when ashore. Sometimes, they prefer to sleep in the low tide pools — perhaps, in their earliest days, because as skin, bone and little else, they are uncomfortable and therefore restless even on sand.

At high water, if there is no beach available, they will remain afloat, swimming and diving for several hours. At these times, the mother is usually close by in the sea. For the most part, she does not intervene but simply behaves as if on-call: she is vigilant. At need, she seeks to lead the pup from the cave to a place (in the sea or upon another shore) of less risk but, as described for pups that have difficulty locating the nipple, she may be unsuccessful in this endeavour.

Where a beach remains available during periods when the sea is rough, it can become mobile. Sand or gravel can be piled in or removed; rocks — even large ones — can be made to dance. Rarely, this leads to pups in the sea caves being partly buried to the extent that they cannot escape. At such times, the seal mother will continue to come ashore to feed the pup. However, such a pup is likely to die, either drowned by an extra high tide or by starvation following weaning.

There are many such ugly ways for pups to die. In the Isles of Scilly, on the shores of small uninhabited islands, pups are rolled by the surf into gullies, are trapped, half-buried, under dancing boulders or are swept down between massive boulders on high spring tides. In all such places, they are likely to drown.

Theirs is a tough start to life. A grey seal pup is tended for just 15 to 19 days by its mother. They have to teach themselves to swim and then to forage for food once weaned — for the seal mothers appear to entirely abandon their young at the time of weaning. Swimming seems to come naturally to them and this appears especially so for the pups of the sea caves who may be required to swim for their lives even on the very first day of life.

Foraging ability, as well as luck, determines whether they will survive or fail in the first weeks of life, or live beyond their first birthday. They can be seen inshore diving repeatedly to the seabed, returning to the surface with stones, seaweed or shells. These they drop, deliberately, so that they can dive and retrieve it repeatedly, much as do adult seals when eating a fish at the surface.

Some post mortem examinations show only a rather sad, small collection of stones as the stomach contents of such a pup. About 50% of grey seal pups may die in the first year of life. A more precise estimate would be obtained by repeating the tagging work of A.L. Johnston, especially as so many pups in the first year of life are taken into seal sanctuaries or drowned as by-catch in set-nets. It would be interesting (and it is important) to discover the fate of cave-born pups, to discover whether — as I believe — seals born in sea caves in learning to swim during the period of lactation have a better chance of surviving the first year of life than beach-born or island-born pups in the same region.

In the sea caves, post-weaning, a moulted pup may remain ashore for up to six weeks without feeding. In that time, it will lose weight, eventually acquiring a wasted look, being thinnest about two-thirds to three-quarters of the way down the length of the body. They will do this where the environmental variables permit — as when above the reach of the tide at all times in all conditions — but it is hard to imagine that they can survive from so impoverished a base.

In writing this, I am remembering seven weeks of one autumn spent based in a lighthouse on an uninhabited island off the north Wales coast. My task was to discover whether it might be possible to identify the age of a pup during its time at the nursery site. Part of my brief was that I was not to handle the pups because there was great concern, which I shared, at the possibility of disrupting the mother-pup bond (although I do believe this to be much more robust than we imagine when in our precautionary, ethically-rooted mode).

My effort was unsuccessful simply because of the variations in the behaviour — primarily — of the seal mothers, several of which are described above. Essentially, some pups expend far less effort receiving much more energy and other care from their mothers than others. These pups may or may not enter the sea during that time. This influences strongly their development to the time of weaning.

What happens post-weaning may be determined by the extent to which the pup has spent time swimming and diving in the vicinity of the nursery beach. In effect, by the time of weaning, these pups have already metamorphosed to become genuinely partly aquatic individuals. They are confident already in the habit of moving between sea and shore.

For the pups that remained land-bound during the period of lactation, perhaps especially because they grew in a nursery beyond the reach of the tide, their habits may be more sedentary. Hunger is said to be the prime stimulant driving the pups to the sea elsewhere but it was not apparent in the moulted pups I watched hardly moving through the course of their days, sleeping most of the time and growing ever-thinner.

I would contrast those pups with another pup on another beach on the same island. This one had, of necessity, been in and out of the sea on most of the days of its short life. On the eighteenth day, it was weaned — abandoned by its mother.

On that day, a big sea was running into its nursery cove. I watched massive forces dragging the moulted pup from one side of the wide cove to the other and then back again but though it could have returned to shore, in fact, it was determined to head seaward. It continued to seaward. By the end of the day, it was no longer in sight.

By chance, I left the island something more than a week later. The following day, out of curiosity, I visited the adjacent mainland shore — a site used by seals that had, in effect, formed an 'annex' colony to the island seals. These seals, I photographed, interested to learn whether any of the island seals were present. Only later, when comparing the images with those I had captured on the island did I recognise the brave little seal that I had watched on its weaning day. It had crossed over the powerful tidal stream and achieved some initial security at least — survival — on the far shore.

Seal mothers in the shallows of a nursery cave entrance resting on rocks painted with Lithophyllum

What I saw in this was, as ever, not the story of *the* grey seal but the story of *a* grey seal. What I have described is one of the things that happen. Others survive by other means. Many die. Some die in fishing nets — two surveys in Cornwall found that, according to the account of the fishermen, about 75% of seals caught in their nets appear to be 'young' — in the first year of life. These have died, in part, because their lungs have not yet fully developed: they cannot remain submerged for so long or as deep as older seals. Neither do they have the power and, perhaps, the sea-wisdom of the older seals that helps some of them burst free of the plastic monofilament nets.

Probably most moulted pups die because they fail to hunt successfully. They starve. As they starve, they lose co-ordination as well as condition. They make mistakes, suffering injuries. Secondary infections set in, and these cause them to die.

Some of the dead seals are discovered by walkers stranded on the shore. Often the young seals are headless. I have heard, oftentimes, a hue and cry raised about somebody 'cutting off the heads of young seals'. At such times, people seem not to want to recognise that when a young seal is dead; its head lolls down in the water. If there is any contact with rock as the seas carry the body inshore, the thin skull suffers massive damage — often it is the first part of the seal to disappear.

People have also pointed out the neatness of the neck-cut, suggesting it could only have been achieved by a blade, but that also is misleading. Gulls can leave just such a fine cut in quarrying their way into the viscera of the stranded seal. Gulls also account for puncture marks that are sometimes taken as bullet holes.

Some seals are still deliberately killed, as happened most horribly a few years back on the Blaskets off SW Ireland. There, local people contacting me very shortly afterwards told me that about 60 grey seals had been killed — most of them being white-coated pups but also including a small number of lactating mothers. They were battered to death, paramilitary-style, with clubs studded with nails. I was asked to intervene with the Irish Government, to have them take seriously the soullessness of the killings but received no answer to my communications. Subsequently, I was told that the police knew who had done it but that they lacked the proof necessary to lay charges.

In SW Britain, here and there, certain people are known for being 'the man' to shoot particular wildlife-related problems away and on extremely rare occasions, groups of men perhaps still kill seals in the old way out of frustration at damage done to their catches. From what I have been told of such ventures, this is done discreetly and remains discreet thereafter, in recognition of the hue and cry that would result from any loose talk.

In the seal caves, after mid-October only a handful of pups are born. The seas are rougher now and the daylight hours are dwindling. No more pups are likely to be born in Sunlight Cave. It will become a station of call for moulted pups seeking rest while migrating away from their nursery site and learning their way around the world. They will most probably rest in the cubby-holes off the main fairway. It may also serve as a resting place for mature males with no wish to get involved in aggressive encounters with the starving and, by now, shabbily emaciated dominant males still patrolling the entrance waters to the nursery caves. For, they do not feed during the long weeks of their fullest power.

The process that leads to mating is fascinating, being as much to do with familiarity as with power.

Once the female has received her aggressive welcome from the dominant male, reached the natal beach and given birth, the behaviour of the male is utterly transformed. He becomes entirely solicitous.

If he approaches the nursery beach, as soon as the female snarls at him, open-mouthed, he turns and swims farther away. He may continue to approach the beach and she will continue to warn him off, but because he has become a familiar and obedient presence, she allows him to swim ever closer to the nursery beach until the day comes when he beaches in the shallows and is not warned off.

Thereafter, he hauls out, over the succeeding days, ever higher up the beach until he is resting close to her without being snarled at or driven off.

Consequently, when she is in oestrus, a condition that he scents, there comes a time when he chases her down into the low water pool or into the cave entrance waters, takes her nape in his mouth — without biting her — and forces her below the waters. There, they achieve coition: they mate. Subsequently, they may remain quiescent for more than an hour, her dorsal surface to his ventral surface, and his fore-flippers resting on her flanks. They rest at or below the surface of the pool. There appears to be total peace between them.

When they do separate, it is likely that the stimulus will be external, such as the hunger cry of the almost grown pup in the interior of the cave or entry into the pool by another seal.

The female is in oestrus for about five days. She may be monogamous, she may mate with several males or she may mate with a male with whom she has formed a pair-bond of long-standing who may not be the dominant male. This is possible because females have the final say as to whether mating will occur.

The sea cave males have access to far fewer females than the 'beach-masters' at the great assemblies such as those at Donna Nook in Lincolnshire, Horsey in Norfolk and the great east coast of Scotland sites. Consequently, many more males achieve local dominance at the mainly scattered sea cave sites. This contributes to the variety of the grey seal gene-pool at SW Britain sites because it allows females ready access to far more males than would be available at any of the main non-cave breeding stations.

If the female becomes pregnant, she will remain so for almost one year. After her egg has been fertilised, a cell forms which divides several times. Just before these cells implant into the uterine wall so that the embryo forms and can begin to grow, the pregnancy is suspended. This is a feature of many mammalian pregnancies, including — for example — badgers, brown hares and deer. In seals, presumably it is because at the time of conception, the female is in woeful physical condition, being emaciated. Consequently, she needs to restore her physical condition. This she achieves by a combination of feeding and rest.

After moulting and having restored her physical condition, the period of suspension is curtailed. At some point in winter, the cells implant and the pregnancy becomes fully active again, for the duration.

Mid-November To March in And Around Seal Bay

This period — the bookend dates of which vary from year to year and from locality to locality — is the time of the winter assemblies. During this time, the grey seals are gathered intermittently in their greatest numbers in the sea caves in order, primarily, to conduct the annual moult. Usually — especially until February - these assemblies are either strongly or totally dominated by male seals along with a handful of immature seals of (visually) indeterminable sex.

The cave assemblies begin to gather very late in November or in December. In the late 20th Century they occurred exclusively in Seal Hole but with the advent of the 21st Century, as numbers have increased slowly, Marshfrit Cave has also become important during the moulting period.

In Seal Hole, seals use the inner sand-hill (as through the remainder of the year), where typically they are gathered in one huge group at and below the high-water mark in the middle of the fairway. Seen from afar, this group always resembles a great rugby scrum. A great mist of warm air rises from their sandy, blubbery bodies. The fishy scent of their perfume is strong. The seals rest close together. Most of their time is spent asleep. Some small amount of time is spent, stretching, scratching, 'doing the banana' or occasionally scanning around them.

At the beginning of my long period of seal cave research, an effort was made to understand the consequences of any disturbance it caused. In this bay, on the day following disturbance, usually but not always — as ever — seals used Seal Hole in small numbers, coming in on the night-time high tide on the day that disturbance occurred but did not remain ashore at the following two low tides. They returned in 'normal' numbers on the second day following the disturbance event.

The same proved true for Marshfrit Cave although more recently they have returned to the cave the same night as when disturbance occurred and were present to be counted in comparable numbers on the subsequent day. However, it has always seemed best to leave the caves unvisited for ten days to two weeks, if the weather permits such a luxury of prediction.

Seals were not using Sunlight Cave with enough frequency for any reliable sense of seal reactions to be gauged. Zawn Cinnabar was not tested as it was never subject to disturbance.

It appeared that many of the seals evidently deterred from using

Seal Hole on the following day then came ashore on the similar substrate and similarly angled sandy slope in Marshfrit Cave. Sunlight Cave was never used as a place of refuge by more than five seals at a time, except during the nursery period. Where five occurred, never more than one was a female.

Of numbers, Seal Hole always sees the largest assemblies, with 102 (males and immature seals with only four females) being the largest counted to date, in December 2016. Marshfrit Cave is always next in importance with a maximum count to date of 44, also made in on the same date that 102 were counted in Seal Hole. With just two males in Sunlight Cave, the total of 148 seals in the three caves on the same day was a record count for the bay for any time of the year.

The months when the largest counts are made are November, December and January. Although unexpectedly large numbers may occur on any single day thereafter, probably owing to sea conditions, numbers dwindle from February onward. However, in some years, smaller moulting assemblies may be found in the caves until and including May.

It is likely that throughout this period, the caves are also being used as lodges by individual seals between fishing trips. It is likely that they are used throughout the period as lodges by moulting pups dispersing from their own nursery sites (perhaps in Brittany, Ireland, and Wales or elsewhere in the West Country). It is also likely these caves are used for just a night or two as a resting place by seals travelling to other sites, in effect 'to visit the neighbours'.

Such sites are rare among the many sea caves used by the grey seals of the NE Atlantic. They have in common that they have spacious beaches although not always a beach at high water that is beyond the reach of the surf. Without exception, they have always been remote from human access. However, remoteness has become ever rarer in recent decades. The coastal footpath, being such a fine leisure resource, means in Cornwall and Devon that almost the entire coastline is overlooked. As the coastal footpath opened, so were more stretches of foreshore made accessible for people with coastal landowners such as the National Trust constructing stairways down to previously inaccessible or rarely accessible beaches. There was an accompanying proliferation in car parks meaning that people had ever closer access to the increasingly accessible foreshore.

On the cliffs, ever more climbing sites have been exploited in recent times. Coasteering has become a popular way of earning a living and of going more or less anywhere at sea level. Coastal kayaking trips offer another opportunity to see the coastline at sea level. These are honourable pursuits. I know and like the people who offer such excursions; but also, I fear for the impact on our last truly wild places, among which surely the seal caves must count. Many sites are unchanged in their use by seals for at least 400 years according to the historical record. I believe it is reasonable to assume, logical to assume, they are unchanged for thousands of years in that regard — since sea level rise more or less stabilised. Now it is on the move upward again, potentially threatening most of the seal cave sites of the islands of Britain.

The exciting ways now available — and others will follow — that allow the exploration of previously inaccessible coasts do threaten the grey seals at the sites that can be called their strongholds. Most of the people offering these adventures will be ethically based, but some will want to go a little farther, be a little different and give people something really special to remember forever. It is a sentiment I recognise very well and one that is very difficult to resist. On the other hand, as the early 21st Century survey (organised with Susannah Curtin of the University of Bournemouth) showed on the wildlife cruises that I was leading, people do understand the need for restraint when treading or water-wandering in places so fragile to our touch — places where life will suffer precisely as cruelly and unintentionally as the cave paintings at Lascaux.

I don't believe in saying 'no!' to people. I don't believe in it being said to me. I don't believe it is a word that works. But this is the time of our watch and the thought of our watch being remembered as the time such wildernesses died is intolerable to me and surely must be to us all.

Let there, by all means, be television moments that are seen — those moments of dramatic highlight that are the Grail for the film-makers. In other words, let the story be told but just very occasionally, on film, informed by the people who know the true stories rather that the partial stories born out of creative minds briefly revelling in the enthusiasm of an interlude rather than long intimacy.

Let the seals and their caves tell their own story, as I have tried to do for them here. Please let us avoid the absurd modern fashion for misplacing presenters into, in this case, the grey seal world. For: it is a private, wild place where we do not belong and which should only be visited — if at all — for the briefest interludes.

David Attenborough can carry it off but it is painfully apparent that, with his intelligence, experience, sensibility and unique gifts as a presenter, he is one of a very rare breed.

Finally, although they are a separate species and although it may be a red herring, some work has been done studying the only other cave-dwelling true seals, Mediterranean monk seals *(Monachus monachus)*. However, their numbers are so extremely small that it is uncertain whether what has been observed in recent studies could be called natural behaviour and therefore can contribute helpfully to their survival from their current critically endangered status. It has long been my instinct that a better understanding of the way grey seals utilise the sea caves and associated inshore habitats might contribute to a better understanding of habitat requirements of Mediterranean monk seals. I regret that the unintended isolation of my working life has thwarted this ambition to make connections, but I would support and wish well anyone so doing.

ANECDOTES 1: The Seal Cave World

Wilderness is a compelling word that I feel wary of using, for it is much misused — for example in the various media, in the advertisement of holidays and just in everyday conversation. It is such a relative word. Is it fair to suggest this potential charlatan-word conjures for each of us a different sense of something natural, dangerous but extremely important to our imaginations? Whether we work there, make occasional visits or simply hold the awareness that it exists, it matters to us all.

For the sea caves of western Britain and Ireland, I would claim the word 'wilderness' is most fitting. Even when the summer sea is at its most placid, to venture into especially one of the greater sea caves — perhaps paddling in on deep, intruding waters upon a wave ski — there can still be present within a malicious, hardly expected wave-break to make perilous a small adventure that had seemed set so fair in the smiling sunlight outside. In so deep a darkness, with only a torch to relieve its totality, the mind veers towards unease, heeding without realising, perhaps, the voices of the ancient ancestors clamouring of caution from the rarely visited core of our being.

Huge dark engulfs the light so readily in these places. Oftentimes, it extinguishes all ambient light. In so great a darkness, the beam of the diver's lamp you have brought along for precisely that contingency can seem unexpectedly small and frail. There is, of course, the problem of how you hold it, with both hands already gripping the stem of the paddle propelling you into this challenging darkness? I clamp it between my bent knees. You might wonder why not use a head-torch? That works just fine in a small darkness, as when perhaps at night you are bent over the car engine or checking to see that the latch to the henhouse is secured. It doesn't work in the larger sea caves, giving there only the thinnest wisp of unhelpful, engulfed illumination.

Venturing into seal caves on a generously quiet sea is, in fact, less common than the alternatives. Most often, the seas that run off the ocean into these caves over the course of a year are moderate or rough. Even people with only a passing interest in them must have winced at the repetitive booming of such waters breaking on cave walls deep within, imagining the forces of Nature there in play. Standing upon a cliff-top gazing down at the endless corduroy of waves running to shore, breaking against cliff faces up which they run or explode, then you are watching a modified version of what is happening in the caves.

Surfers know well how it feels to be tumbled in the white water of a breaking wave. It felt to this surfer always that I was helpless as a leaf in a gale; for all that, it is a tame way of describing it. Other people have likened it to being tumbled in a gigantic washing machine.

Imagine, then, the added refinement of it all happening in confined space. There can be no living with it — not for us humans, at least. That is the root of what makes such places 'wildernesses'. Wind, surf, tidal streams, submerged or emergent obstructions, sea-floor gradients and darkness are the major elements that make it so. The mobility of local offshore marine substrates also plays its complicating part: temporary accretion of sand or even boulders can make the surf break closer to or farther from shore, rendering inaccessible what may previously always have been accessible — something I have observed periodically over 30 years of seal cave studies at the so-familiar sites closest to home.

These forces generate great mobility for the cave substrates, too. Overnight in winter, if the heaviest seas of the year are running directly into a seal cave, then that refuge can be entirely stripped of its sand. If so, it will be stripped to the bones of itself — becoming a darker place of boulders and bedrock in the process, for the sand always reflects something of any light within while it yet remains.

Here, even in such a wild and shifting habitat, some of the grey seals do dwell. Even when the storm seas are most violent, if they coincide with the breeding season then small, apparently helpless new-born seal pups enter that world of darkness, thunder and surf. They may be rolled first up the beach before the churning chaos of white surf, often heavily-laden with quartzy grains of sand, and then sucked back down again into commotion. Especially in the first half of a suckling period that varies between 15-19 days, most (not all) seal mothers are usually particularly solicitous of their pups. A minority of mothers behave solicitously throughout this period of lactation and utmost dependency on the part of the pups. They insert their blubbery bulk between the weakly crying pup and the tongues of surf, making blubbery breakwaters of themselves. If that fails, then they accompany the swimming pup out of the cave and, if it be their fate, along the coast until they find a safer haven.

Not all pups survive these ferocious interludes. Not all mothers are solicitous of their young. A very small proportion of them abandon their pups at birth. Some others appear extraordinarily wary of venturing ashore to suckle their young. Such mothers tend to curtail the suckling bout soonest rather than allowing the pup to drink its fill of fat-rich milk with the texture of runny mayonnaise. If the pup is under-fed, it becomes more susceptible to injury and the debilitating infections that stem from it. Usually, pups that die during the period of lactation do so from such infections rather than because their bodies are broken by the violence of the conditions. Underfed pups that survive to weaning are unlikely to survive long thereafter. They lack sufficient reserves of fat to see them through the do-or-die interlude during which pups learn to swim and succeed or fail in learning to forage for themselves. Most of these pups will die or will be taken into care at seal sanctuaries.

Seal sanctuaries are marvellous havens for each individual pup that, otherwise, would have died; however, what is the effect on a species that has existed for three million years — according to the genetic record — of helping to survive those that would have failed? This is a species renowned for its hardihood. But for the intrusion of hunting, it is a species that has prospered over time.

Today, apparently, it prospers again, albeit in the context of a world that closes with remorseless inventiveness in on the once remote haunts they yet occupy. We are not in a position to identify what beaches they used before they learned to shun them due to increasing human access and numbers. Grey seal numbers today would appear to have returned to pre-Bronze Age levels — to what they were before the easily-found, easily-killed individuals were slaughtered to provide needy people with clothing, oil to light the hours of darkness and flesh the Church classified as 'fish' so that it might be eaten on every day of the mediaeval week.

Is the species weakened because those that would have perished are helped to survive? This is the ethical question underlying our acts of kindness and altruism. I have an open mind on the subject but would observe that it is a small 'indiscriminate' altruism set beside the similarly indiscriminate millennia of the slaughter of their kind that continued even after Parliament made the grey seal the first British wild mammal to receive some protection from the law. Also, I would invite you to consider what you might do, chancing upon an emaciated young seal on the beach. Whether the nearest seal sanctuary is of the highest order, such as Exploris in Portaferry, Northern Ireland, or is one that has too much the flavour of a zoo or circus about it, I think you would be hard-pressed to leave the seal where it lay, choosing to allow it to die.

But as seems right in edge-of-the-world places so violently harsh, there is also enchantment to be found. I have learned to try, at least, to time my visits to various caves so that the fullest sunlight is pouring through their entrances while I am exploring within. Then, if I look back over my shoulder, I can see the illuminated maroon baize of algae, the raspberry-coloured glistening of the pock-marking sea squirts and perhaps the turquoise leaching of copper carbonate all painting the seal cave walls. Mauve *Lithophyllum* algae everywhere at low tide encrust the boulders underfoot and thereby facilitate a good grip. A strawberry anemone sags fatly to one side at the retreat of the waters. High overhead, the bottle-green shag sitting on her nest of seaweed and man-made marine debris passes creaky comment in a voice reminiscent of a football rattle slowly wound from bygone days. Deeper within the cave, in the gloom beyond the reach of sunlight, a seal mother raises her voice to wail the song of lonely places or perhaps it is her pup making a breathy, insistent cry, demanding the next feed.

But, on a sunny day, I am not sure whether the best part of every adventure isn't when I re-emerge, still safe, back from whatever delights or fears were discovered within into the restoring sunlight.

ANECDOTE 2: The Sea Cave Death Chambers

I cannot say that I cherish a few seal caves above the others; although I do. All of them have extraordinary stories stretched back across an epic geological scale. Some of the longest-known have been the stage for local events across historical time — mostly in the form of bloody 'battues'. 'Battues' is a dainty name for such bloodthirsty deeds. Across the mediaeval period (almost certainly from much earlier) and even into the twentieth century, local men have taken advantage of the calmest seas to row or clamber into the slippery glooms. Long ago, in one hand each man held aloft a flaming brand. More recently, he held aloft a lantern. In the other, across the ages, he has carried a club, firearm or a hammer. They were there to kill the seals.

The men would have been mainly fishermen and farmers (until the 18th and 19th centuries when, for example, on Lundy pilot or tug-boats, captains and crew would participate for the 'sport' of it). In many instances, as from at least the 18th through to the first half of the 20th centuries, they would have become first acquainted with these natural cathedrals as boys. Determinedly daunted by nothing, on summer days they would have swum into the caves as the feral children that often once they were.

No amount of experience would have enabled the men with the clubs to enter the seal caves with ease. The light they brought would have served to blind them as much as to help them to see. Where smoking brands were used, eyes would have stung and watered in the smoke. Each step would have been perilous, laden with the prospect of misadventure, slipping and stumbling at the bottom end, cracking heads against unguessed protrusions at the top.

Now and then, they would have fallen over — it is easily done. As described earlier, once it happened to me. I was very lucky. It was precisely the unexpected event that I have always sought to school myself to anticipate — the worst mistake I have ever made in a seal cave. It is inevitable that the men with the torches and clubs would have had not only similar but far worse encounters. Almost certainly, they would have known that usually the first instinct of a seal disturbed in a cave is to mill around but then to stampede toward the refuge of the sea. It is evident from all they do that the sea is home, is safety, while the very margins of the land are apparently a necessary evil frequented upon occasion.

A stampeding seal uses no finesse. It galumphs in a direct line — it appears to be a habit-line, such as a badger might follow (except badger-trails are marked — as if by cats-eyes — by secretions from scent glands in their paws) — for the cave entrance. The natural response of a person in that cave is to flee what appears like an undulating and entirely irresistible torpedo (more typically, a fusillade of torpedoes, as there may be a considerable company of stampeding seals).

The seal-hunters would have learned to expect this and to use it.

Surely, they learned to step to one side — to the wall on the farther side from the line of the stampede. They would have clubbed at the seals in passing. Blows would have found their mark, whether or not to lethal effect. Oftentimes, they would miss. Then, they might fall. It is easy to imagine that there would have been collisions amid the wailing terror of the seals and the belligerent, frightened bellowing of some men while those others beyond immediate danger doubled up with helpless laughter. It is easy to imagine a seal blocked in its line of intended escape, wheeling around heavily to snarl blood-curdling defiance against those men at closest quarters. A blow intended to strike the seal might strike, instead, the wall or some rocky protrusion, jarring the length of an arm. If the seal managed to bite a man, then it could have been a gruesome business. A seal often tears at the same time as clamping together its teeth. Fighting one another, it is not unusual for them to tear out a cooking-apple sized chunk of blubber or to tear away half a fore-flipper.

The worst of the bite of a seal, however, is the bacterial flora around their teeth, which are highly toxic to humans. It is very likely that some seal-hunters died slow deaths or at least suffered amputations of gangrenous limbs after having been bitten during such forays.

For the aftermath, if there was purpose beyond the killing, seal-skins were valued for gloves, boots and jackets: for their water-resistant qualities. The blubber was rendered down for a smudgy kind of oil used for lighting. In times of hardship, the flesh was eaten.

A very small number of massive seal caves that once were turned into death chambers are remembered today on the finest scale local maps as 'seal holes'. Every such cave but (possibly) one that I have visited remains in use by seals today.

ANECDOTE 3: The Turquoise Cave

Discoveries of places such as the Turquoise Cave serve better than any guess to demonstrate that seals were using sea caves almost certainly back for thousands of years. It was ever thus. These are not gloomy places of refuge to which they have been driven by the current mania for residential and leisurely life at the seaside with its attendant sprawl. Neither do I believe such places to be sub-optimal sites for seals, as one expert memorably explained them. I would assert, on the contrary, that often they are the precise opposite: seal caves are places that advantage most seals and their prospects of flourishing.

It was mentioned previously that just one important and well-known seal hole of which I had learned may no longer be used by seals. Long use by the seals may have ceased in my time: in 2010; however, before we reach the 'why' or 'how' of it, there is a story to be told.

I heard of it first through stories told by local men after an illustrated talk about seals and their neighbours that I had given one evening. They told of a place that had been mentioned to me already by a local boat operator and of which I had read in an historical novel (*The Angry Tide,* by Winston S. Graham). They told a story of feral children, of how they had swum into the 'great seal hole' as boys, along the way meeting with seals, back in the 1950s.

Later, I explored every sea cave along that section of coast, locating Great Seal Hole without yet being able to explore it owing to the heavy play of surf action onshore.

As soon as the sea calmed sufficiently, I went to the cave entrances — there were two of them — which soon I discovered merged into the one long tunnel insinuating itself in narrow, serpentine fashion more than 60 metres into the cliff. My use of the paddle was cramped. I needed to hold it steeply to avoid clashing it against the cave walls, thereby alerting anything within to my ever-wary approach.

It was one of the many caves with a deep-water entrance. While I was leaving the light behind, I had already seen the ghostly forms of two female seals, seaward-bound, streaming swiftly by below me in the opposite direction just above the boulder-strewn bottom through the clear water. I cannot pretend that I reached the interior with any confidence. The confining walls and my inability to turn about, at need, in the high-walled but narrow entrance tunnel were oppressive — are always oppressive. Twice I ventured part way in, a little further the second time than the first, before I wearied of my cowardice and struck out more deliberately into the dark interior.

The serpentine nature of the tunnel ensured that it was true darkness about 80 metres in. There, the atmosphere about me altered. No longer were the tall walls confining me. Clearly, I had arrived in a chamber whose extent and shape, as yet, I could not see. I did not want to switch on my torch until I touched the cave floor or until the skeg on the underside of the tail of my ski scraped against rocks. Rather, it was my hearing that painted for me this more spacious picture. In the dark, hearing — or the use of that sense — comes into its own. You can 'hear' space, where it becomes sufficiently altered. If it is there, you can hear the irregular breathing of the seals. You can scent, too, their fishy perfume.

I progressed very much more slowly now, slowed by a sensation of imminence. My skeg touched noisily upon what must have been a large but barely submerged rock, jolting the ski so that it wobbled alarmingly. Somewhere not far ahead of me in the total darkness, there was a massive, slithery stirring. I sought to turn but already they were upon me: massive shapes that, of a mercy, I could not see. They came undulating all about me through what turned out to be the shallows. Bodies buffeted me from side to side without quite tumbling me from the rocking ski. There was a great commotion of white waters wherever they surged by. In the confusion, I was unable to switch on the torch, having quite forgotten to unlock it.

I counted a minimum of 24 seals by the bumps and near misses that I experienced during that very prolonged and alarming interlude. In

201

the aftermath of the stampede, having belatedly switched on the torch, I dismounted from the ski. I dragged it ashore on to what turned out to be an exceptionally slippery beach of middling-sized boulders and found a place to stow it some distance in from what would very soon become a rising tide.

Only now did I turn in a slow, full circle, splashing torchlight all around and above me to discover the nature of the seal hole. Only then did I begin to discover the full miracle of what I had blundered into.

It is relevant that I was there primarily, as on all initial cave visits, to make a crude map of the site. For a measuring device, I was using my trusty paddle. Using a 2B pencil, after that initial scan I sketched a likeness of the shape of the cave on one of three white plastic boards given to me by the Bretons while undertaking similar pathfinding work with them in the seal caves of Île d'Ouessant. As I worked my way farther into the cave, I added annotations — mainly measurements but describing significant features where appropriate.

At home afterwards, I would draw a neater, proper plan view of the site approximately to scale. When I looked at what I had drawn, I saw the shape resembled nothing more than what might have passed as the effort of a child to sketch a three-legged elephant. The long, serpentine entrance was the trunk. What was revealed as the great main chamber, from which the seals had stampeded, was the body. Where the serpentine entrance entered the main chamber, there were legs — in effect like creeks running off the mainstream — to left and right culminating in small beaches, one of which was of sand. At the back of the great chamber, there was another more truncated creek, or leg, which proved to be a sandy beach where a lone seal mother lingered beside her new-born pup: the placenta lay close by on the sand, indicating it had been born since the last high tide, less than six hours before.

Lastly, leading straight into the deepest interior off the back wall of the chamber ran a long, body-width, 'tail'. About 20 metres in, there was what resembled a caisson of freshwater falling from what proved to be a blocked hole leading to the surface. Beyond this screen of water, I was able to count at least 5 seals, at rest there, nose to tail, snarling into the light my torch had brought.

It didn't show initially on the plan view but later I marked the existence of massive rocky boulders and ledges that could be used by the seals during the high-water period.

By any measure, this was one of the most memorable caves that ever I had entered. There was another feature that I have kept from relating until now because it had a bearing on what proved to be an even greater story.

The splashing around of torchlight at the outset had revealed that great patches of the walls of the cave were deeply turquoise.

Although that sight remains an abiding memory, in fact it was not quite so. Thick turquoise pastes of leaching copper carbonate seeped down the walls in massive patches but the greater area of the walls was as in any other seal cave. Rough-hewn or gleaming with wetness were these high walls with slimes of orange here and there left by the leaching of iron; sea-polished in places.

Later, when I had made good my escape, I went searching through books about the local mining effort in St Agnes museum and it was there I discovered one version of the larger story. Before it is related, it should be stated that some people regard this tale as invention while others hold it to be true. Therefore: it may be so. I hope it is.

Two centuries before, tin plus a lesser amount of copper were being mined very close to this site and, as was the custom, to keep the waste-water pumping to a minimum, a tunnel was dug from the extensive and labyrinthine nearby mine-workings to the seal cave in order that it be used as a 'natural' drain.

It is said that some of the best quality tin ore extracted from any mine in Cornwall was extracted here. Great riches were made by the shareholders. In celebration of this, at some time in the middle of the 18th Century, it is written that they had lowered down a stope (the considerable hole from the surface that, today, survives as the caisson of falling freshwater mentioned above) a banqueting table and chairs. The shareholders had men ferry in, by means of a narrow skiff, the food for the banquet while themselves they were winched down the stope in large buckets. Thereafter, there was feasting and merriment on that one memorable day around the hours of low tide.

The story tells nothing of the seals but already at that time it was known as the seal hole.

Great Seal Hole formed part of Polberro Mine, itself an amalgamation of many smaller mine-workings from earlier times. Seal Hole and North Seal Hole were named as two of these. While exceptionally rich yields of tin ore were extracted from Polberro, copper ore was associated primarily with North Seal Hole. Of the adits used to drain this mine, none were as important to the mine as that which drained into the Great Seal Hole. It is said to have stretched about one-third of a mile inland in order to be connected to the main Polberro engine shaft.

The mine-working continued. After initially finding tin, they went on to find copper. Lastly, they had thirty years of income from the arsenic that was extracted, before the adit fell into disuse and the seals came back into their own; until 2010. That was the year when part of the cliff above the entrance collapsed, leaving the entrance tunnel blocked by a massive boulder.

The seal hole itself has not been destroyed. The question soon to be answered was whether the seals can still enter and depart the cave, perhaps by means of a submerged gap below the boulder or on the high tide. It is so made that it cannot be clambered over — or at least over and back again — around the hours of low tide, when normally I make my entry to the caves.

ANECDOTE 4: Challenging Devonshire Caves

There is an innocuous cave, or so it appeared to me when first I explored it at low tide on a tide part way between springs and neaps. I paddled my way in through shallow waters, weaving through a dense maze of large, barely submerged and emergent boulders against which the paddle loudly clattered now and then, in no great hope. It had about it only the feeling of a routine check of a previously unexplored site doomed for disappointment. Likelihood was that it would prove to be as it had seemed from without: a 25- metre deep hollow in the low cliff. Likelihood was this would prove to be a dead end.

So it was, or seemed to be, at first. The ski grounded, was beached and made secure above the slack waters while I made the brief check of nooks and crannies. That was when I saw what might have passed as the bouldery entrance to a badger sett.

Under the low, angled roof of the back of the cave, over to one side, there was a hole. At that unpromising entrance, I squatted and thus was able to make out a pool of water below me leading to the interior. At that first visit, the pool seemed to have no end for the waters reached almost to the angled roof. Now I know it runs in for no more than 15 metres. However, on that day, I spent a long time on the brink, knowing it needed to be explored, but disliking enormously the murkiness of the waters and the possibility of something lurking there.

There has never been the least desire in me to intrude into a murky cave pool to find it occupied already by seals. Perhaps they would tolerate such intrusive proximity but if I can avoid it, I mean to avoid putting the question to the test. I know myself for an intruder at all times and the first principle is that I keep my line of retreat clear at all times. I do not intend ever to be trapped by an angry seal resting between wherever I am and the sea cave entrance.

This is due in part, but not exclusively, to a passage I read long ago in *The People of the Sea,* in which David Thomson had recounted an anecdote related to him by a seal-killer named Sean Sweeney. He came from near Ballinskelligs Bay and Bolus Head in Ireland:

'His name was Murphy and all the latter part of his life when I knew him, he had only the one tooth. It was he used to go killing seals with my father. It was into the cave they went those times for seals — into the darkness of the cave on the headland above the house here. And a big crowd of men used to go there together. They used to leave their boats outside at the mouth of the cave and swim in there with every man a flaming torch of bog deal stuck in his hat to give him light. Every man had a mattock for to strike the seals and kill them, and every man carried a stocking filled with black fire coals for to throw to the seals when they were angered.'

'Oh, they did, they did,' said Tadhg, 'but myself I heard it was in the sleeves of their coats they put the burned coals.'

'Some put them in their sleeves, and some in their trouser legs.'

'They did,' said Tadhg Tracy, 'for they know that if a seal caught a hold of you, she wouldn't be satisfied with squeezing you until she heard the bones cracking, and if she heard the coals cracking, she'd let go her hold thinking 'twas the bone.'

That tale has lived long in me and continues to do so, despite the fact that I have never allowed myself to be cornered in a cave by a seal and so have never verified it. I do know of others who have been cornered in a cave for an extended period of time, but none of these — so far as I know — has suffered the crunching of their bones. My experiences indicate seals may brush by you in a narrow fairway but also that they make no attempt to snap or nip in passing — this far, anyway. Nevertheless, I continue to strive to avoid the kind of encounters described by those Irishmen from another time.

In the Devonshire cave, probably I waited for a quarter of an hour. By then, had a seal been sleeping or otherwise resting in the pool before me, it would have needed to surface in order to breathe. Stepping three or four steps downward, I began to swim slowly, seeking to make no sounds, across the pool. My torch cast its illumination from one of my hands. At the same time, I was listening intently for the sounds of seals within — in particular, for their breathing.

Reaching a far shore of boulders, I emerged very slowly, trying to keep the giveaway water sounds cascading from my body muted as possible while focussing the torch beam on my feet — keeping the intruding illumination to a minimum. I remember a flight of large and heavy flies driving into my face at that point; hurting. My first thought was that something dead might rest stranded within but that proved not to be so.

Broadside on to the pool and the short slope that rose from it, a long tunnel ran in both directions. Drawn in plan view later, it resembled a lower-case letter 'h', albeit with the left vertical greatly extended in both directions. Thereafter, I would always know this as the h-cave.

Having scanned the boulder-floored tunnel to my left and glimpsed no seals, I chose to explore first the right wing. Here, the floor was sandy. It ran for about 30 metres, curving at last out of sight to the right. The ceiling seemed high at first but very soon I was forced to crawl forward for, by then, it was no more than a metre high and dwindling. Most exciting then was that there was the track of an adult seal in the sand with the chevrons of flipper marks indicating it had been moving toward the then-submerged exit of the cave apparently in the middle two hours of the tidal cycle. Nevertheless, my heart was in my mouth until I came around the final bend and found myself alone.

Having returned the way I had come, I checked behind the largest boulders at the other end of this tunnel, finding no seals — although on other days when I was monitoring the site during what proved to be a regionally belated breeding season, I found up to two pups at any one time. In fact, this most secret place proved to be the main pupping site for that locality.

My great good fortune that day was that I explored the cave on a tide that allowed the full potential of the cave to be recognised. Subsequently, when seeking to monitor the cave on a neap tide at low water, I found the sea waters covered the badger's sett entrance. I would not have known there was a tunnel to follow. My prejudice for making all my sea cave surveys based on low-tide visits on a spring tide was confirmed: it means everything is exposed. Few surprises remain to emerge on subsequent visits.

This cave is associated with another that lies more than a kilometre farther along the coast but is, in seal site terms, where the next-door cave-using neighbours live. The reason I am linking them here is because of the number of occasions that I have 'followed' the first sea journey of the pups suckled, moulted and weaned in the h-cave, subsequently discovering them to be hauled out in the small assemblies of seals using the much more spacious neighbours cave.

The neighbours cave is another that has many times daunted me, kept me out, far more often than the h-cave with that unpleasant little swim with just enough head-height below the roof to reach the far shore. Oftentimes, I have struggled, wallowing along the coast in what might appear from the cliff-tops to be a negligible force 4 swell, hoping I can manage to enter the cave while being all but certain that the gate would be barred against me, even so.

This cave is entirely different to the h-cave. It has a simple, high-roofed tunnel entrance that opens within, after about 25 metres, to a vast, high-roofed, watery chamber. More than 50 metres farther in, there is the main, swiftly-narrowing sand-hill to the left that has a tiny beach remaining even at high tide. A much more stunted beach, always submerged at high tide is situated to the right.

Within this great chamber, if there is any sort of swell, sea conditions are confused. Under the greater part of the watery chamber on the left side, the centre and even intruding over to the right, there is a flattish stone reef with gullies over which a surf-break forms and re-forms. There is a very narrow deeper water channel — not much deeper in fact — that may be essayed by staying close as possible to the slowly curving right-hand wall. At low tide, this may become perilous for it is precisely the habit-line taken by seals when departing the cave. Once, on a low spring tide during summer, I was carried backward on the bucking back of one such seal for several metres in what I remember as an unwanted magic carpet ride.

The water just off the beach is deep, rising in a large step at the last moment to the sloping sand hill. Here, if the sea is sea state 3 or more, a confused cross-break will form with ballooning surf ricocheting across the entire beach frontage. This means you land under fire, in expectation of being knocked hard from one side or the other. Thereafter, the hill of initially very soft sand or gravel curves to the left as it rises with a moderate gradient toward the back of the cave.

However, the place where the main drama is played out is where the entrance tunnel yields into the seaward end of the main watery chamber. It is possible to enter this cave even when a force 4 sea is piling into the cave, even when the confined and heightening lump of water is cresting almost to the roof. This I discovered on one of my tentative days, one of my probing deeper and ever deeper into the entrance tunnel until I decided that because the wave was not breaking in a massive commotion of surf within the cave, entry (and the all-important exit) must be possible. In relation to seal cave exploration, the worst dangers have lain in my imagination, usually.

I paddled in — at the last allowing the main swell to pass under me and riding in on its backside — and found that no sooner had I reached the main chamber, all the height and power of the swell was dissipated. Within no more than a few metres I was able to turn the ski about and consider the way I had come. It wasn't a pretty sight. Wave after wave humped in massively, almost brushing the roof. Rather more sinister at the time was that every time a wave almost touched that ceiling, it extinguished much of the light that was otherwise reaching into the cave.

However, once the watery challenges are surmounted and the eerie vocalisations of the seals are set to one side, I paddle to shore as swiftly as I can go (hectic action keeping the fear away). That means I can beach the ski and maybe have just enough time to extract my camera from its dry-bags to capture images of any seals within.

Their favourite resting place is at the top of the sand-hill, in one straggling assembly. The moulted pups do not form part of the assemblies, which tend to be either exclusively or mainly male. Rather, they are to be found sleeping, maybe shivering a little, at the base of one of the sand-hill walls, much closer to the tide-line.

Having described the challenges of this cave, by way of a post script, it must be added that on a rare day when the sea is calm and sunshine is pouring in through the cave entrance, this is a lovely, even balmy, place with a scant but interesting fauna to be found associated with the reef when it is exposed by the lowest tides. It has, also, the distinction of being the principal sea cave moulting assembly place in Devonshire as well as being the easternmost such site on the Channel coast of England.

ANECDOTE 5: A Long-known Cave

Of all the seal caves I have come to know, few — possibly none — boast so long a human record of exploration, adventure and misadventure as one that delves into the cliff for more than 150 metres from its double entrance. The cliffs thereabout are pock-marked with holes scoured by the sea along with others higher up the cliffs — in the form of adits — delved by men over the past three hundred years. More disturbingly, there is much evidence of rock-falls and cliff-collapses of both small and large scale, historical and, too often, since the last visit.

Once upon a time, it was possible to crawl along an adit into this cave from an entrance in the cliff slope. Sometimes, people still feel moved to unblock its now sealed entrance in order to explore not only its length but the sea cave down into which it opens. There, a knotted rope — oftentimes replaced — yet dangles down to the cave floor about 100 metres in from the sea and the distant memory of daylight.

The stories that follow were related to me following a chance meeting at the home of friends on Dartmoor by a lady called Jessamine. Hers was a generous Cornish childhood that allowed her to run wild and explore the local coasts. Thus, she came on the allotted day to the adit entrance in its cliff-slope hollow in the company of an older brother, some ninety years ago or so. She did not mention that they brought torches to light their way but the two of them made their mole-like way to the opening in the cave ceiling where the knotted rope dangled down.

Here, Jessamine would go no farther but her brother somehow eased himself out over the overhang and down the length of the rope below to the cave floor.

The twin entrances to the cave converge into the broad cave

fairway, forming the shape of a letter 'Y'. The cave itself runs mainly straight for its entire length, narrowing about two-thirds of the way in — making it an extremely elongate 'Y'. Both entrances are always submerged by waters that still rise up to 5 metres up the cave walls on the lowest tides. On such tides, elegant painted topshells can be seen crawling slowly up the entrance walls. Within, the cave floor is a jumble of mainly massive boulders and bedrock basins, many of which contain low water tidal pools of varying dimensions and depths.

Deep within — beyond the knotted rope and the narrowing — the fairway continues to one final shallow, low water pool. Beyond lie the seals quarters. They occupy, intermittently through the year but mostly during the season of pup production, a shallow-sloping beach of sand and gravel through which protrude occasional boulders. On most tides, they are able to use this for a resting place even during spring tides at high water, so it is ideal for, in their season, the pups to enjoy an unthreatened nursery period. Beyond this, there is one final, quite deep but much narrower chamber. It is but rarely used by the seals. As with most seal caves, it serves as a resting place for marine debris as well as offering anchorage points for the webs of marine and other spiders.

Here, so far from the sea, the darkness is not entire but what light remains is scant indeed. It is little different at the foot of the rope down which Jessamine's brother climbed. He reached a floor of jumbled boulders and knee- deep pools. If he had a torch, its small beam would have been swallowed by the vast space and the vast darkness that engulfed him there. Nevertheless, it would have been seen by the seals resting in the innermost deeps of the cave, for their eyes have evolved to make maximum use of least light, usually while foraging at the bottom of the sea but also in the sea caves where they took their rest.

Mouths opened. An eerie, unearthly wailing began. A rhythmic slapping began as the seals began to move over the sand down toward the shallow pool and the long escape from whatever the thin light signified to the mouth of the cave and the saving sea. A single seal moved alone at first but almost immediately triggered a general stampede. Splashing through the shallow pool, they began to make their laborious way up and over the 150-metre field of boulders that separated them from the cave entrance waters. This was no cavalry charge but a remorseless grunting-gasping slog. No matter how much effort had to be expended surmounting the boulders, no matter how long they needed to pause to recover dwindled energy, they proceeded. Sometimes they would bump into one another. There would have been growling and open-mouthed snarling along the way.

The lonely boy was frightened. Not knowing, perhaps, what monsters were bearing down on him, yet he managed to clamber slowly back up the knotted rope, all the way to the overhang — almost all the way to safety. But there he had to pause, for he could find no way to continue upward, up over the overhang. With nothing to grip, with the rope being pressed taut against the rock, he froze and so remained for what was remembered as a quarter of an hour. He would have been sweating, trembling with fear, his strength ebbing away. The torchlight would have begun to fail.

Below, quiet returned — or perhaps a single seal made a belated exit from the resting beach. The horrible sounds dwindled and ceased; and still the frightened boy clung there, urged upward by his equally frightened sister.

In the end, helped by his sister, the chastened boy managed to achieve the safety of the adit and soon thereafter the joy of being back in unconfined, unthreatening daylight.

Although that was their story, she told me of yet another event that occurred in the same cave, the following summer. A man brought his four children and their nanny across the cliffs to the adit entrance. All of them made their way along the adit to the same knotted rope. There, using his own rope brought along coiled over one shoulder, he lowered first the nanny and then the four children down into the cave.

Whether they encountered seals was not known. They explored the cave and, when their curiosity was sated, they returned to the knotted rope up which the man shinned. However, at the top he found he lacked the strength to draw up the others after him; so he was forced to return down into the cave. They made their way now toward the cave entrances and there he bade them wait for there was only one alternative available to him.

He slipped into the sea and swam along the coast until he came to a place where local men sometimes came for some fishing off the rocks.

Here, he clambered out and managed to scale the cliff. He began to run in the direction of the nearest farmhouse, more than a mile away. From there, he was able to put through a call to summon the St Ives lifeboat.

While he returned to the place where he had emerged from the sea, the St Ives lifeboat was drawn across the harbour sands by horses so that a launch could be achieved. She drove across the bay and, in time, made rendezvous with the wet man and thereafter with the family waiting not far within the adit cave. This story, too, had a happy ending.

During two summers, in 1961 and 1962, Ray Fordham and Dave Lewis made a pathfinding study of the seals using this cave. They took photographs rather than, as had been the tradition, bludgeoning the seals to death. Subsequently, these they shared with me to see whether any of the seals I had been able to photograph had the same pattern of markings of the head and neck area — to see, in fact, whether any of the seals they had photographed had survived so long. Alas, no matches were made: it would have been a long-lived seal that survived to the age of about 40 years in the wild — although, to be fair, not enough life studies have yet been made that anyone should sound overly confident about average lifespan.

This is one of the easier caves to explore. It is relatively wide and there is sufficient cover to approach quite close to the seals without giving yourself away. The only daunting aspect is really the nature of the rock. Being slate and shale, it has a tendency to rock-falls. Indeed, there is a considerable stretch of coastline stretching west from Perranporth as far as St Ives Bay where an unusual glut of erosion events occurred in a cluster of years from the first decade of the twenty-first century onward to the present day. Perhaps it was related to the continuing spate of relatively extreme weather conditions, saturating and desiccating everything in turn. I was working away on the Welsh coast for much of that time but still was concerned to see seal cave after seal cave — nursery site after nursery site — had been destroyed. Where would the prospective seal mothers go? Would new sites be opened up or would existing sites be subject to greater use?

ANECDOTE 6: The Lonely Twins

Greatest of all the caves in terms both of size and of the numbers of seals that use it throughout the year is one of the twins while the other is so formed that its assemblies of seals remain largely undiscovered on secret boulder beaches. Strikingly different in character despite being kindred in geological structure, they stand side by side under a deep dip in the high cliffs. Here at sea-level, fewest people stray, for the caves are far from safe havens in the event of a rapid and severe deterioration in weather conditions that are characteristic of this coast. Indeed, there is a well-deserved traditional rhyme that should always be heeded, warning: '*Between Padstow Bay and Bideford Light, tis a watery grave by day or by night*'.

They are caves best explored when the comparatively rare south-easterlies are blowing their gentlest, laying a calming hand across the elastic surface of the Atlantic, and when no storm out to sea is sending in a pulsing swell to render inaccessible these exceptional places. Such periods do occur in winter but are most likely between late spring and early autumn.

The south cave has a great portal. Like the h-cave, first impressions can be misleading. The very narrow tunnel leading off to the left has always looked too narrow for my taste. Perhaps it could be swum and perhaps, somewhere within, a chamber might open up where the seals could take refuge. I have not explored it and neither have I seen, ever, a seal in those uninviting tunnel waters.

What daunts me about the narrowness of such tunnels is a story I was told by one of two men who had paddled unwittingly into a seal cave on the Calf of Man. Part way along just such a narrow tunnel, they heard seals ahead of them stampeding toward the entrance that they were blocking. Somehow, they managed to clamber up the walls sufficiently far that they were able to span the tunnel cross-ways, hands against one wall, feet braced against the other, while the seals flowed by underneath them.

Unlike the h-cave, second impressions can be misleading, too. It seems that, after all, the great portal is just that: a great entrance hall leading in no farther; but that is not so. If you paddle in slightly on the diagonal to the left, you will come to a tunnel entrance. It is narrow but not as narrow as the other entrance tunnel. If the paddle be kept angled steeply, it is possible to paddle along its length, curving to the right as you go. It is sufficiently narrow that you can propel yourself toward the interior by using your hands to make your way along the tall walls of the tunnel. This ensures that you will make the quietest possible entry, causing least potential disturbance to the seals within.

Perhaps it runs for 20 metres. Then, with all light extinguished but for the lamp you will have brought with you, it yields — at low tide, at least — on to a sliver of beach composed of fine sands below a head-high rampart of rocks. At this point, I have always acted silently with speed, stowing the ski upright at the right wing of the beach before making my way with torch and paddle up on to the rocky rampart. By that time, if there are seals within — and I have never found the cave to hold less than twenty of them — they may have started to begin their movement toward the rampart and the tunnel opening beyond. Always, I make a very quick scan by torchlight of the two tunnels that lead to the interior, the one to the right being both longer and more attractive to the seals.

The shorter, broader tunnel of the two, which leads off to the left, is usually the lesser-used by the seals. I have learned to take refuge there — in order to avoid blocking or impeding in the least way the seaward flow of seals. In so doing, every time I break my long-standing rule never to allow seals to come to rest between myself and the cave entrance. The reason is that the very first time I visited this wonderful place, I teetered on the rampart while the avalanche of seals came undulating toward me. Unlike in most caves, these seals did not, in effect, keep to one side of the fairway but came toward me across the broadest front — the full breadth of the cave. Uncertain what to do in

216

so novel a situation, I thought first to make the swiftest possible getaway, but the leading seals were already pouring over and through the broken rampart on either side of where I stood, making escape impossible. That was when I realised what I might have done but could not now do: make a dash for the left-hand tunnel.

Instead, I climbed as high as I could go on to the highest point of the rampart where seals seethed around me and poured down on to the margin of wet sand. One large bull seal (seals always seem 'large' at close quarters in the sea caves, especially the bulls) seemed intent on over-running the place on which I stood, being just two strong undulations away before he turned to one side, looking left and right before taking an easier but more crowded course. That was the worst moment.

Because it is part of what I am there to do, I continued to make a running count of males and females throughout their passage by me. In their wake, after the thrashing through the shallows and the settling of the waters when they were gone, all was quiet.

Once safe, I made a swift reconnaissance in an atmosphere utterly transformed, jotting down the measurements of wall lengths and estimates of height. I noted the extent of boulders, bedrock and sand. I checked closely for 'cubby-holes' or kennels — passages off to left or right of the fairways wherein single seals have a taste for resting. I checked the walls, especially above head-height, for ledges large enough to accommodate seals between the high water and low water marks must always be sought. I checked for seal or fish- bones and for marine debris.

Then I made my getaway, back through the great entrance chamber and out into the lovely sunlight beyond. The first half of my exploration was complete.

I rested for long enough on the glass-calm sea to drink some peach juice in the sunlight, watched reproachfully — or so I imagined — by wet seal heads at various distance from where I rode, in effect, at anchor. For that little while, I tried not to think of the other entrance hall awaiting me. There is something of shock and exhaustion in exploring some caves for the first time. What becomes exhausted, I cannot know for certain. I think the imagination, informed both by instincts and the evolving reality, works in over-drive. Fear plays its part: I suppose some deep ancestral instincts must be provoked by such adventures in the dark, far from hope of help in the event of misadventure — for who would know, who — knowing — would know where or when, specifically, I needed help; and all the while, the tide would be rising and the torch batteries would die soon enough.

It is not a matter of over-egging an ordinary exploration. I notice I feel almost no fear when I have been accompanied by a companion, even though these are times when I know I stand responsible for their safety. I notice also that I suffer far more injuries when accompanied that when alone. Clearly, something subconscious is happening. If I could drag it kicking and screaming into the light, I would suppose solitude to be so dangerous in such places that I dare not make a mistake and this I achieve by behaving with, by my own lights, extreme caution.

I am very often afraid when alone at the entrances into the seal caves, being concerned primarily about the dangers of the swell I can hear turning to surf deeper inside the cave; concerned likewise about being surprised by the unexpected. That is why I have always chivvied myself to expect the unexpected — whatever that might be.

I write of fear at this point because the cave I was to enter next was the penultimate cave I identified as being used by the seals of the Cornish coast. I had achieved entry several times previously without ever daring to paddle all the way to the beach some 350 metres or so within. It is a cave in which the light is lost after about 120 metres. Deep water runs all the way to the beach of fine sands. Often there is a swell or at least choppy waters. The walls are high. As you paddle in, there are seals extremely close by in attendance from the outset until the beach is reached. Their eyes reflect the torchlight. They dive languidly just under the ski, sometimes gently bumping it — not suggesting menace but apparently in play only.

The great darkness of this cathedral-scale cave quells the brightness of the beam emanating from even my torch, making me doubt the charge in the batteries. It may seem like a small, feeble fear but to make the long journey back through such intense darkness to the light would be deeply unpleasant to me. Perhaps I will simply switch off the torch one day on the return journey from the beach and see what it does feel like — to inform myself that lack of light need not be a fatal affliction.

I have learned to circumvent my doubts about battery charge failure (they are always fully charged at the outset and claim a 45-minute period of illumination on full beam) by carrying always two torches and ensuring that both are secured to the ski or to my body by straps: available at need!

Hence my interlude of quiet soaking up the warmth of the sun and the peace of the sea.

Thereafter, I paddled literally straight into the neighbouring entrance hall. For 60 metres, it runs in between tall walls in a straight line before turning sharp left for the next 60 metres. That is the easy part always, unless the sea conditions are confused to the extent that the longer journey appears impractical, in which case I turn back.

The next abrupt turning to the right leads to the almost immediate extinction of any remaining ambient light and requires thenceforward that torchlight be used. With the honour guard of seals gently playful in the waters about me, I scan not only the waterway ahead of me but the walls above me. My very first attempt to explore this cave was quite unique in my experience of sea caves. From the entrance, it had seemed I had to brush aside webs trailing down from the cave roof to the waters — not the webs of spiders but the threads of time itself. For the only time ever in my life, I had a sense of being abroad in a place never before known to man. I had a sense of disturbing for the very first time the threads of Time itself.

Such was my fancy. In fact, I would imagine G.A. Steven and Midshipman Blake, R.N. swam into this cave in 1934 and doubtless many others will have chanced upon it. That, however, was my true impression, felt only on that occasion and never subsequently on other visits.

It was while brushing through these threads that there was the most terrific and shocking splash in the waters just ahead of me. A seal, sleeping on a ledge above and ahead of me, was wakened by my quiet progress and immediately telescoped its neck down toward the waters and fell rather than dived in. My response was to turn about and drive out of the cave as quickly as I could go, back into the reassuring daylight. And though I tried twice more that day to venture as far as the cave beach, my courage failed me to the extent that I didn't even ascertain that there was a beach at the back of the cave.

On this day, I had reached maybe 175 metres in when, because it was low water on a spring tide, I found a low-lying, rocky skerry blocking the way ahead of me. In following visits, it became clear this was a spring tide but not a neap tide feature. On this occasion, I had to haul myself on to it, dragging the ski behind me only to re-launch on the far side. Now I was paddling at the left-diagonal to the way I had come, an unexpected draught on my face. This proved to be coming from an extremely narrow tunnel, fluctuating in width and perhaps barely wide enough to be paddled, that leads from a little farther north up the coast to the same interior in which then I found myself. Unexpectedly, this high tunnel also admits a minimal ambient light, which always lifts the spirits.

The sandy beach — the sand-hill — is about 250-275 metres into the cave by the way I had come. Composed of finest grains of sand, it is used for a nursery place, a moulting place and as a lodge through the year: the greatest and most impressive of all the Cornish seal caves.

I cannot — would not dare — know how wave action is expressed at this place but suspect it is less heavy than might be imagined, because of all the twists and turns the wave pulses must take to reach in so far and also because of the skerry that obstructed me that day (that does not show on the least neap tides at low water). I suspect it functions as a reef, causing waves (at least for the main part) to break and lose what remains of their main power before they reach the beach. I think that the seals use it in such numbers through the year is also indicative that this must be a refuge rather than a death-trap.

I love the nature, the inhabitants and perhaps above all, the privacy of these caves and their neighbourhood. Although the ocean often comes to shore hereabouts with the greatest weight and violence, it can also be a place of greatest peace.

ANECDOTE 7: An Ynys Wair Gateway to the Otherworld

Many of the islands strewn down the western seaboard of Britain, Ireland and Brittany have strong traditions, faded almost to nothing now but important in their time, of being gateways to the Otherworld. Solitary monks and, before them, druids lived lives there of lonely contemplation but for the company of seabirds, seals and cetaceans. Often, islands were named for them and some names have survived renaming by the Saxons and Norsemen to the present day. One such is Ynys Seiriol, off the south-east tip of Ynys Môn (Anglesey) — otherwise known as Priestholm and today best known as Puffin Island. Two more are, collectively, the Tudwals, situated south of the Llŷn Peninsula. In their time, Île de Sein off the west tip of Brittany and Ynys Môn itself, off the coast of north-west Wales, were of particular importance to the druids: their most sacred places.

The next cave I would describe is situated at an extremity of one of the debateable islands, ownership of which was so long disputed between two of the old regional kingdoms of post-Roman Britain that it is named separately in the two tongues. It has a front door marvellously well-sheltered by a neighbouring headland as well as by a screen of skerries that also serve as haul-out sites for the seals. There is also a weak tidal stream that deters some potential intruders but not the harbour porpoises.

The cave itself has a narrow, vertical-walled deep-water entrance. Within the cave, the water yields initially on to a very steeply angled rampart of massive boulders — so steep that during a pathfinding exploration, there seemed to be no easy way to achieve a landing. However, at low tide it widens a little immediately to the left and here was the possibility of making a somewhat awkward landing. The ski can be lodged to the left, upright, leaning against the cave wall.

The boulders seem all to be painted in colours orange and mauve — the mauve being the lovely encrusting lithothamnium, ubiquitous at low water along all the rocky western shores. Careful to leave no silhouette, making a way along the left-hand wall, it is an easy clamber of something more than five metres up to the plateau of boulders that waits at what must be the mean high- water mark. From here, a shallow shelving plateau rises most gently towards a jumble of gigantic boulders piled up in the rear of the cave.

On the plateau, there are often two or three shallow tidal pools and here the fairway-proper narrows somewhat and leads to the interior, floored with smaller, even-sized boulders interrupted near the seaward end by emergent bedrock and a few much larger boulders. Everywhere, the cave roof is high while the quality of light is good in the front half of the cave and fair even in the deep interior by seal cave standards.

The seals use this place throughout the year, mainly in considerable numbers — rarely less than twenty being present at a time. Moulting assemblies gather here for, unlike virtually every other seal cave on the island, the cave is only at risk of inundation during major storms that coincide with a wind blowing directly into the entrance. These are very rare events; such are the natural defences of this place. However, pupping here occurs only exceptionally. That is unsurprising, in that when a site is being used as a nursery, all 'non-essential' seals — meaning excepting pups, mothers and an attendant male who seeks to deny other prospecting males access to the site and the female seals using it — disappear; they keep out of the way. However, because pup production at this site is so rare, it serves mainly as a peaceable communal refuge for those non-essential seals.

The seals arrive mainly during the period of high water and tend, customarily, to remain hauled out through the tidal cycle. There is enough spaciousness in the interior that bickering — common cave behaviour among seals — can be kept to a minimum. There is a broad enough field of access to the sea at the top of the rampart that it can be achieved without aggravating seals resting closest to the water's edge.

Whereas most of my research effort over the years has been made at the low water half of the tidal cycle, this is a place that allows behaviour to be studied over the full tidal cycle. This is because the quality of light where the seals most commonly congregate is better than in most caves. What happens most of the time, as at non-cave haul-out sites, is that they sleep. Occasionally they might stir, scratch, curve their bodies into the banana-shape or even scan to see what is going on about them. The only period of general agitation is when the tide is high, when the surf runs white against the dry, warm pelages of the seals. They stir, waken, fidget, grumble and occasionally go through the motions of provoking brawls with their neighbours. It can be noisy. There may be open-mouthed snarling, flippering, the eerie, drawn-out wailing that in seal-tongue means: I am adamant; leave me alone!

Seals depart. Other seals arrive. The comings and goings cause more displacement, more likelihood of bickering and half-hearted brawling. At high water, along the water's edge twitches a restive fence of seals, many of their bodies curved into the banana. The duration of the unrest depends on how strongly the surf is running. As the tide ebbs, when it reaches them intermittently no longer, the peace which marks the great majority of their time ashore in the cave settles upon them once more for perhaps as long as 9–10 hours.

There was an exceptional day — not for the seals, necessarily, but for me. While watching from without the cave, I heard a familiar monotonous bird call that seemed quite wrong for this kind of habitat at this time of year. As I peered about me, I glimpsed the sun-bright kingfisher flying higher than usual above me under the blue sky before dipping low and, all the while playing out behind it a long line of turquoise, disappearing into the glooms of the seal cave. And then: dashed out again, like a wave that had run in, boomed against a wall, only to come ricocheting out again.

Kingfishers are not strangers to the sea. At need, they will abandon pond, stream, river or estuary, coming down to (most often) the winter sea to take what plunder is to be found in the pools along the shore. This one seemed out of place and time but was not less welcome than ever they are.

ANECDOTE 8: How Martin's-Finger Cave Came by Its Name

Without quite yet meeting him, I encountered Martin Hunt one summer's day while trying to find a new way to clamber down to the sea into the bay of my soul. As I pondered my way, during one of the lengthy pauses I became aware that a party of people had settled themselves on the sea-slopes of the headland to the west. They spread about them and were enjoying a packed lunch while the fulmars drifted in from the sea to their narrow cliff ledges, there to take up their resting or nesting places somewhere between us.

At the time, I found it exasperating to have my pathfinding effort overlooked. I have always had a horror — most especially while venturing into the almost secret places of the seals — of showing the way to others. I know precisely how much of an intruder I have been there. I know that it is virtually impossible to share a cave with a seal without the seal becoming entirely aware of the alien presence. I know that their response is often to stampede from the cave any time from immediately to within a quarter hour of coming to that awareness.

The way I have justified my own intrusions has been by furnishing the results of my studies to the science and environmental oriented organisations primarily responsible for coastal management — the names have changed so often over the years but I have known them most fruitfully as the Countryside Council for Wales, Natural England and Scottish Natural Heritage. The Sea Mammal Research Unit also receives copies of my results. It has the responsibility for advising governments about sea mammals and fisheries.

Ethically, that may or may not be sufficient justification but it must serve until others find their way to the sea caves sufficiently well-funded to install devices capable of remotely monitoring seal behaviour over the full tidal cycle and extended periods of time.

That balmy summer's day, I managed to clamber down to the sea, thereby giving myself one more variation in the small suite of approaches — my efforts to outwit forbidding wave action: one of the main stories of my life — I could take to attempt to access the most remote cave in the bay. Later, I made my way eastward, checking other seal sites: skerry haul-out sites and water resting places and then simply seeking whatever there was to be found — mainly butterflies and day-flying moths, flowers, beetles labouring in brilliant armour along the footpath, palmate newts in the holy well, a dead common shrew and birds: whatever birds were to be seen in what was by now the early afternoon.

That was when Martin and I met. He was standing with his retinue of adventurous walkers pointing out a nest in the tumbling, sloping ground below the cliff-top. Recognising them, I would have hurried by but Martin is a man of great good nature. He hailed me and drew me over to where he stood, pointing out for me the nest of a carrion crow in which the topsides of four mottled blue eggs were showing; like treasure. Afterwards, he verified that it was indeed I who had been clambering down among the roots of the cliff and we did, after all, fall into conversation and, soon enough, into enthusiasm.

We became friends. Since that day, so fortunate for me, many are the adventures we have shared. In the field, he is a bold, brave, very well- informed and above all a happy and usually a devil-may-care companion. His spirit, to do rather than to hold back, has been enormously cheering for me, causing me to attempt more than I would ever have dared do, were I alone.

I know of no person better able to bring alive and make fascinating, often by novel, idiosyncratic means, anything at all pertaining to geology. If I see a boulder beach, he finds there all manner of minerals whose names end with '— ite'. I have in mind as I write the rock painted brilliantly with a little spur-dog of peacockite that he picked up and showed me one day, down at Cligga.

There was a winter's day. The sea was sufficiently lacking in malice for us to swim and clamber to one of the less-visited sea caves. Three of us swam in high hopes of seeing a large assembly in the cave for we were well into the season of the moulting assemblies. We gained the safety and relative warmth of the cave. We were there stripped of anything superfluous. We had brought no dry bags, no cameras, nothing that would encumber. I don't remember why. Probably my flash unit had experienced a misadventure or a malfunction. Camera equipment does not flourish in the attritional environment of a seal cave. Neither have I been sufficiently careful with my gear.

That late morning in January, simply, we were there to make a count and then be gone: smash, grab and run.

It began as one of the great cave visits. Fifty-one seals lay within, mostly sleeping soundly. Nearly every seal was a mature male. The small remainder were too young to sex accurately. Although the numbers were greater than ever I had counted in this cave before, that all the mature seals were males was predictable for this particular month. Females sometimes shared these assemblies but only ever in small numbers.

This cave has two main beaches, one being a whale-back, the other forming a sand-hill. There is a third with a scattering of large boulders emergent from the sand the closer you get to the sea that forms the floor of a second entrance. It has come to be known in our private parlance as the Seal's Entrance, as they largely shun the one we had used. However, the main fairway consists of the outer whale-back and the inner sand-hill, the latter being by far the longer and steeper of the two.

That day, with so many seals present, they made a fantastic spectacle. Our arrival was sufficiently distant from them and discreet that we were able to make a very surreptitious way to the foot of the inner sand-hill without drawing the least attention to ourselves. There, we were able to watch at our leisure; and what we saw was this:

The seals, as usual, were massed in the one great spread about half to three quarters of the way up the sand-hill. As such, they were spread out some small distance below the high-water mark. From memory, it seemed they covered the full width of the cave (approximately 4 metres wide) and 25 metres of length of the sand-hill. As usual, steam rose from the great, stranded hulks of their blubbery bodies and we could smell strongly the fishy perfume emanating from them. While nearly all the great hulks lay still, and mainly upon one side, there were three seals in the first year of life that were not sleeping. These appeared to be playing a game of tag. That is to say, they appeared to be chasing one another through the great maze of their elders' bodies, through any gap where those bodies were not touching. From the sightings we have made, before and since, this appears to be, by far, their favourite game. Two pups on a strandline of By-the-Wind Sailors in a granite cave

Their spirited fun was not passing unnoticed. Not everywhere but oftentimes, the nearest mature male would stir, maybe find sufficient energy to make a half-hearted, open-mouthed growl or else vibrate an admonishing fore-flipper in their direction. In fact, it resembled nothing more than a crowd of grumpy old men being teased by young teenagers.

This behaviour continued perhaps for the fifteen minutes we had watched, the three of us crouched against the cave wall, when at last the three youngsters found themselves at the seaward margin of the slumberous company. What caused them to do what followed is unknown. Perhaps they caught our scent. Perhaps one of us made a betraying movement. Perhaps what they did was a wicked variation in the game they had been playing — if, indeed, game it was. The three of them, almost as one, began a high-speed race down the sand-hill toward either the Seal's Entrance or toward us. It was high-speed because their bodies were lightweight.

Whether stimulated to life by their movement or by the rapid, light slapping of their bodies against the wet sand, the assembly came to life. Heads were lifted. Necks were craned. As if moved by one mind, the great company of males began to move partly down and partly up the sand-hill, according to where they lay. By the time the three youngsters were swerving around at the bottom of it into the passageway leading to the sea, the full assembly was galumphing down the sand-hill behind them to a much heavier drumming of the sand. They came slower for their bodies are not made for speed over land; but they came across a broad front: heavy cavalry on the move. We shrank before this eruption out of the cave gloom. Having met the like often enough before, I persuaded my companions to stay still and not to run. As I was the most forward of the three, they decided to give my counsel the benefit of the doubt; just.

That was how the count came to be made, for the mass of bodies thinned as they came wheeling around the corner at the bottom of the sand-hill into the sunlight.

Three youngsters had led the way. All but last in the stampede there came a fourth youngster that I counted, moving on to count the next and last seal, being in counting mode. It was Martin, beside me then, who cried out: "Look! That one has netting caught around its neck!"

Even as I jotted the count total on to my slate, he was up and running in pursuit.

Belatedly, I chased after him. By then, Martin was restraining it having caught the considerable shawl of monofilament netting in one hand. The unexpectedly muscular young seal was throwing itself about all over the place in its desperation to escape.

Martin was superb that day. He started breaking the strands of net immediately. I joined in but the seal did not begin to calm down, continuing to throw itself about until I said to him: "Let me get out of this wetsuit! We'll cover its head, and then one of us can sit astride it while the other breaks the remainder of the strands. We mustn't get bitten. The bacterial flora around their teeth could be catastrophic for us!"

He ignored me. As I tried to slip out of the wetsuit, he continued to break the strands. Then he cried out and leapt up and down on the spot, wringing a hand. The young seal had nipped him. I grabbed the shawl of netting lest the seal made good its escape, breaking a few more strands before Martin set aside his hurt and joined in again with renewed vigour.

The shawl was entirely removed in that cave entrance. I doubt I could have achieved so happy an outcome had I been alone. He was possessed of a beautiful, irresistible determination that day.

The young seal was able to escape. Only afterwards did Martin examine more closely the blood dripping from his finger to find that the finger nail of his fore-finger had been nipped off. I said let's get to hospital and have the correct drug (doxycycline) administered immediately.

There would be, of course, no 'immediately', I was thinking. We had to swim back to the mainland. We had to cross a boulder beach some 300 metres wide, clamber up a cliff, and walk across the maritime heathland about a mile and a half back to my cottage and then make a twenty-minute drive to the hospital, there to queue for however long.

Martin must have been thinking the same thoughts.

Perhaps you are curious to know more of the third member of our company? Perhaps he had felt there was no room for him to help during the efforts to release the seal. Now, he left us as soon as we reached the beach, having not enjoyed his finest hour; but Martin said, irrepressibly: "Let's explore this cave while we're here."

In the end, we explored two more caves and checked other skerry haul-out sites and water resting places before we retired for lunch at my cottage. It was four hours after the event that we drove into town and, later still, that he received the cleansing shot of doxycycline at the Penzance hospital.

That wasn't quite the end of the story and neither was it allowed to remain so small.

The nail grew again in time but forever afterwards, even last weekend when he displayed it to us yet again, there has remained a measure of misshapenness about both the fingertip and the nail. While showing it off, he regales us with another retelling of the story. If you are lucky, perhaps one day he will tell it to you.

Of course, we renamed the cave. Forever thereafter, for us at least, it will be Martin's Finger Cave.

A local newspaper got hold of the story but somehow managed to make more of it than any of us could have stomached, relating that a man had lost a finger, bitten off by a seal. One of the national tabloid newspapers improved the story still more by reporting to the nation that a man had his arm bitten off by a Cornish seal.

ANECDOTE 9: The Serpentine Cave and the Pool in an Islands Heart

To me, there is no rock-type more alive that serpentine — so many maroons or greens shot through with straight white lines or speckled with black. There are few stories more wondrous in the natural world than where and how serpentine comes to be made, along with all the transitions it goes through including serving as the seabed for a geological interlude before finally being thrown up as stretches of coastline or otherwise erupting from the interior.

It is a marvellous rock, named for its supposed likeness to the skin of a snake. It is a rock created at great depth in the earth's crust, an area of high pressure as well as high temperature, by the interaction of heated seawater with peridotite. The olivine component of peridotite is hydrated, with most of it being transformed into serpentine. This is subsequently squeezed upward through fractures in the earth's crust.

However I describe serpentine, it won't be a patch on the way Martin Hunt described it, drawing pictures in the partly serpentine gravels one day on Pentreath Beach. Using the tip of a stick that had been washed ashore by the tide, I recall him describing how, once upon a time, the serpentine we had seen spread all around us was to be found south of the equator aeons ago but had sailed slowly north and emerged here. Geology stories are as wondrous as fairy-tales.

Backalong the way we had walked, there is a serpentine cave. It is not easy to see from the coastal footpath or to reach from the shore because its situation is remote from any launching place — and the reaching of that launching beach is a wearisome yomp. Its entrance is sheltered from the prevailing winds by a headland and, at low tide, by a small trickle of skerries. As with so many of the most interesting seal caves, it has a tall-sided, deep-water entrance that runs in for less than ten metres before yielding into a seawater pool that varies in extent and depth according to the cycle of the moon. Paddling in, it is not uncommon to see one or more pale grey seals, usually females, ghosting out fast and submerged. Their eyes are open as they swim. As they close on and pass by under the wave ski, always they are looking up before they accelerate the few remaining metres to achieve the safety of the open sea.

Within, landing is rarely easy because usually the rocks, aside from being sea- polished, are mucous-covered and slippery. In effect, you arrive on the left side of the cave. To the right, the wall bellies and there is water of varying depth where, often, seals yet linger, heads at the surface; watchful. Diagonally to the right, there is a lesser tunnel which yet is that used most commonly by the seals. Occasionally during the breeding season, up to two pups can be found on this beach, from which there are cubby-holes leading off, which are their favourite resting places: off the main fairway.

This is not a cave of importance to the seals. The locality is of only minor importance to them, but they do use it through the year while the cliffs, promontories, headlands and coves are beautiful, varied and even awe-inspiring. The serpentine cave is most beautiful on account of its walls that reach up to the perimeter of a rough-hewn ceiling. Over the centuries and through the storms of its existence, the walls have been polished to a natural sheen that might belong more to fantasy than harsh reality. Yet so it is. The seals and the occasional choughs are but a grace note here.

There was a memorable adventure one February day made to and from this place. Jenny Glanville, a Devonshire naturalist, was down visiting. With a film-making companion, Matt Ruglys, who filmed, in effect, over my shoulder for a companionable year, we decided to visit this cave because there was an idyllically sunny day that was promised to stretch from dawn to dusk.

We launched from a harbour in the middle of the day in full wetsuits. We paddled down the coast, dipping into caves to check whether there were any visitors using them and came in time to the serpentine cliffs and coves. The trouble was that there was too much companionable ease in our adventure. I know that the time of the tide and then, as the sun sank lower in the sky, the time of sunset were ever-present keynotes in my thoughts. As ever, I was struggling to balance the imperatives I know these things to represent. Proper haste versus leaving people sufficiently alone that they can enjoy in each their own way the adventure without me treading on their heels.

The simple fact is we arrived too late at the cave.

It was a long paddle and for those not used to it, a tiring one. The entire passage back to the harbour was a struggle. We were only a third of the way back, the heat of the sun was waning as it sank ever lower in the sky, when I suggested to Matt that he simply paddle at his natural speed, get back safe to harbour so that in need he could call up help for us.

Jenny and I came on slowly behind; then, very slowly. I didn't enjoy the moment that Matt was lost to view. I don't suppose Jenny did either. I do know that I tried to urge her on but she said she was already going as fast as she could go — which made me feel like an insensitive, blundering clod.

The sun sank entirely away. The world changed from being idyllically warm and pleasant to becoming suddenly very cold.

Next, the dark came and still we stopped and started, progressing ever more slowly. By now, despite the wetsuits, we were freezing — the extremities most of all. The moon rose and then the February stars, bitter-bright above the great black mass of the high cliffs.

It was an hour after dark that we came to harbour. Mercifully, Matt was still there, along with my (then) wife, Fijke, who had brought a flask of sweetened tea. We could hardly straighten up to dismount from the skis. Our feet were frozen. Our fingers, for so long curled about the stems of the paddles, refused to drag the skis to shore. Matt helped. Afterwards, Fijke helped first Jenny and then me out of our wetsuits. Without that help, we would still be wearing them.

As Matt departed, Fijke drove us the ten miles or so to home with the car heater blowing at full blast. There, I think Jenny had a shower while Fijke made soup for us. Afterwards, I showered. Our bodies began to feel their way back painfully to working order thereafter.

Meanwhile, another lesson was learned and written in lead: set out earliest and finish earliest when undertaking explorations on glorious winter days: never lose the winter sun. The principle applies equally when exploring under high east-facing cliffs, when the sun departs very early in the day.

The polished cave we had visited that winter's day is not the only exceptional cave in the locality. Farther still along the coast, there is an island upon which seabirds make their nests. On its seaward face, there is a crooked slit of a tunnel that it is just possible to squeeze along upon the ski if you are prepared to angle it rather steeply to pass through the narrowest points. At its inner end, it opens into a great dwarf's hat of a cave, illuminated by a natural window open to the sky set high above on the south side. Within, there is nowhere to land. You find yourself upon the calm surface of a very deep seawater pool. The water is very clear. You can see all the way to the pale bottom, which may be of sand or of bedrock.

The very first time I squirmed into this unique place, while I gazed down through the clear waters, there was an immature seal of between one and two years of age swimming round and around below me, all the while staring up at me staring down.

Maybe he or she followed me in. Probably the entrance underwater is more substantial than that at the surface. For the seal, there was nothing there but refuge, privacy and peace. I would guess it is a place where just one seal comes at a time to sleep, bottling upright in waters that are hardly ever disturbed by the noise we folk tend to bring with us.

ANECDOTE 10: Ogof Morlo

Alone among all the sea caves I am remembering as anecdotes, this cave is most interesting when reached from the land — although it requires that first you reach an island well-guarded by tidal streams (as most islands seem to be: the nature of the beast). There are many marvellous stories and legends associated with this place.

Today, the island is a year-round regional stronghold for the grey seals, as well as being a place visited by a handful of harbour seals through the year. The grey seals use these shores for a resting place between fishing trips or during longer peregrinations that serve either to help make a map of their world or else take them to visit neighbours or distant relations.

They give birth to their pups here, although the number of potential nursery sites was considerably greater than the number of pups being born here annually. In fact, most recently there has been an explosion in pup production here, which will be interesting to observe. The seals also congregate here in large moulting assemblies during the winter months. The sites they use are sea caves, skerries, an islet and, above all, beaches.

The sea cave is on a side of the island from which walkers are banned partly for their own safety — for the sea-slopes are very steep and there are no footpaths but for wispy sheep tracks that can be treacherously slippery whenever the ground is wet. They are banned also on account of the birds that nest here, especially the thousands of burrow-bound Manx shearwaters: a quite strict and effective effort to prevent disturbance.

The sea hill is very high. On its seaward face, running down the scree is always an option but I tend to make at least a small part of the journey down to the low sea cliffs on my bottom. This is partly because I want to take in the life that everywhere about me seems to be burgeoning. Also, there are the skulls of Manx shearwaters to be found.

It is not difficult clambering down the lowest skirts of the sea cliff to the bouldered shore, by the nesting razorbills. It is not difficult to cross the boulders of the beach, angling upward at the end to arrive outside the small hole in the cliff maybe some 10 metres above the high-water mark. It is not an inviting hole.

It may not be the most sensible way to go about it but I have learned to enter it head-first, worming my way through until I am doing a bent-bodied hand- stand on the cave floor within. There, I drag in the remainder of my body and resume a more normal posture: it is possible to stand up. Immediately before me to the left, behind a thin angled screen of rock, there is crammed the disused nest of a chough lined with wool; but my progress is not in that direction. Leading out downward from the small chamber, there is a short, narrow tunnel of less than 10 metres that curves a little before opening into the chamber below.

Again, there is a choice and again I go along this tunnel head-first. At the end, I emerge into the cave proper but at ceiling level. At this point, there is no choice but to step down on to a great solid sheet of rock sloping massively downward toward a lower edge that is set above seawater. The first magic is in seeing that water, inside the cave: it is always coloured purest jade-green and is always crystal clear.

The second magic is the feeling of squatting there under the ceiling below maybe 1000 feet of rock. Squatting with thighs and knees drawn up to my chin, there is a wonderful timelessness to the atmosphere. It might be that 20,000 to 30,000 years before, Stone Age people knew this place and squatted likewise. If so, did they experience anything of the sense of wonder that was upon me and always is in that place?

There is one little tunnel that runs along below the left side of the sloping massif of rock, becoming a small, narrow stony beach at low water. The remainder of the cave floor has usually been covered by water, although other miniature, pebbly beaches form at low tide. These allow seals to haul-out for brief periods. Pups may be born here or else take refuge here occasionally, but I have yet to find them.

Amid so much that pleases about that extraordinary place, I love best just gazing down into the clear, jade-green water, illuminated by the sunlight outside, from under that ancient roof. If I could choose, I would be watching — as so often I have — the black silhouettes of submerged seals swimming, drifting or else upright and sleeping in the jade depths. Then they seem to be more the impressions of seals rather than their own substantial selves — a dream of seals. Being in the habit of capturing images that identify an individual seal or a place, there is a rare pleasure in photographing them as these magical impressions of themselves.

ANECDOTE 11: The Island-Perilous and Awkward Annie.

The final anecdote strays from the seal caves, but I couldn't resist including it.

Islands, especially uninhabited islands, have always exerted great allure upon me, despite D.H. Lawrence's cautionary tale. Britain, Ireland and, to a lesser extent Brittany, are blessed with a multitude and wonderful variety of them. Rare, however, are the uninhabited seal islands that are not protected to some extent by tidal streams. The negative side of this is the degree of extra toil and perhaps unease that this introduces to my work. The positive is that I am very familiar with the edges of the tidal streams as being the haunt of (usually but not always) small groups of harbour porpoises. Nick Tregenza, who knows much more about harbour porpoises than I, has often referred to them as 'Tidal Streamers'.

Of all the wildlife that associates by chance with the grey seals and their haunts, for me the closest associations are with the shags and porpoises.

Shags very often nest just inside or just outside seal caves. Where they nest outside, because they are so site-specific in their choice of perching places, over the course of the year, heavy deposits of chalky patches of guano accumulate about them. From afar, this has always looked to me like the base for the name-plate for a house. In effect, I think of it as meaning: 'seals live here!'

The association with porpoises is more substantial. Grey seals and harbour porpoises are not greatly different in size and their ranges overlap very substantially. Most especially, that is true of their foraging areas. Although I have never been in a position to have satellite relayed data loggers attached to either species to inform such an assertion, I have worked with fishermen. Primarily in west Cornwall, we collaborated in an effort to describe grey seal by-catch as well as grey seal damage done to netted fish. Working primarily with set net inshore fishermen, we found both seals and porpoises caught in the same kinds of (tangle and trammel) nets in the same places — that is, on and just above the seabed. At the same time, fishermen I worked with described much bigger by-catches — especially of seals — being made by the hake boats farther out to sea. This I absorbed without being able to check for veracity.

There is nothing deliberate about it. It is simply a consequence of so much net being set, with a soak time often massively extended due to bad sea conditions or other fisheries coming into season and the fact that nets are so good at what they are designed to do. Certainly, no fisherman wants to haul up a dead seal or porpoise. For as long as such nets are used and seals and porpoises live along our coasts, the problem will continue for tangle and trammel nets would be the best way of deliberately catching seals — as was initially confirmed by the experience of fishermen around Barra in the Outer Hebrides in the 1970s.

This island is on the porpoise-road. It is necessary to paddle quite far out across a shallow sea to reach it but always the sea-track is decorated with a wide variety of seabirds. The island itself rises to no great height and has but one pebble and cobble beach joining the main island to the largest outlier that appears around the hours of low water.

For the greater part of the year, turnstones and purple sandpipers forage over the rocks and there is a low water pool that is much frequented by teal. Of nesting birds, there are only gulls and shags, the latter decorating their nests lavishly with ex-fishing line as well as floats and coloured fishing weights in particular. On one occasion, I found there, tried to catch and failed to catch, a nesting shag that had a fishing hook in one of its eyes.

The gulls have a roosting place there the year round. Mainly herring gulls nest on the low-lying, jagged rocks beside a large number of foetid green pools. I am always surprised that the seals hauled out there on the rocky shores pay such scant attention to the cacophony they make when I begin my exploration of the island.

The island is used by more harbour seals than use any other west British site south of Scotland excepting only (outside the people-hours in summertime) North End Haws, at the north end of Walney Island, Cumbria. They are not ever-present but were observed there in every month of the year during the period that I was studying the seals there. This made it the most important year-round harbour seal site on the west coast of England and Wales.

This dominant position was only displaced in 2019 by a small number of harbour seals discovered to be using the estuary of the Dart in Devonshire.

They seem to prefer to occupy a position at or near the edge of one of the sub- groups of grey seals that assemble there, usually (but not always) very close to the water's edge.

I have watched the same behaviour by mature harbour seals at a Devonshire archipelago site. They were always close to the water's edge, entering the sea more readily than the attendant grey seals — although there was a particular yearling grey seal that seemed to want to copy everything that the summer resident harbour seal did. Consequently, when the two of them crashed into the sea, this tended to set off a chain reaction among the other grey seals yet remaining ashore: always, they followed them abruptly, abandoning the haul- out rocks for the remainder of that tide cycle.

Usually, the island is easily reached, for there has never been much malice in the tidal stream. However, there were two occasions, both occurring after prolonged periods of rough sea conditions that had kept the island inaccessible, when I chanced my luck and paddled there in marginal conditions. On both occasions, there was an offshore wind blowing at force five. The sea was full of short steep waves, many with frothing white crests. Paddling with the wind, the pace was swift but uncomfortable because the nose of the ski repeatedly dug into the wave ahead or had to be manoeuvred over the top of it. It was a corkscrewing kind of progress but I reached the Island in record time (for me) — less than 20 minutes — despite my discomfort and a paucity of seabirds to pause for and watch.

It was in the month of October. Assemblies of seals tend to vary at that time of year. This day, the assembly, divided into small sub-groups, was not large although, as usual, females predominated —in all the sub-groups but one. This, too, was gratifyingly typical.

The surf was exploding along much of the rocky shores so the seals were not sleeping. As usual in such conditions, they were more watchful and alert than usual. Consequently, there were few opportunities to capture the images that would identify them. Soon enough, I was re-launching the ski.

The problem was that the wind, locally, had increased to at least gale force, being channelled and accelerated down an adjacent sea-valley. I had to launch with spray lashing my face through choppy surf. Then, as is my custom, I spent about 15 minutes making what headway I could without glancing back over my shoulder. I was wearing a peaked cap, to try to keep to a minimum the discomfort to my eyes done by the surf spray. I was trying to bend myself near-double to offer least resistance to the wind but the short waves running so close together broke repeatedly into my lap or upon the dry bag that was angled there while also being anchored to one of the toe-loops.

It was uncomfortable, but I supposed I was making progress. Therefore, it was an unpleasant surprise when I risked the first quick glance over my shoulder to see that I had made only about 200 metres in that time.

I redoubled my efforts and kept my head down. Nevertheless, the spray still filled my eyes and stung. My nose was running. I wasn't a pretty sight.

To cut the long story short, I reached safety but where I had run to the island in 20 minutes, it took two and a half hours to return to the launch-beach. I think the one cheering detail of that struggle was that the sky was entirely blue throughout: there wasn't a cloud to be seen.

I learned three important things that day.

Of general importance: even in such a wind and sea, nothing is constant. I think it is fair to remember that for at least 90% of that horrible passage, all I could do was attempt to hold my position, digging the paddle blades into the sea to serve for some kind of anchor, trying to stop myself losing ground. During the other 10%, I paddled while bent double with all the power I had. In effect, I paddled hardest every time there was a hole in the wind; and the wind is full of holes. When I paddled, I tried to head directly into the wind, toward the nearest shore, hoping the land beyond would offer some little shelter against the full force of the wind — and it did.

Secondly, the gale was not general but localised. There was a valley running directly toward the sea precisely opposite the island launch point. I think the wind was funnelling down that valley, gaining speed and then running over the sea like an aerial delta of some great river of wind. As I neared the launch beach on that return passage, conditions eased mainly because I had moved into a lee position caused by the proximity of the land.

Lastly, I could have fallen back on the island and besought help from the RNLI. Had I done so, I wonder if any environmental agency thereafter would have considered funding aspects of my work. It is one thing being thought a little crazy by people sitting behind desks, especially while there has been no other cost-effective way of collecting the information. Forever afterwards, they would remember the one false move I made rather than the decades of quietly going about my chores. Besides, I never felt in extremis: it was merely a long, trudging struggle home. At least when I had reached the car park behind the beach, when I looked back to the sea, I had the deep pleasure of beholding the full simplicity of wet yellow sand, a dark blue and white sea, the warm blue of the sky and a great rainbow arching over it all.

Bearing in mind the uniquely exhausting nature of that passage, you may be astonished to learn that I repeated the mistake just one month later. Similar conditions prevailed with a force five offshore wind and a swift passage to the Island. Until that day, the penny hadn't dropped, about being subject to highly localised weather conditions associated with the local coastal landform adjacent to the island. I think the penny dropped when I recognised the previous conditions were being duplicated precisely.

Knowing what awaited me, I did my island round, checking the seals and finding them as before, restless and in even lesser numbers exclusively along the lee shore. However, this time when I tried to launch, I found myself locked in. I couldn't launch.

December. A cavalcade of seals issuing from a moulting cave

To the NW, the sea was notably calmer, being under low cliffs and the hills beyond. There was a long swell, bigger than before, but if I could drive across in a straight line, I thought I had a fighting chance of reaching the adjacent beach. Then, if need be, I could drag the ski back home behind me for a mile or more along the shore.

I was nervous. I wasn't sure about the status of the tidal stream off that shore and I felt acutely disturbed at the prospect of being picked up by the swell working with a notional tidal stream and being carried up the coast to a too- near headland where conditions would be horrific. This was no jaunt. I launched, paddled hard as I could without looking to left or right, feeling myself being carried in precisely the direction I didn't want to go. I was so frightened that my mouth was dry but I kept up the drive for the shore because it was the only show in town. However, this time, after all, I made it with ease and without, in the end, much drift due to swell and stream. Again, it took two and a half hours to get back, but this was because the walk was a slow slog. At least it wasn't life-threatening.

I shall, of course, never venture out to the island in such conditions ever again.

There was one other even more memorable day at this place in conditions altogether different.

A friend — let her be called Awkward Annie, after the song by Kate Rusby — wanted to accompany me to the island but asked before we departed whether we might first walk along the local lanes and down to the sea through the lovely local countryside. As the adventure was, in effect, hers I agreed, although on every sea jaunt, I remain uncomfortably aware throughout of the timing of the tide. To insist on leaving at the planned time felt churlish, under the circumstances; and it was a lovely walk. Had we paddled directly to the island, we would not have met red-legged partridges, brown hares and even a large dream-fox that came galloping over the hill at full tilt even as I was predicting him. The dog fox, very soon glimpsing the startled stillness of us, paused and then wheeled about in that clever disappearing kind of a way that they have.

Having walked in sunshine, later we paddled in sunshine across an April sea blue and almost glassy calm. We saw the lovely variety of seabirds in their breeding plumage as well as some belated great northern divers who must soon be northward-bound to their own nesting country. We landed discreetly on the island, hauled our skis a reasonable distance from the sea and set about the scripted part of our adventure. This consisted mainly of seals, of course, but the flamboyantly crested shags were especially beautiful in the bright light in their gleaming bottle-green plumage, with every feather seemingly outlined sharp and clear so that they might have been wrought in metal by a jeweller. There was fine maroon tracery on the yellow of their gapes. Their nests are rarely dull, always seemingly decorated with something. That day, I recall a white plastic fork being one of the more conspicuous components.

At the end of our round, Awkward Annie asked whether we might just sit for a while — I suppose I had hustled her around the Island, mindful that the tide was turned. She was neither the first nor the last to suffer that particular tyranny at my hands. At the time, I thought: be fair. This is her adventure, too, not just my routine site visit. So; we clambered across to and sat on one of the seaward promontories gazing out over the sea and toward distant mountains ranged along that horizon. It was idyllically warm, one of the smiling days that can make April such a glorious month. I don't think much was said, but there came the moment when I realised — and did say — that the cap of kelp that had been floating on the surface of the sea some distance to seaward on top of a submerged reef was gone.

In sudden alarm, I rose, looked behind me and saw that on our long promontory, we were almost cut off and had become an island. Then the more alarming thought occurred. There was no gallantry offered to Awkward Annie. I set off down into the trough behind us and waded chest- deep through the water where earlier it had been but ankle-deep. On the far shore, I began to run upon the slippery rocks over which I had never thought to run before. I suppose I ran for more than 50 metres back toward our landing place over the slippery boulders.

It was submerged. So was the tidal bar that connected it to the main part of the island. With an appalled cry, I saw one of the wave skis about 400 metres out to sea. The other one was even farther distant. My dry bag was in the shallows, no longer dry but half-submerged and full of water, as I had left it gaping open. My mobile phone was in there, now useless to us.

Awkward Annie caught up with me. By then, I was beginning to strip off my 'shorty' wetsuit. She was asking me what I was going to do. I had already experienced my moment of doubt and indecision. I said I was going to swim after the wave skis. She said the water is freezing. I said I'd swum most days in the sea this winter past so I'd be OK. She offered to go in my place, saying she was a strong swimmer. And so she was; but even wearing the full wetsuit, she hadn't been swimming most days the year round. By then, I was naked — not having imagined the need for swimming trunks under the wetsuit, and because I swim faster without the encumbrance of a wet-suit. Apologising for it, I waded into the water and began my pursuit.

It turned out to be a very long swim. After five minutes, I shouted back to her, asking whether I was gaining on the skis — the perspective from sea-level being unhelpful in that regard. Yes, she called back. I swam on at the same speed. Another five minutes or so passed when I called back with the same question. No, was her answer this time.

I intensified my effort. With hindsight, I think the tidal stream came into play, accelerating first the skis and then me. I was a long time in pursuit. There was plenty of time to think. Along the way, I experienced a moment of doubt because after swimming so far, I was still too far out to sea to achieve the safety of the shore at need. The improbable occurred to me as no longer at all improbable: I might die. More than anything, what troubled me about that thought was that if I did, it would be without having said goodbye to Sophie, my daughter. The thought lingered, troubling me; but all the time I was, it seems, closing on the more laggardly of the skis.

I didn't reach the ski until I was somewhere off one corner of the launching beach. I must have swum for a minimum of three-quarters of a mile. The relief was enormous as I hauled myself out of the sea and on to the ski. With intense exasperation and frustration, I found the ski had no paddle. Normally I tie my paddle to an anchorage point when on the ski and I had done that day for both of us, so that did either of us capsize, ski and paddle would remain together and the situation could be more swiftly recovered. I suppose Awkward Annie had untied hers when first we came to shore. Without a pause, I prostrated myself face-down on the sculpted surface of the ski and began paddling after the other ski using my forearms for flippers, like a surfer paddling out to catch a wave.

In time, I caught the other ski which, mercifully, had the paddle still attached. I have always carried extra twine for no particular reason other than it might be useful one day — always attached to some point of the ski. Now I used some of this to tie the rear end of my ski to the other one upon which I had made the final chase. With that done, I began the long paddle back.

All the while, I was wondering what was best to do. Do I go directly to shore, borrow a phone to call out a friend, asking that a spare paddle could be unearthed from somewhere? Did I have such a friend, indeed! Do I go back to the island, talk things over with Awkward Annie while keeping her company while marooned? I don't know that I came to a decision, but all the while, I was paddling back toward the rapidly shrinking island on the rising tide. I paddled gloriously (as I prefer to remember it) naked in the sunshine.

At least if the worst came to the worst, at high water there would remain plenty of dry ground, so at least inundation wasn't a risk.

I was perhaps 250 metres short of the Island when I heard a RIB tearing along behind me. I flagged it down, calling it over. Once more apologising for my nakedness, hoping I reassured them that I was not some weirdo, I explained the predicament and asked them if they would mind picking up Awkward Annie from the Island and dropping her ashore so that she could walk back to the car while I brought back the soggy remains of our gear. As I pointed toward her, I saw that she was waving the spare paddle aloft: it was not, after all, lost! Greatly relieved, I thanked them — and do thank them — so they continued on their way. No longer chilled through but warmed through now by the glorious sun, I paddled back to the island and stumbled ashore, barefoot over the pebbles. It may not be something Awkward Annie prefers to remember but despite my embarrassment, she hugged me and we were laughing at the 'get-out-of-gaol-free' of it all: the happy ending.

She told me that as I had swum from the island, I was accompanied by a chevron of about a dozen seals spread out in the waters near to but behind me. I had noticed two or three but hadn't realised there had been so many.

When I was more properly dressed, we paddled slowly back to the yellow sands. Indeed, together we had the last laugh. My car keys were not waterlogged and probably rendered useless in the dry bag but were in the camera bag I had carried with me on our jaunt around the Island; so we were able to drive home without making a greater complication of things.

Three Case Studies: Some of My More Interesting Research Efforts

Year-round grey seal (Halichoerus grypus) abundance and distribution at inshore sites near Land's End, Cornwall, England: 1994-1997.

Summary

During a four-year period, between January 1994 and December 1997, grey seals were studied at sea cave and other sites in the Land's End locality of Cornwall, England. A total of 144 visits were made to eight sites south of Land's End in the four-year period, with three randomly timed visits being made every month.

These sites had not previously been identified as being used by grey seals. The timing of the season of pup production and of the annual moulting period for this locality was established. The occurrence of occasional out-of-season births was noted. The pattern of site use, close to shore or onshore through the year is described. Largest counts of seals ashore or close to shore were made during the winter months. Lowest counts of seals ashore or close to shore were made in late spring/early summer. September and October were the main months for pup production. At the most, only pups (both weaned and un-weaned), seal mothers and attendant mature males were present in the caves during the season of pup production. Moulting began at the end of November with the main element of the season continuing until February, although some moulting continued in some years through to May. Moulting assemblies were overwhelmingly single sex and predominantly male, especially in the period late November to

February.

Annual un-weaned pup mortality was 20% or less.

The three sea caves in the study area were used by seals through the year with largest assemblies being recorded in the largest cave. Use of the other two caves was intermittent. Of these, one cave served as the main nursery cave overall. The other cave became the main nursery cave in the latter part of the season of pup production and was a moulting site of intermittent importance. Except in 1997, when there was a crash in pup production and of numbers of seals using caves, seal use of caves outnumbered seal use of non- cave sites in this locality.

Interpreting seal tracks in all caves, it was evident that seals were ashore at high tide even during spring tides and during storm sea interludes, when available haul out space was least. It was evident that seals commonly re-entered the sea two to four hours after high tide. This suggests that such seals did not enter the sea as a result of disturbance caused by wave action upon the confined space available at high tide when, typically, bickering occurs between the seals.

Tidal pools within caves as well as deep waters penetrating the entrances to caves were important. These were commonly used by seals as both resting places and mating sites.

Introduction

Grey seals in Cornwall, Isles of Scilly, Lundy and Devonshire (the region of SW England) are very close to the southernmost limit of the breeding range (in 1997, in l'archipel Molène, Brittany) for the species in the NE Atlantic (Summers, 1974; Prime, 1985). However, prior to 1991, their year-round abundance and distribution, moulting period, majority of nursery sites and number of pups born were unknown, as was the timing of the breeding season (Summers 1974; Prime 1985).

Scant previous research into grey seals in SW England has concentrated exclusively on the identification of grey seal nursery sites and counting the number of pups present at those sites (Steven, 1935; Summers, 1974 and Prime, 1985). Of these, the most successful was in 1935, insofar as for the first time, the importance of sea cave sites to grey seals in the region was published in the scientific literature, along with first drawings of those sites, in addition to confirming the one seal breeding species in Cornwall was the grey seal and not the harbour seal, as previously (incorrectly) identified.

Annual population estimates for grey seals in the UK are made by the Sea Mammal Research Unit (SCOS, SMRU). In the 1994-1997 period during which fieldwork for this study occurred, these were based on an extrapolation from the number of pups born, taking account of grey seal life history data (Hewer, 1964). Very crudely, this entailed multiplying the number of pups born by 3.5 to 4. However, there was no scientific basis for figures given for SW Britain.

SMRU (initially SRD) deployed two expeditions intended to identify breeding sites and pup production in SW England (primarily Cornwall), in 1972 and 1981. Both expeditions failed due to not knowing the location of some nursery sites and, more crucially, to known sea cave breeding sites being rendered inaccessible by sea conditions, as was acknowledged (Summer, 1974; Prime, 1985). Consequently, SMRU was left in no position to make reliable pup production estimates. In fact, Prime (1985) said that any future efforts to produce figures for pup production should be locally based.

This and all subsequent work on seals in the region has recognised and responded to Prime's injunction.

Prior to fieldwork for this study, scoping visits made to known and potential seal sites in Cornwall, Devon and Lundy between 1988 and 1993 made evident that seal numbers at each locality vary through the year (Westcott, 1993) — that some caves are used through the year, others are used exclusively as natal/nursery sites, while some others appeared to be used intermittently as resting places.

Regarding etymology, the sites where seal pups were seen are here described as nursery sites, as neither the birth of any pup or the nearby presence of a warm placenta was then observed (although subsequently warm placentas were located beside new-born pups on the sandy fairways of all 3 seal caves visited in this study). Nursery site here describes what might elsewhere be described as a breeding or a natal site. Relevant to nomenclature, also, is the fact that nursery/breeding/natal sites are sometimes inundated by destructive sea conditions. These can trigger an unacceptable level of conflict between seal mothers sharing a cave site. In these events, seal mothers do swim in company with their pups to a more secure site — that cannot be described as a 'breeding' site but certainly continues to be a nursery site until the pup is weaned.

Aims

The primary purpose of this study was to describe year-round seal distribution and, if possible, abundance at sites on shore or visible from the shore in the Land's End locality.

It was hoped this would establish a basis for localised year-round monitoring of seal distribution in the region and thereby contribute to effective regional seal management.

Methods

The fieldwork was carried out over four years in order to identify any variations that may have been present in the timing of the breeding and moulting seasons.

Eight sites south of Land's End had been identified as being regularly or seasonally used by seals (Westcott, 1993). They are located between Gwennap Head, in the east, and Land's End.

The sites consist of three sea caves (BGC, BLC and RC), one group of 3 rocky islets (Gwennap Islets) and one group of skerries off a headland (CLB Skerries) as well as two inshore water resting places — stretches of water adjacent to shores where seals gathered as they might at a haul-out site, in order to rest or interact (BSk and ZK). There was also a relatively long, narrow boulder beach below high cliffs at ZP.

Of the sea caves, BGC and BLC are located on the north-west side of the bay, and RC on the south-east shore. Plan views were drawn of each cave prior to the research period. These identified length and breadth of the fairway, the extent to which the sea ran into the caves at low tide, features within and without (notably extent of different sub strata, dimensions of tidal pools and other waters and the height of important stacks inside the caves. They also indicated the orientation of the cave entrances).

The inshore water resting places at ZK were just to seaward of RC, off a large boulder beach. BSk were situated north-west of Nanjizal Bay.

Of the two rocky islet haul-out sites, one main and two subsidiary islets together comprise Gwennap Islets, below the lookout station to the north of Porthgwarra. The other is CLB Sk, situated at the north-western limit of Seal Bay. There is another small rock very rarely used by seals outside the entrance to BGC that runs along the headland. This is The Islet. On the rare occasions that seals were seen there, they were included in the count for CLB Sk as both skerries were located outside the headland entrance to this cave which, uniquely in the study area, had two entrances.

The boulder beach at ZP was located on the north side of CLB headland — a long, wedge-shaped inlet with almost sheer-sided high cliffs on 3 sides. It appears to continue the same geological feature that was exploited to become BGC but from the opposite side of the headland. Although apparently inaccessible from the land, it is accessible by a combination of clambering and swimming from the landward side of its entrance, ideally in dry weather during spring tides when sea conditions are calm.

Observations were made by a lone fieldworker.

The procedure used was to begin survey work overlooking Gwennap Islets, about 150 minutes before low tide. There, the observer made a count of the seals. Separate counts were recorded for males, females, immatures, moulted pups and whitecoat pups. In the event that sex could not be ascertained, it was to be recorded as unidentified. A separate count (included in the site count) was made of any seals in the water adjacent to the site.

There is a coastal footpath that links the sites: that is, it allows access to the shore to achieve access to the sea caves or to make remote observations of the islet and sea sites.

After trotting westward along the footpath to CBa, the cave site there was scanned for seals before continuing on the cliff-top overlooking ZK to count any seals in the sea off that beach.

Having gained access to the shore of Seal Bay by clambering down the tumbling stream bed in the south-east corner of the bay, the 300m wide boulder beach was crossed to reach the entrance to BLC.

When sea conditions permitted, BGC was the first cave site to be accessed following the combination of a swim of less than 50m interspersed with clambering, in order to make the first seal cave count. Another entrance to the same cave was not used but is accessible by swimming only.

Having made the swim back to the departure point, seals in BLC (which is directly accessible from the boulder beach at low tide) were counted. The reason for counting the BGC seals first was to avoid complicating that count by possibly double-counting any seals flushed accidentally from BLC. After re-crossing the boulder beach and swimming into RC, the final sea cave seal count was made. Exceptionally, the deep-water entrance to RC becomes sanded up during the summer months, making it possible to walk or wade in, but that did not occur in the study period.

In the sea caves, at each visit annotations to a plan view of each cave were made, recording changes in the substrata and in any tide-pool dimensions, in order to clarify whether such changes affected seal use of the sites.

Least possible time was spent in the caves collecting data, both to keep disturbance to a minimum and to avoid losing track of time, as the effort was time consuming.

Having clambered back up to the coastal footpath and trotted to the tip of the next headland, it is possible in benign sea conditions to clamber down to the shore and access a headland cave.

After returning to the cliff-top, the next viewpoints were halfway down the cliff slopes overlooking either side of ZP, where observations were made without needing to access the shore, using binoculars to scan the beach from the cliff-top. It was then necessary to run NW along the coastal footpath to visit the small caves inside BSk and to make observations of the water resting place of the same name, to complete the search.

The entire survey effort took about 5 to 6 hours.

Notes were made using a pencil and notepad or a plastic board. Kowalski diving lamps were used to provide illumination in the caves, where it was also essential that wet suit boots were worn, so as to render walking reasonably comfortable. A bandana was worn in preference to a helmet in the caves because although it offered only a fraction of the protection offered by a helmet, it allowed clearer hearing — this being pertinent to locating seals as well as self-orientation in the deep gloom before the lamp was switched on. A Nikon F301 camera body with a 70-200mm. lens and a Megablitz flash unit were used to capture photographic images of seals. It was essential to point the torch near to but never directly at any seal photographed in order to achieve good focus while also avoiding the irradiation of the subject.

Equipment was carried inside one dry-bag folded down and locked inside a second dry-bag. The outer bag was liable to puncture — always did puncture, nearly always sooner rather than later — but always preserved the inner bag against the same fate.

Previously, seal pups had been observed using four sites as nurseries in the district: ZP, BGC, BLC and RC (Westcott, 1993). A fifth site was identified as being of particular interest to moulted pups making their first independent swim from the nursery site: BSkC.

Although (at least) three visits to each site were made each month, the choice of days upon which visits were made was random, being determined by sea conditions. In moderate to rough sea conditions, generally prevalent in the winter months, seals used none of the rocky islet sites either because they were awash, therefore impossible to use, or because wave action caused them intolerable levels of discomfort. It became impossible to access BGC in moderate sea conditions because waves struck the cliff wall with such power that heavy runs of white water ran up the walls. Also, wave action varied annually due to the shifting nature of the bottom topography: every year, the shape and position of the sandbanks in Seal Bay and its neighbour varies, thereby influencing the size and position of the wave-break and their impact on the study sites as well as access to them.

Access to RC became impossible when a moderate sea was being driven to shore by a northwest wind on a neap tide but the cave was accessible always on spring tides except when the heaviest winter seas were running. BLC was always accessible at low tide except when the heaviest seas were running. Consequently, visits were nearly always made when sea conditions were sea state 4 or less, although in the winter months, when the windows of opportunity were sometimes scarce, visits were made sometimes in sea state 5 during spring tide periods.

The reason for conducting the search for seals in the six-hour period around low tide was that then least disturbance to seals might be caused by survey effort at their sea cave sites and also when there would be least confusion about the number of seals present (for example, some seals may have been submerged when the tide was higher). Effort was made to achieve access to the caves at intervals of not more than 10 days, to minimise the prospect of missing pups, although this was not always possible during the winter months (due to rougher and colder seas, to shorter day length and lesser light quality: greater risk).

Great effort was made, by using good field-craft, to avoid causing disturbance to the seals, especially when in the sea caves (Westcott 2010).

Visits were never made on consecutive days, except once, because the impression had been formed that seals do not use a sea cave site, or else use it in greatly reduced numbers, on the day following a visit (Westcott, 1993).

Where pups were found, they were taken to be new-born where a warm placenta was present. Otherwise, in efforts to age them accurately, reference was made to the 5-stage age class system (Radford, 1978), although this was found useful as a reliable guide only for the first few days of life.

In addition to making the random site visits each month, visits were made to neighbouring sites between Porthgwarra and Sennen Cove through the same period, to check whether pups were being born elsewhere. None were found.

Where opportunity allowed, photographs were taken of the head and neck markings of seals.

Where seal tracks were found on sea cave beaches, they were always eradicated, the sand being smoothed with a piece of driftwood. This was to help avoid confusion when making subsequent visits in interpreting the use seals made of cave sites when rough seas were running.

Results were always written up at the end of the day.

Results

During a four-year period, between January 1994 and December 1997, a total of 1152 visits were made to the 8 sites to locate adult, immature, weaned and un-weaned grey seal pups, at a rate of three randomly timed counts every month, at sites used by grey seals in a locality south of Land's End.

Abundance and Distribution (see Appendix One)

Grey seals are present in the inshore waters and sea caves through the year in the Land's End locality.

Highest counts of seals, and of seals assembled in sea caves, were made during the winter months, between the last week of November and the end of March, but especially in December and January. Seal assemblies at this time were almost exclusively male in composition. Individuals were of all ages. At these times, very small numbers of immatures or mature females were sometimes present.

The moult was taking place during this period, this being apparent from the large quantities of hair found on the sand on the sea cave beaches at and above the high-water mark. At this time, the pelages of the seals had a patchy appearance.

There was a secondary peak in daily sea cave use from late August to October, when nearly all of the pups were born.

Lowest counts were made between April and early August, especially in June and July.

Occasional large assemblies of seals were recorded for RC in the winter months. Some small exclusively female assemblies were observed in late February and March.

BGC was used throughout the year but was the cave least- used for pup production in this period. A top count of 39 (all male) seals was made in December 1994.

BLC was only ever very lightly used through the year. Predominantly, it was used only occasionally by solitary animals outside the season of pup production, for rest. It was used mainly as a place for pup production. A top count of 12 seals was made here in September 1994, exclusively consisting of pups, their mothers and one attendant male. It was the main nursery site in the locality during the four-year period.

The pattern of use for RC at this time was less distinctive. Although it was an important site for pup production later in the season, it was very little used between late March and the end of August except for occasional influxes of small numbers of seals. Although this cannot be demonstrated, there seemed to be a connection between use of BGC and RC — the possibility that the RC site may be preferred occasionally to the BGC site by the same seals, perhaps due to surf action or lack of it in the caves.

As noted above, it was of intermittent importance as a winter assembly site. A top count of 17 seals was made in January 1996.

Gwennap Islets haul-out site was exclusively used on the low tide part of the tidal cycle, being at least partly submerged at other times. In most conditions, seals preferred to use the low-lying central 'saddle' of the island. However, when the wave action came from a SE direction, they would transfer to sites at the N tip of the island. Therefore, wave action, strongly associated with wind speed and direction, appeared to be the main determinant of whether and where the seals hauled out.

In the survey period, the largest assemblies of seals used the island in May and June. A top count of 13 was made in May 1996.

CLB Sk was only ever lightly and rarely used as a haul-out site, with a top count of 7 seals being made in December 1996.

ZP was also only rarely and very lightly used, notably between August and October, when it was used for pup production in three of the years — although of the 4 sites so used, it was the least important. A top count of 6 was made in August 1994.

At the water resting places, use by seals through the year at ZK, near RC, was fairly constant, being almost exclusively used by males and immatures. A top count of 14 was made in April 1996.

Prior and subsequent to this survey, much larger low tide counts of seals have been recorded for BSk, especially during the winter months. However, during this survey, a top count of 21 was made in November 1997. An impression was formed that it was used by seals emerging from BGC during the low water half of the tidal cycle because the seals swam across the neighbouring bay just to seaward of the wave-break from the headland of CLB. Other casual observations by the author from CLB saw seals issuing en masse from the BGC entrance which is situated alongside the CLB headland.

Sea cave use at times when sea conditions were rough

In visits made on the first low tide after sea caves became accessible following interludes of rough sea conditions, large numbers of tracks and depressions were often discovered in BGC above the high-water mark. These indicated that some beach remained beyond the reach of the waves inside the cave even when sea conditions were rough.

The depressions in the sand showed where seals had rested for prolonged periods above the high-water mark (at all times through the lunar cycle and through the year) in BGC and RC. Confused tracks in the same locality indicated the presence of seals at the same time, albeit not necessarily in a restful state. This shows that seals are able to continue to use certain sea cave beaches as resting places even when sea conditions are rough.

Other tracks yielded information about the approximate state of the tide, therefore the time, that seals had departed the cave since the last high tide. Below the high-water mark, the sea leaves the sand smooth from the time of the last high tide. Fresh tracks marking the smooth sand, and then ending abruptly due to water entry, show when seals have abandoned the cave. This can be confirmed as departing the cave, as against arriving from the sea, because seals in effect make a breast-stroke movement through the sand with the fore-flippers, causing sand to build on the hind side of the flipper marks.

Whether these tracks are straight and singular or are braided, they all end at a similar point some way down the sand-hill. The height of this point either below the high-water mark or above the low tide mark can be estimated. Then, taking account of the tidal range for the day, it is of a combination of factors:

Cave topography: the steeper the sand-hill slopes, the more limited is the band of impact of breaking waves as well as the spent run of the surf thereafter up the sand-hill.

Copper sulphate leaching down a seal cave wall

Protective accumulations of 'dunes' of kelp: especially between late summer and winter, kelp fronds are torn from their anchorages, carried through the water column and deposited on the shore. Particular accumulations appear to be concentrated on sea cave beaches. They may be spread thinly, either patchily or as a carpet, or in accumulations resembling dunes in appearance and function. Dunes of up to three metres in height were noted during the survey at one site (in RC) and up to one metre in height (in BLC). They are deposited at the (variable and mobile, according to the lunar cycle and the vagaries of barometric pressure) high water mark. Where it eventually settles at the high-water mark (neaps), this leaves stranded a number of significant lesser 'dunes' or spreads of strewn kelp in the interior of the cave.

What follows sometimes, especially where the dune accumulates at the high- water mark on a spring tide, is that a plateau of sand becomes established. It remains beyond the reach of waves or runs of surf because of the soft barrier of accumulated kelp that bars its progress. As the tidal cycle swings from spring to neap tides, the plateau is left 'stranded' at high tide at the back of the cave. The same powerful wave action that deposited the kelp may continue to scour the sand substratum to seaward of the dune of kelp. In effect, it erodes progressively the substratum while continuing to deposit kelp and, thereby, 'raises' the height of the dune.

The plateau may continue to be used by any adult seals and pups stranded there throughout its period of isolation — or at least until the following spring tide. Consequently, through this period, the plateau becomes a refuge of extraordinary security for the pups.

While most massive (and essential) in RC, smaller dunes of about one metre in height have been seen on several occasions accumulated in BLC, where it was possible to use the wave ski to enter the cave at high tide and observe the 'behaviour' of the dune in relation to the surf. What happened was that as each successive wave beat upon the soft wall of it, the dune yielded fractionally before settling back in place. On the inner side of the dune, at the base of the wall of the sea cave, a varying number of white-coated and moulted pups lay sleeping, untroubled by the proximity of such commotion.

The kelp dunes at these times are structures of extraordinary resilience, absorbing and staunching the power of heavy surf that would otherwise inundate the cave beaches. In effect, they are an effective form of protective soft engineering.

It is noteworthy that where dunes do not accumulate (and such accumulations were observed in one year only of this survey), the mother of one pup was observed on four occasions inserting her body broadside-on to the run of the surf, apparently protecting her pup against being sucked into the sea by the backwash of the surf pouring back down the beach. Indeed, the mother was not always successful, in which case she was observed swimming in company with her pup out of the cave. Subsequently, pup and mother re- entered the cave when the tide and therefore the effect of the waves had fallen or they sought a new site.

Geological features emerging from or leading from cave fairways, such as the tower of rock ('The Tooth') obstructing the central part of the BLC fairway, about 50 metres inside the 100 metres long cave, also contribute to the security of the beaches for seals that haul-out there. It ensures that the inner half of the cave fairway receives a considerably staunched run of surf. Seals were also commonly observed to use tunnels leading off the main fairway when that fairway was otherwise empty.

The Season of Pup Production: Numbers

This study resulted in the first identification of the timing of the full season of pup production, the first estimate of pup production and of pre-weaning mortality described for any Cornish (or southwest England) locality.

In the four years of the survey, nearly all of the 59 pups were born between August 28 and October 19, with most pups being born in September. However, in two of the four years, two pups were born outside what became recognised as the main breeding period. One was born in mid-April and the other was born in early June (see Appendix 5).

All but 3 of the 59 pups were born on beaches at sea cave sites. The 3 exceptions, born to the same mother in successive years (see Appendix 5), were born on a narrow, north-facing boulder beach in ZP.

Mortality

Annual mortality among un-weaned pups was consistently low, amounting to 20% or less.

Determining the Age of Pups

The use of the 5-stage age-class system (Radford, 1978) to distinguish the age of pups was found to be unreliable and therefore not useful, except for part of the description of pup features during the first week of life. Thereafter, it was of little value, insofar as the descriptions of pup development did not tally with what was seen or else were subjective and therefore not reliably repeatable.

This is especially so where the pelage of the pup is wet, because it has the effect of 'shrinking' the pup and 'accelerating' the moult — or, at least, the impression of the moult because, from birth, the white natal hair is growing ever thinner while the next pelage becomes ever more apparent from the second week of life. In effect, the 'veil' of the white lanugo grows thinner causing the underlying next pelage to show through ever more clearly. Initially, the effect when the pelage is dry is of 'dirtiness'. Soon thereafter, the black blotches show through ever more strongly.

Make-up of nursery cave seal community

During the season of pup production, at all nursery sites used in the locality, the only seals ever found using the sea caves were un-weaned or weaned pups, the seal mothers and, sometimes, an attendant male seal. Where the males were tolerated ashore, they remained closer to the water's edge than any other seal there present. However, for the most part, the attendant males waited in the sea, either in the entrance waters of the cave on the high tide part of the tidal cycle, in tidal pools within the caves over the low tide period or in the sea approaches just outside the cave.

The same female was seen in all four seasons having given birth to a pup at RC. Two other identifiable females were observed in two of the four years at the same site. Identification was based on sketches made of the head and neck pelage markings of the adult females.

The number of adult seals at sea cave nursery sites was always low. At no time were more than 6 pups (including moulted pups), three seal mothers and one attendant male seen on any beach.

Seal Tracks and Marks

Seal tracks consisted of, in adults, a broad central 'wake' of churned sand made by the body being dragged over the sand flanked, at 45° to the wake, by chevron marks made by the fore-flippers which perform a movement similar to the breast-stroke. Small rims of sand are piled at the trailing edge of the chevron marks, so it is always easy to tell whether the seals were moving to or from the sea. They are much more clearly defined in wet sand, as are those of the immatures. In profile, such seal locomotion resembles the locomotion of a caterpillar along a twig.

In immature seals, the central wake is slender, as if drawn by a stick flanked, at 45° to the wake, by chevron marks made by smaller fore-flipper marks.

During this study, confident differentiation could be made between up to seven seal tracks, at least where individuals were moving in the same direction.

Favourite resting places were marked by approximately oval- or comma-shaped hollows in the sand, always above the high tide mark.

Seal Cave Behaviour

Agonistic behaviour did occur sometimes between seal mothers, especially where one tried to move by another. This would engender open-mouthed snarling, the darting of heads threatening to bite or actual biting resulting in bloodshed.

The behaviour of the pups at these sites is noteworthy in two particulars: Most pups were observed swimming during the period of lactation. This appeared to be predominantly a behaviour of choice, only rarely of necessity. They were observed playing with other un-weaned pups in sea cave tidal pools. They were also observed sleeping in sea cave tidal pools, apparently out of choice during periods when sea conditions were calm.

Where a high tide at spring tide totally covered the nursery beach with water the pup swam, but remained in the cave. As the tide receded, the pup settled back on the nursery beach. At times, pups did swim out of caves, remaining outside for periods of several hours, mainly in the sea, but only one example of a pup transferring from one nursery site to another, accompanied by its mother, was observed during this survey.

Males appeared to keep a fairly low profile throughout the nursery period, regards the females. No inter-actions were observed here between males and pups.

Inter-male conflict did not occur at the surface but may have occurred while submerged. From time to time, a male seal would visit the locality, apparently prospecting for females in oestrus. It seemed that underwater engagements between the males then occurred, followed by underwater chases.

At RC and BLC, the same males (one at each site) served as the attendant males in consecutive years. They were recognised by a combination of snout shape (from both broadside-on and head-on), scarring and pattern of (scant) markings. In addition, the Bosistow Lesser Cave male had only one eye.

It seems that cave breeding by grey seals offers the opportunity for a greater percentage of local males to mate with females than happens where there are large beach-breeding assemblies.

Mating was observed on 14 occasions, always in water — 12 times in the tidal pool inside BLC and twice in the deep-water entrance waters in R C.

In BLC, on every occasion, the male pursued a female down the main fairway from the interior cave to the tidal pool. Near the pool's edge or in the shallows of the pool, he grasped her nape in his mouth, but without biting her hard enough to break the skin. The seals then engaged in coition at or just below the surface. Following the completion of the encounter, on every occasion the seals remained together with the male resting his fore- flippers along the flanks of the female. On every occasion, the female broke off the encounter — usually apparently in response to hunger cries uttered by her pup. The duration of these encounters was for between 37 and 76 minutes.

On several occasions in RC, the male was in the entrance waters adjacent to the cave fairway, apparently cajoling the female into the water. Nearly always, the female resisted the appeal either by 'flippering' — the rapid waving of one fore-flipper in the direction of the male: a gesture of rejection — or by extending her neck toward the male and either uttering open-mouthed snarling or prolonged ululations (eerie wailing sounds).

However, where the female entered the water, the male

manoeuvred so that he was able to grasp her by the nape and coition followed. Again, there was a prolonged interlude of post-coital contact lasting for 44 and 51 minutes.

Comparison of Sightings: Inside Caves v Outside Caves

In 1994, 59.6% of seals were counted inside caves.

In 1995, 51.5% of seals were counted inside caves.

In 1996, 55.4% of seals were counted inside caves.

But in 1997, 34.2% of seals were counted inside caves.

The dip in cave use in 1997 was reported by fishermen as being due to an unusually high capture of seals in local bottom set nets, between late winter and early summer. This appears to have caused a crash in pup production (see below) as well as a reduction in moulting assembly numbers in the following winter, 1997–1998.

Discussion

As this was a first examination of seal abundance and distribution through the year at seal cave sites in the British Isles, there is no comparison that can be made with earlier work. However, much of the variation in abundance appears similar to that described for the beach, skerry and island sites in l'archipel Molène off the west coast of Brittany (Vincent, 2001). There, the highest counts of seals were made in the winter months at the time of the annual moult, and with males predominating, as was the case here.

The sharp decrease of seal numbers counted in the April to August period in Brittany as well as N. Wales (Westcott, 2002; Westcott and Stringell, 2003; Westcott and Stringell, 2004) was likewise apparent in the Land's End locality. However, the importance of the offshore LR haul-out sites, west of Land's End, could not be verified although it is likely to be significant during periods of quiet sea conditions. The Reef is known from historical references, going back at least to Ray (1667), to have been used by grey seals for hundreds of years. There was no funding available during this survey to buy equipment necessary to monitor that site – the seaward side of the rocks being invisible from the mainland. Including the numbers of seals using the LR is certain to modify the impression here of low seal counts in the April to August period. During not more than 5 visits made to the Reef at times of quiet sea conditions, using the wave ski, always between 30 and 45 seals were present, hauled out or else in the sea adjacent to the haul-out sites.

The timing of the season of pup production is similar to that described for sites in SW Wales (Baines, 1995) and N Wales (Westcott, 2002; Westcott and Stringell, 2003) but differs from that described for Breton sites (Vincent, 2001), although the fact that only extremely small number of pups (<10) are born there each year may account for the difference.

This study shows that seals use some sea cave sites through the year, as shown for north Wales's sites (Westcott, 2002; Westcott and Stringell, 2003) but they use them in the consistently largest numbers during the season of pup production and of moulting. At other times, they serve as resting places for single seals or small groups of them.

It shows the seemingly improbable importance of the sea cave sites during the winter months, when to the casual observer, seal numbers appear low and sea conditions often appear to make the use of caves by seals impossible. In fact, these investigations show that winter is the time when grey seals rest ashore in the largest assemblies of the year in the Land's End district. It is noteworthy that the sites they use on the LR become almost impossible to use when anything more than a slight sea is running: at Beaufort Scale 4 or more. By contrast, cave topography (the steepness of the sand-hill slopes, the protective accumulations of 'dunes' of kelp — in effect, structures of extraordinary resilience, absorbing and staunching the power of surf that would otherwise inundate the cave beaches — and other geological features emerging from cave fairways) all help to maintain the security of the beaches for seals that haul-out there.

However, it remains possible that in this locality, perhaps due to environmental variables, seal distribution and site use is anomalous for the region. Therefore, it is recommended that another locality be subject to an equivalent intensive examination.

As only three visits were made each month, it is possible that the sample of counts was not representative.

An updated, more objective and less inaccurate system for assessing the age of pups than that of Radford (1978) needs to be devised. This would enable greater precision about the time of birth for each pup. Effort was made to this end in 2005 (Westcott, 2005, unpublished report to CCW Bangor) but it found that variation in maternal investment in pups made production of such a reliable key impossible.

Appendix 1: Tri-monthly seal counts for the Land's End district (excluding LR)

BGC

1994

Jan	32	09	31
Feb	05	10	06
Mar	13	07	10
Apr	08	09	08
May	06	07	07
Jun	07	02	02
Jul	03	07	01
Aug	04	07	07
Sep	03	02	03
Oct	04	04	04
Nov	04	04	02
Dec	29	39	15

1995

Jan	26	21	02
Feb	17	14	15
Mar	04	05	05
Apr	02	07	07
May	06	06	06
Jun	02	04	03
Jul	01	07	04
Aug	07	04	03
Sep	03	09	08
Oct	07	06	10
Nov	03	04	07
Dec	27	06	16

1996

Jan	04	27	15
Feb	21	16	18
Mar	03	27	05
Apr	06	11	07
May	03	02	03
Jun	03	05	05
Jul	02	03	07
Aug	03	02	12
Sep	02	07	08
Oct	08	02	02
Nov	02	07	24
Dec	25	22	23

1997

Jan	28	33	16
Feb	09	10	01
Mar	04	02	03
Apr	13	03	07
May	04	0	01
Jun	01	02	0
Jul	01	03	01
Aug	01	0	0
Sep	03	03	02
Oct	0	01	01
Nov	05	0	02
Dec	18	06	26

BLC

1994

Jan	01	01	01
Feb	02	01	01
Mar	0	0	01
Apr	0	02	01
May	0	0	0
Jun	0	0	0
Jul	0	0	0
Aug	01	02	04
Sep	07	12	07
Oct	05	04	06
Nov	04	04	02
Dec	05	02	01

1995

Jan	0	01	02
Feb	0	0	0
Mar	0	0	0
Apr	0	0	0
May	0	0	0
Jun	0	0	0
Jul	0	01	0
Aug	02	03	04
Sep	02	03	03
Oct	02	03	03
Nov	03	04	07
Dec	03	01	02

1996

Jan	02	01	01
Feb	02	01	0
Mar	0	01	0
Apr	0	01	02
May	01	0	02
Jun	0	0	0
Jul	0	0	0
Aug	0	01	01
Sep	03	02	10
Oct	07	04	02
Nov	03	0	01
Dec	03	03	03

1997

Jan	0	03	0
Feb	0	03	02
Mar	01	0	0
Apr	01	0	0
May	0	0	02
Jun	0	03	03
Jul	0	01	05
Aug	02	01	01
Sep	03	02	03
Oct	01	0	0
Nov	02	02	03
Dec	02	01	03

RC

1994

Jan	03	04	01
Feb	04	16	13
Mar	13	11	07
Apr	0	02	01
May	0	0	0
Jun	0	0	0
Jul	0	0	0
Aug	01	02	04
Sep	08	12	08
Oct	05	05	06
Nov	04	04	01
Dec	04	03	02

1995

Jan	13	01	03
Feb	03	06	05
Mar	05	02	02
Apr	0	05	05
May	0	0	0
Jun	0	01	0
Jul	0	01	0
Aug	02	03	04
Sep	08	11	10
Oct	05	06	06
Nov	05	01	04
Dec	03	05	09

1996

Jan	09	07	17
Feb	02	01	01
Mar	07	05	09
Apr	06	08	09
May	06	07	05
Jun	04	03	04
Jul	0	0	01
Aug	0	03	0
Sep	02	06	04
Oct	04	03	02
Nov	02	02	04
Dec	03	03	03

1997

Jan	02	02	16
Feb	12	0	11
Mar	04	04	01
Apr	01	0	03
May	0	0	0
Jun	03	0	08
Jul	0	03	0
Aug	0	01	0
Sep	03	02	03
Oct	03	01	0
Nov	0	10	03
Dec	0	03	05

Gwennap Island

1994

Jan	0	0	0
Feb	0	0	0
Mar	01	0	05
Apr	02	02	02
May	01	02	01
Jun	01	02	01
Jul	0	03	0
Aug	05	03	05
Sep	05	0	03
Oct	02	05	02
Nov	01	02	03
Dec	0	01	0

1995

Jan	0	0	0
Feb	0	0	0
Mar	01	04	03
Apr	02	05	01
May	08	05	05
Jun	08	05	03
Jul	02	02	03
Aug	04	03	02
Sep	01	01	01
Oct	09	03	02
Nov	03	0	01
Dec	0	0	0

1996

Jan	0	01	01
Feb	01	02	03
Mar	0	0	07
Apr	04	02	03
May	13	11	09
Jun	08	06	03
Jul	01	06	02
Aug	04	05	05
Sep	04	02	01
Oct	02	01	05
Nov	0	0	0
Dec	0	0	0

1997

Jan	04	02	07
Feb	0	03	08
Mar	0	0	06
Apr	08	15	12
May	03	02	13
Jun	0	09	13
Jul	14	12	20
Aug	03	07	08
Sep	07	03	01
Oct	07	03	01
Nov	06	02	03
Dec	0	08	0

CLB

1994

Jan	0	0	0
Feb	0	0	0
Mar	0	0	0
Apr	0	05	0
May	0	04	03
Jun	03	03	04
Jul	02	02	0
Aug	02	01	0
Sep	02	02	04
Oct	0	01	0
Nov	0	0	0
Dec	0	0	0

1995

Jan	0	0	0
Feb	0	0	0
Mar	0	0	0
Apr	0	0	0
May	0	0	0
Jun	01	01	01
Jul	0	01	0
Aug	0	01	01
Sep	0	0	0
Oct	0	0	0
Nov	0	0	0
Dec	0	0	0

1996

Jan	0	0	0
Feb	0	0	0
Mar	0	0	0
Apr	0	0	0
May	0	0	0
Jun	01	03	03
Jul	04	02	03
Aug	04	03	04
Sep	02	02	02
Oct	02	05	01
Nov	01	01	02
Dec	07	06	01

1997

Jan	07	0	0
Feb	0	0	0
Mar	0	03	03
Apr	05	0	0
May	0	02	0
Jun	0	0	05
Jul	0	0	04
Aug	01	05	0
Sep	0	02	01
Oct	0	01	05
Nov	0	0	0
Dec	0	0	0

ZP

1994

Jan	0	0	0
Feb	0	0	01
Mar	0	0	0
Apr	0	0	0
May	01	0	0
Jun	0	01	02
Jul	01	0	0
Aug	02	06	03
Sep	02	02	04
Oct	0	01	02
Nov	01	0	01
Dec	01	01	0

1995

Jan	0	0	0
Feb	0	0	0
Mar	0	0	0
Apr	0	0	0
May	0	0	0
Jun	0	0	0
Jul	0	0	01
Aug	02	01	01
Sep	03	02	03
Oct	02	02	02
Nov	03	02	03
Dec	0	0	01

1996

Jan	0	0	0
Feb	0	0	0
Mar	0	0	0
Apr	0	0	0
May	0	0	0
Jun	0	01	0
Jul	0	0	01
Aug	01	02	01
Sep	02	0	02
Oct	02	02	03
Nov	02	01	02
Dec	0	0	0

1997

Jan	0	0	0
Feb	0	0	0
Mar	0	0	0
Apr	0	0	0
May	0	0	01
Jun	01	0	0
Jul	0	02	0
Aug	0	02	01
Sep	01	0	01
Oct	01	03	02
Nov	01	0	01
Dec	03	0	01

ZK

1994

Jan	04	05	03
Feb	01	03	03
Mar	07	06	12
Apr	01	02	03
May	03	04	03
Jun	02	02	04
Jul	06	07	05
Aug	04	06	04
Sep	03	03	06
Oct	07	07	04
Nov	05	08	05
Dec	01	03	01

1995

Jan	04	08	07
Feb	05	05	03
Mar	03	03	03
Apr	06	08	07
May	09	06	08
Jun	04	03	03
Jul	08	07	07
Aug	07	05	07
Sep	04	06	12
Oct	06	08	07
Nov	09	09	09
Dec	08	12	09

1996

Jan	06	05	06
Feb	03	04	03
Mar	04	04	04
Apr	04	14	02
May	04	04	05
Jun	01	0	02
Jul	07	01	01
Aug	06	06	03
Sep	07	03	02
Oct	03	03	07
Nov	04	04	03
Dec	02	05	03

1997

Jan	02	01	04
Feb	02	01	0
Mar	0	02	03
Apr	06	04	0
May	03	03	03
Jun	04	0	0
Jul	04	04	08
Aug	0	03	05
Sep	05	02	01
Oct	07	10	06
Nov	02	0	0
Dec	03	02	0

BSk

1994

Jan	01	02	02
Feb	05	10	06
Mar	02	02	04
Apr	02	02	03
May	01	03	01
Jun	02	03	03
Jul	01	0	02
Aug	0	0	0
Sep	01	0	0
Oct	0	0	0
Nov	0	0	02
Dec	02	02	01

1995

Jan	04	04	03
Feb	0	01	01
Mar	03	05	02
Apr	02	02	01
May	03	05	02
Jun	02	02	01
Jul	02	01	01
Aug	03	01	01
Sep	03	01	0
Oct	01	0	01
Nov	01	0	04
Dec	0	02	0

1996

Jan	01	05	04
Feb	04	02	01
Mar	04	06	04
Apr	05	03	04
May	04	03	04
Jun	02	05	03
Jul	04	04	06
Aug	04	05	06
Sep	0	03	03
Oct	04	04	03
Nov	03	04	03
Dec	05	04	04

1997

Jan	06	12	03
Feb	02	14	11
Mar	06	05	04
Apr	01	05	06
May	11	03	01
Jun	05	10	05
Jul	04	08	17
Aug	10	06	04
Sep	03	03	05
Oct	09	17	11
Nov	21	15	16
Dec	20	16	19

Appendix 2: Tri-monthly total counts of seals in the three sea caves (in brackets) set beside the daily total count of seals at all 8 sites between Gwennap Island and BSk, 1994-1997.

1997

Jan	41 (36)	44 (14)	39 (33)
Feb	17 (11)	40 (27)	30 (20)
Mar	36 (26)	26 (18)	38 (17)
Apr	13 (08)	24 (13)	18 (10)
May	12 (06)	20 (07)	15 (07)
Jun	15 (07)	13 (02)	16 (02)
Jul	12 (03)	19 (07)	08 (01)
Aug	19 (06)	21 (11)	27 (15)
Sep	31 (18)	33 (26)	35 (18)
Oct	23 (14)	27 (13)	24 (16)
Nov	19 (12)	22 (12)	16 (05)
Dec	41 (37)	51 (44)	20 (18)

1994 total: 905 (540 in caves: c.59.65%)

1995

Jan	47 (39)	35 (23)	17 (07)
Feb	25 (20)	26 (20)	24 (20)
Mar	16 (09)	19 (07)	15 (07)
Apr	12 (02)	27 (12)	21 (12)
May	26 (06)	21 (06)	21 (06)
Jun	17 (02)	16 (05)	11 (03)
Jul	13 (01)	20 (09)	16 (04)
Aug	27 (11)	21 (10)	23 (11)
Sep	24 (13)	33 (23)	37 (21)
Oct	32 (14)	28 (15)	31 (19)
Nov	27(11)	20 (09)	35 (08)
Dec	41 (33)	26 (12)	37 (27)

1995 total: 887 (457 in caves: c.51.5%)

1996

Jan	22 (15)	46 (35)	44 (33)
Feb	33 (25)	26 (18)	26 (19)
Mar	18 (10)	47 (33)	29 (34)
Apr	25 (12)	39 (20)	27 (18)
May	31 (10)	27 (09)	28 (10)
Jun	19 (07)	23 (08)	21 (09)
Jul	18 (02)	16 (03)	21 (08)
Aug	22 (03)	27 (06)	32 (13)
Sep	22 (07)	25 (15)	32 (22)
Oct	32 (19)	24 (09)	25 (06)
Nov	17 (07)	19 (09)	39 (29)
Dec	45 (31)	43 (28)	42 (29)

1996 total: 1032 (571 in caves: c.55.4%)

1997

Jan	50 (31)	55 (40)	31 (17)
Feb	25 (21)	31 (13)	33 (14)
Mar	15 (09)	16 (06)	20 (04)
Apr	35 (15)	27 (03)	28 (10)
May	21 (04)	10 (0)	09 (01)
Jun	13 (03)	24 (05)	34 (11)
Jul	29 (01)	36 (07)	55 (06)
Aug	17 (03)	25 (02)	19 (01)
Sep	25 (09)	16 (06)	14 (05)
Oct	28 (04)	36 (02)	26 (01)
Nov	37 (07)	29 (12)	28 (08)
Dec	46 (20)	36 (10)	54 (34)

1997 total: 1031 (343 in caves: c.34.25%).

Grey seal pup production at two localities in west Cornwall (Land's End: 1994 to 1998 and 2012 to 2014; North Cliffs: 1996 to 1998 and 2012 to 2014

Summary

Having identified the timing and shape of a SW England grey seal breeding season for the first time in 1994 at Land's End and repeated the survey between 1995 and 1997, it was important to discover whether results were locality-specific or whether they might be described as approximately typical for the region.

The nearest substantial mainland grey seal breeding locality to Land's End is situated between Godrevy Point and Bassett's Island — hereafter described as the North Cliffs locality. However, the section of coast between Godrevy and Navax Point, notably Godrevy Island and Mutton Cove, was excluded as it was already being observed.

To begin the examination of whether the Land's End results were anomalous, seal nursery sites in this locality were subjected to examination while continuing to examine pup production at Land's End.

Variations were found between the two localities in number of sites used, the timing of the period of pup production, the pattern of pup production and the fate of weaned pups — so far as it was possible to track them.

Strong similarities were identified between the two localities. Primarily, nearly all the pups at both localities, including the firstborn, were born in sea caves and nursed to weaning at the sites in which they were born. Pre-weaning mortality at these sites was always very low.

The season began earlier and was more compressed at the North

Cliffs sites, where, between 1996 and 1998, it peaked between mid-August and mid-September in contrast with the Land's End locality, where it peaked in mid- to late September. In two of the three years, no pups were born after September in the North Cliffs locality (although 5 pups — 20.8% — were born in October 1998).

More sites were used and more pups were born at the North Cliffs locality than at Land's End. Sites in the North Cliffs locality are more remote from easy or casual access than those at Land's End, being almost exclusively accessible from the sea.

During and following the season of pup production, more moulted pups are taken from North Cliffs to Gwithian Towans sites into care in the seal 'sanctuary' at Gweek than from the Land's End sites (Barnett and Westcott, 2001). The North Cliffs to Gwithian locality, provided the largest component of pups removed from the natural environment of the Cornish coast to the 'sanctuary' (Barnett and Westcott, 2001). This is not because the locality is the principal breeding area along the Cornish coast. The Boscastle locality currently has that distinction (Westcott, 2007). It is because many beach resting sites used by moulted pups having departed the North Cliffs nursery sites are either more easily overlooked (popular and well-publicised viewpoints overlook Hells Mouth and Mutton Cove) or accessed (Fishing Cove, Castle Giver, Kynance Cove, Mutton Cove, Godrevy Cove and the three-mile sandy beach extending west to the Hayle estuary under The Towans) than at other seal breeding localities in Cornwall. Nowhere else in SW England are seal pups so readily encountered and nowhere else (except for the Eastern Isles in the Isles of Scilly) is the presence of grey seals using local haul out sites better known or more widely publicised.

The two localities were revisited in the 2012–2014 breeding seasons, using the same methods. This examined trends in pup production at both localities. In the case of North Cliffs, these years followed a major headland collapse in autumn 2011 that totally destroyed four nursery sites and affected the seal use of two more. In the same year, major rock falls inside a neighbouring cave (+C) also affected pup production. Seals appeared initially to make greater use of HMCO and its associated cavelets. Subsequently, +C was reoccupied and to an extent not previously seen while PC saw a more tentative but increasing occupation during the breeding season. It seems from these observations that when old seal caves die, the seals that had previously used them move to neighbouring sites in the same locality.

At Land's End, between 2012 and 2014, pup production appeared to be restored to levels existing prior to the crash recorded in 1997. The same caves were used, but choice of preferred cave site had changed.

Contents

Introduction

Land's End and North Cliffs districts accommodate the two most westerly grey seal breeding site clusters on the English or Welsh mainland (Westcott, 1993, 2010). They are also the most southerly of the substantial breeding localities — that is, where annual pup production occurs repeatedly at known sites) in the NE Atlantic except for uninhabited island sites in the Isles of Scilly, more than 30 miles WSW of the Land's End site cluster and on the SW Lizard coast about 25 miles SE of Land's End (Westcott, 2006 and 2010).

Grey seal pup production is known to occur also at very low levels at sites in l'archipel Molène and in l'archipel Sept-Îles off the west and north coasts of Brittany (Ridoux, 1997; Vincent, 2002), where the number of pups born each year is understood to vary between 2 and 10 (Liret, pers. comms.). A similar range and variability in numbers is observed for pups born at sites on the Lizard Peninsular (Westcott, 2010).

Prior to 1994, the timing of the season of pup production at SW England sites in general, Land's End sites in particular, remained unconfirmed (Westcott, 1993). Steven (1936) had initiated research into grey seals in SW England by identifying a number of sea cave sites and categorising them as breeding sites and/or as lodges (resting places). His work was elaborated remarkably little by the two expeditions made by the Seal Research Division (Summers, 1974) and by the Sea Mammal Research Unit (Prime, 1985) even though their purpose was to confirm breeding locations and to count the number of pups present at those sites. These frustrated efforts delivered acknowledgements that survey work had been inhibited by lack of knowledge of the timing of the season of pup production although the primary problem while attempting to conduct fieldwork was found to be adverse sea conditions. However, it is evident when reviewing Summers and Prime that their knowledge of the location of nursery sites was substantially inhibited by their uncertainty of the timing of the season of pup production.

Summers (1974) concentrated effort on visiting 'reputed' breeding sites, while noting that there were so many sea caves along the coast that a complete investigation would take several weeks even in calm weather. He acknowledged that a short expedition made before the timing of the breeding season had been established was 'unlikely' to provide a precise estimate of total pup production. He was able to confirm only four breeding sites.

Prime (1985) correctly recognised that the timing of the breeding season was earlier than had been supposed previously. Based on anecdotal accounts, he suggested up to 40 pups were born annually. He made the recommendation that regular surveys be conducted at all pupping sites through the breeding season.

This study was inspired by, and formed the initial component of, the locally- based response called for in Prime. Locally-based research will achieve the best results for as long as there is no remote monitoring of sample breeding sites. It allows best use to be made of the environmental variables and enables recognition of variation in the timing and shape of the seasons of pup production. Such variations can vary dramatically, from locality to locality and year to year in the SW region. This is most emphatically evident when comparing the Boscastle locality with that at nearby Lundy, where three months, sometimes more, separate the onset of pup production although numbers of pups born each year are relatively similar (Westcott 2007; 2009).

In 1985, some of the North Cliffs sites were particularly well-known due to previous studies — descriptions of battues in local caves by local naturalists in the 19th century, observations made by the visiting naturalist and author W.H. Hudson (1909) and subsequent observations by Fordham and Lewis (1963). By contrast, no survey had identified the cluster of breeding sites just south of Land's End, although one sea cave site may have been described without being named in Tregarthen (1909). These were identified in 1989 (Westcott, 1993).

All nursery sites currently used in the two localities had been mapped already (Westcott, 2010). At both localities, to ensure that no sites were overlooked, repeat checks were made of other candidate sites (sea caves and remote beaches not confirmed as being seal nursery sites) during survey work.

Aims

The primary aim was to compare the timing and shape of the season of pup production at the Land's End and North Cliffs localities. It was achieved by locating and comparing how many pups were born where, when and by noting the number of mortalities.

Methods: Land's End

The sole purpose of the study was to count grey seal pups, estimating the date of birth as well as the location, while also examining their fate to weaning.

The methods used for examining the Land's End sites were as described above, where eight sites south of Land's End had been identified as being used during the period of pup production by grey seals (Westcott, 1993), but not in every case by pups.

The nursery and 'leaving home' sites used by seals in this study consisted of three sea caves in Seal Bay. The fourth site, ZP, is a narrow boulder beach surrounded on three sides by steep cliffs at the SE end of the neighbouring bay while the fifth site is BC, inshore of the BSk water resting place.

There is a coastal footpath that links the five sites: that is, it allows access to the shore to achieve access to the sea caves (it also overlooks the zawn site), along with four candidate sites where pups were never located: CBC, ZK, CLBC and PC.

The procedure used throughout was as described in the Lands End 1994 – 1997 study (above). In addition to making the random site visits each month, visits were made (usually in the form of cliff-top scans where access could not be achieved easily) to neighbouring potential seal sites between Porthgwarra and Sennen Cove through the same period, to check whether pups were being born elsewhere or these sites were being used as resting places by moulted pups beginning their journeys of dispersal from natal sites.

Males, females and immatures present at any site were counted separately at the time, but because these data were collected so long ago, detail of the breakdown by age and sex has been lost. In the few cases of uncertainty, the sex was recorded as 'indeterminate'.

The survey was duplicated between June and December, 2012–2014, in order to discern trends and changes.

Methods: North Cliffs

It had been necessary to make preliminary scans of sites between Navax Head and Bassett's Cove in 1994 and 1995 to identify sites used for pup production as well as others where conditions appeared favourable for pup production.

The methods for data collection at the North Cliffs sites were different from those used at Land's End only insofar as every site had to be accessed from the sea, making use always of a wave ski.

There were sixteen candidate sites between Navax Head (east of St Ives Bay and Godrevy Point), and +C, east of HM and HC, where pups had been seen previously (Westcott, 1993). All were visited during every survey period. Twelve are sea cave sites, two are beach sites backed by steep cliffs. Several are subject to occasional, usually quite small, rock-falls.

One beach plus cave site is situated at CG, separated by a rocky promontory from a beach used by the public: FC. Especially at low tide, CG is accessible from FC. There is also a fisherman's track down to CG from the cliff top. There are two small caves at the back of this beach that make it necessary to access the site to ascertain whether pups are present rather than just to scan from the cliff top. The other beach site is at HM, although it is backed by cavelets and flanked by substantial caves.

One sea cave site (AC, in the headland) is mentioned in descriptions of battues made in earlier centuries. The cave is sometimes accessible via an adit and then down to the floor of the cave using a knotted rope — of which currently one remains in situ. Although access to the adit is normally blocked, from time to time it is unblocked and used by adventurous people — this being known because the rope changed during the survey period.

There is a coastal footpath that runs close to the edge of the cliff-tops above all the sites in the North Cliffs district. However, access to the shore is possible and permitted only at FC and CG. In fact, the cave entrances are generally visible only from long range.

The procedure used was to launch a wave ski at FC and to paddle it eastward along the coast, visiting the several sites en route as far as Bassett's Island. Thereafter, there was a long paddle back to explore the Navax caves.

The intention was to make at least 3 and preferably more site visits each month, to maximise the chance of locating every pup born in the district. However, the choice of days upon which visits were made was random, being of necessity determined by sea conditions. The ideal wind direction for making site visits here was SE. Access to the caves became impossible when onshore winds (clockwise from SW to northerly) blew above force 4 (onshore), because surf channelled into the narrows of the cave entrances was intensified by the compression, making them bigger than those outside the caves. There was also the complication of paddling into the dark through increasingly boulder-strewn approaches to the cave beaches. The bigger the surf in the caves, the more confused and dangerous were the conditions and the more difficult it was to exit the cave.

The search for seal pups was conducted in the five to six-hour period around low tide, as this was the time when least disturbance to seals might be caused by survey effort at their sea cave sites and also when there would be least confusion about the number of seals present. This is a longer survey period than for the Land's End sites, this reflecting the much larger number of sites to be visited (16 at North Cliffs compared with 7 at Land's End).

Methods (Both Study Areas)

The fact that the two study areas could be surveyed under different weather conditions was helpful when choosing which locality to survey on any given day. The weather forecast (as well as the effect of current conditions) was another crucial element in the organisation of the fieldwork.

Notes were made using a pencil and notepad. The use of a good quality Diver's lamp was crucial both for safety (the terrain under foot usually included large, jagged boulders as well as smaller rocks that were slippery and pools of various dimensions with rocks in the bottom) and for locating pups (and other seals) in conditions of darkness. A Kowalski 1250 diver's lamp was used, with another being carried for use in an emergency. It was imperative that wet suit boots were worn, to offer some protection for the ankles and against stubbing or cutting the feet.

A Nikon F301 camera body with a 70-200mm. lens and a Megablitz flash unit were used to capture photographic images of seals.

Equipment was carried in one dry bag folded down inside a second (slightly larger) dry bag that was liable to puncture, but entirely able to preserve the inner bag against the same fate.

Results were always written up at the end of the day.

Observations were made by a lone fieldworker.

Results: Land's End

Four sites were used as nursery sites in 1996, 1997, 2012 and 2013, of which three were sea caves and one was a cliff-backed beach accessible only from the sea. Three were used in 1998 and 2014, all of which were sea caves.

BLC appeared to shrink in importance between 1996 and 1998

while RC grew in importance and BGC seemed the least attractive nursery site throughout. Between 2012 and 2014, BLC and RC became identical in importance whereas BGC had become the most attractive nursery site, and exceptionally so in 2014. Through the two survey periods, there were only minimal changes in cave substrates, so this does not account for the relative changes in importance of these sites.

The number of pups born at these sites crashed during the survey period between 1996, when fifteen pups were born, of which three died and 1997, when five were born, all of which survived. There was a small recovery in 1998, when ten pups were born, of which one died (Appendix 1). Pup numbers rose between 2012 and 2014, resembling counts for 1994 and 1995 (not included here in the interest of making direct comparisons). However, the 11 seals born in BGC in 2014 was the highest count for any site in any year of this survey.

Either one or no pup births were recorded for ZP in every year except 2013, when three were born there. Therefore, 100% of pup births were recorded in sea caves in 1998 and 2014, 92% in 1996, 1997 and 2012 with 82.5% in 2013.

Only one pup was born outside the survey period. In 1996, a pup estimated to have been born on 16 April died three days later, having apparently been abandoned immediately after birth.

If the April-born pup is excluded, pups were born exclusively in September and October in 1996 and 1997 and between 30 August and 26 November in 1998. In each year, September was identified as the peak month for pup production, with October being second in importance.

The longest period, over which births occurred, was in 1998, coinciding with the minimum number of sites used.

A total of twenty-nine pups were born between 1996 and 1998, of which four died prior to weaning. A total of forty-nine pups were born between 2012 and 2014, of which one died before weaning.

Generally, pup numbers at any one site were low or very low, but the highest number of pups (five) observed at any one site per visit was found in RC in 1996.

The mother who gave birth to pups on similar dates at ZP (06 October 1996 and 05 October 1997) was the same individual. She was identifiable by her distinctive markings as well as by her choice of nursery site.

The 5-stage age-class system (Radford, 1978) was found to be mainly unhelpful, as described above for the Lands End 1994 – 1997 study.

The location of the 'dominant' male was also contributory to attributing age to a pup. In general, seal mothers using sea cave sites always displayed aggression where male seals attempted to haul out ashore on nursery beaches. This behaviour was particularly pronounced while pups were in the first seven to ten days of life. It had the effect of keeping the male from hauling out on the nursery beach. Subsequently, dominant males were tolerated in achieving, initially, a seaside resting place ashore. In succeeding days, the male tended to move up the beach ever closer to the female.

This behaviour was complicated where more than one seal mother was using a beach. Then, the position of the male on the beach became less helpful in working out the approximate age of the pups.

Results: North Cliffs

The preliminary scan of potential and actual nursery sites made in the Navax district between July and November 1995 confirmed recent discoveries of seal nursery sites (Westcott, 1993).

Altogether, sixty-seven pups were born at the ten different sites used as nursery sites between 1996 and 1998. Eight sites were used in 1996, all of which were sea caves (including HM). Eight sites were used in 1997, of which seven were sea caves (including HM) and one appeared to have been born on a beach surrounded by high cliffs and backed by three sea caves (and therefore may have been cave-born). Seven sites were used in 1998, of which six were sea caves (including HM) and one — CG — is accessible with some difficulty from the land but otherwise is a beach backed by two caves, one of these being substantial. Six sites were used through all the seasons of pup production.

The two consistently most important caves were +C, in the east of the survey area, and AC in the central part of the survey area (N headland). Neither is overlooked by the coastal footpath (although the entrance to AC is visible from afar) and both are accessible exclusively from the sea.

Pup counts were accurate but potentially erratic and misleading in the period 2012 to 2014. In autumn 2011, a major headland collapse had occurred on the NE side of HC, obliterating four caves previously used for low level pup production and altering a fifth to the extent it was not used by seals in the following year. In addition, at the same time, there was a considerable internal rockfall in +C that also deterred seals from pupping there the following year. Pups that might have been born at the 'lost' sites appear to have been born at HMCO and in the associated caves.

The number of pups born at the North Cliffs sites varied very little over the first three-year period. In 1996, twenty-three pups were born, of which two died (one being stillborn). In 1997, twenty-one pups were born, of which one died. In 1998, twenty-three pups were born, of which two died.

In 2012 to 2014, the great majority of seals were born each year in September with just five being born in August and ten born in October, suggesting the breeding season was becoming later.

In the subsequent survey period, 11 pups were born in 2012 (apparently influenced negatively by the H rock fall), 23 were born in 2013 and 32 in 2014, totalling 66 pups for the period. Although the overall three-year counts are similar, 2014 saw a spike in pup production for the North Cliffs sites just as there was in the Land's End locality.

Unlike in the Land's End district, at North Cliffs no pups were born outside the August to November period of pup production described for Land's End (Appendix 2). In 1996 and 1997, pups were born exclusively in August and September. In 1998, pups were born between August and October. The peak in pup production varied slightly between seasons. In 1996, the spread of births was almost equal between August and September. In 1997, births took place almost exclusively in September. In 1998, the spread of births between August and September was again almost equal, with a few births in October.

However, the total number of births fails to support this impression of near equality, insofar as thirty-nine pups were born in September, twenty-four in August and five in October. In this period, just one pup died, in 2013.

The most extended season of pup production occurred in 2014, coinciding with another cave interior rock fall event in the nursery area of AC. Despite this major collapse and a massive pile of rubble accumulated on the nursery beach, all three pups then present, as well as their mothers, survived to the time of weaning.

Overall, the peak in pup production here appeared to have edged later in the year from mid-August and mid-to late-September (1996–1998) to September (2012–2014).

A total of sixty-eight pups were born between 1996 and 1998, of which five died prior to weaning, one of these being stillborn. All were born in August, September and October — identified at Land's End as the season of pup production. In 1996, 95.5% of births were in sea caves compared with 85% in 1997 and 91.5% in 1998.

Of 66 pups born in the second period, eleven were born in the 2012 season, twenty-three in 2013 (with the one mortality) and thirty-two in 2014. Of these, 91% were born in sea caves in 2012, 65% in 2013 with 90% in 2014. 2014 also saw the largest nursery of nine seal pups at one time in +Cave, which had not been used in either of the preceding years. There was a slow but increasing return of seals to PC. HM and its adjacent caves were important in 2013 and 2014, seemingly functioning as an alternative to the 'lost' or 'disturbed caves.

Where seals went in 2012, if they did produce pups, was somewhere beyond the surveyed locality.

The mortality rate was very low. Between 1996 and 1998, only five pups died prior to weaning, of which one was stillborn. There was only one pup mortality between 2012 and 2014.

Generally, pup numbers at any one time at any site were low or very low, except for the nine found in + C in 2014.

Therefore, the season of pup production appears to be earlier and more compressed at North Cliffs than at Land's End. At North Cliffs it starts and finishes earlier, peaking earlier also, sometimes in late August to mid- September, sometimes (more recently) in September.

More pups were born at the North Cliffs sites, where the mortality rate was also slightly lower than at (the more exposed) Land's End sites.

Discussion

In contrast with the sandy beach and island sites (in the Hebrides and Scotland) that accommodate the largest grey seal breeding colonies in the NE Atlantic (e.g. SMRU, 2012), as well as with the island sites in the rocky Farne Islands and sandy beach sites at Donna Nook (LWT 2012) and Winston Dunes (NWR 2012), which accommodate the largest grey seal breeding assemblies in England, the great majority of seal pups born at the two Cornish study sites was born on beaches deep inside sea caves. There was also contrast in the timing of pup production between the non-cave breeding sites noted above and the Cornish sites surveyed here in that in every year it began and concluded earlier in Cornwall (LWT).

The propensity for using sea cave beaches as nursery sites at the Land's End and North Cliffs localities is similar to, but even more extensive than, that recorded for seals at sites throughout Wales (Baines, 1995; Westcott 2002; Westcott and Stringell 2003). Nevertheless, sea cave sites usually form the principal nursery habitat at Welsh localities, Lundy (Westcott, 2009) and Devon (Westcott, 2008), the Isle of Man (Sharpe, 2011) and Donegal (O' Cadhla, 2002), as at the Cornish sites.

At least during the three years of this survey, while pup production peaked in September in both localities, in the Land's End district October was the month second in importance whereas in the North Cliffs locality August was the month second in importance between 1996 and 1998. Between 2012 and 2014, October became the month second in importance for both localities. At both localities, the most extended season of pup production occurred in 1998, coinciding with the minimum number of sites used.

The collapse in pup production for the Land's End locality, reportedly due to a higher than usual by-catch of seals in local bottom-set nets, appears to have skewed the impression of the timing of pup production for the 2 years during which the consequences were most acute (1997 and 1998).

The collapse in pup production for the North Cliffs locality in 2012, seemingly due to the cliff collapse in HC in 2011, was followed by, initially, the use of other sites — mainly HMCO and attendant cavelets and subsequently by what appeared to be a 'creeping' re-occupation of initially abandoned sites along with a continuing 'new' use of the HM sites.

Although the events influencing falls in pup production cannot be predicted with any precision, it should be noted that the Cornish bottom-set net fishery is the principal one of its kind in UK waters. One well-known Looe fisherman noted decades since that there were now more nets set than ground to fish. Therefore, while this fishery thrives, there will always be the potential for significant local by-catches of grey seals (and harbour porpoises).

Similarly, in the context of climate change and stormier, more erratic weather conditions (and therefore sea conditions), cliff collapses and internal erosion events inside seal caves will continue, doubtless affecting seals and the sites they feel able to use — this along a coastal zone most attractive to/heavily used by holidaymakers and those local people pursuing leisure interests detrimental to seals.

Although the timing of the breeding seasons for Land's End and North Cliffs districts includes considerable overlap, the impression gained from this survey is that the season at North Cliffs starts earlier, finishes earlier and is more compact than at Land's End. However, while this survey confirms that the pups were born at both localities in August, September and October, in this period, pups were never born in November at the North Cliffs sites — in contrast with the Land's End sites.

The pattern and timing of births for the Land's End locality more closely resembles that of SW Wales (Baines, 1995) and N Wales (Westcott, 2002; Westcott and Stringell, 2003) than those from the North Cliffs locality.

Altogether, this study leaves some doubt as to how precisely established was the timing of the season of pup production at these west Cornwall localities. There is variation in the timing of the breeding season at Cornish sites from year to year. Results for individual sites sometimes vary significantly, sometimes hardly at all — as here. It did not become evident during this survey whether this is due to natural variations — perhaps due to pregnancy failure, failure to become pregnant, mortality among mothers in certain years most likely due to occasional significant fisheries by-catch (as in 1997), or even due to site fidelity being less strong than is generally assumed.

The starting point for achieving sufficient detail to begin to test this thesis would be to identify every seal mother producing pups in the study area and thereafter to track her through the years.

Results gained through this study were made exclusively by means of, at most, weekly site visits, in the course of which disturbance occurred regularly. This disturbance consisted of seal mothers and attendant males departing the nursery sites more often than not, although no instance was ever recorded of such disturbance leading to the abandonment of pups or the abandonment of sites controlled by 'dominant' males. Adult seals nearly always returned into the caves within three hours of the initial disturbance.

Most accurate results would be achieved by continuous remote observation, making use of cameras (including thermal imagers) capturing still or moving images, especially in relation to the daily cycle of the tide. Remote observation would ensure that disturbance to the seals caused by the research effort during this critical period would cease.

Recommendations

It is necessary to examine other sites — especially at Boscastle, Lundy and South Devonshire — in order to examine the degree of variation in the timing and pattern of pup production in different localities in SW Britain.

Future studies should use remotely operated observation tools to examine the fine detail of seal behaviour at the sea cave sites. However, relevant only to future studies is the certain prospect of substantial rock-falls continuing to occur at coastal sites in SW England and particularly in the predominantly slate and shale North Cliffs locality. A number of seal caves have been swept away or rendered inaccessible by these events in the past two decades while the interiors of other seal cave sites (+C and AC) have been subject to lesser rock-falls that appear to have influenced the degree to which seals make use of them during the nursery season.

Relevant, also, to future studies will be prevailing sea conditions.

Where the sea state reaches or exceeds Beaufort 4, access to sea cave sites becomes problematic or impossible. This is particularly so where the wind is onshore. In the wake of storms, even where the wind dies away entirely, it takes at least two to three days for the sea to settle to the point where sea cave access becomes possible again at SW England sites. The formation and mobility of sandbanks likewise influence the impact of waves on sites used by seals by altering the location, size and weight of impacts.

These factors, along with the evidently highly variable timing of the season of pup production at localities across the region combined with the high cost of mounting a full survey to examine sites from Lundy and Dartmouth in the east to Land's End and the Isles of Scilly in the west — the current breeding range of grey seals in the region (Westcott, 1993; 2010) - provide the explanation for the current failure to examine all the seal localities in the SW England region in one all-encompassing research effort.

I hope that cave-born moulted pups will be tagged, along with non-cave-born moulted pups, to discover whether they follow similar dispersal routes as well as to discover and compare each their own fates.

Consequently, this would enable the various missing or partially understood elements regarding understanding grey seal use of the region's coasts to be examined effectively and at least cost.

Appendix 1: Land's End: Number of births per month, with mortalities in brackets)

BGC

	Jun	Jul	Aug	Sep	Oct	Nov	Total
1996	0	0	0	0	01	0	01
1997	0	0	0	01	0	0	01
1998	0	0	0	01	0	01	02
2012	0	0	0	03	01	0	04
2013	0	0	0	05	01	0	06
2014	0	0	0	04	06	01	11

BLC

	Jun	Jul	Aug	Sep	Oct	Nov	Total
1996	0	0	0	04	02	0	06
1997	0	0	0	01	01	0	02
1998	0	0	0	01	0	01	02
2012	0	0	0	02	02	0	04
2013	0	0	01	03	01	0	05
2014	0	0	0	03	0	0	03

One pup was born (and died) in April 1996

RC

	Jun	Jul	Aug	Sep	Oct	Nov	Total
1996	0	0	0	04(02)	02	0	06
1997	0	0	0	01	0	0	01
1998	0	0	01	02	01	02	06
2012	0	0	0	03	02(01)	0	05
2013	0	0	0	02	01	0	03
2014	0	0	0	03	01	0	04

ZP

	Jun	Jul	Aug	Sep	Oct	Nov	Total
1996	0	0	0	0	01	0	01
1997	0	0	0	0	01	0	01
1998	0	0	0	0	0	0	0
2012	0	0	0	0	01	0	01
2013	0	0	0	0	03	0	03
2014	0	0	0	0	0	0	0

Appendix 2: North Cliffs: Number of births per month, with mortalities in brackets.

+C

	Jun	Jul	Aug	Sep	Oct	Nov	Total
1996	0	0	04	02(01)	0	0	06
1997	0	0	01	04(01)	0	0	05
1998	0	0	03	02	0	0	05
2012	0	0	0	0	0	0	0
2013	0	0	0	0	0	0	0
2014	0	0	01	06(1)	02	0	09

HE(Pebble)C

	Jun	Jul	Aug	Sep	Oct	Nov	Total
1996	0	0	01	01	0	0	02
1997	0	0	0	02	0	0	02
1998	0	0	02	01	0	0	03
2012	0	0	0	0	0	0	0
2013	0	0	0	0	0	0	0
2014	0	0	0	0	0	0	0

HNWC

	Jun	Jul	Aug	Sep	Oct	Nov	Total
1996	0	0	01	01	0	0	02
1997	0	0	0	0	0	0	0
1998	0	0	0	0	0	0	0
2012	0	0	0	0	0	0	0
2013	0	0	0	0	0	0	0
2014	0	0	0	0	0	0	0

PC

	Jun	Jul	Aug	Sep	Oct	Nov	Total
1996	0	0	01	01	0	0	02
1997	0	0	0	02	0	0	02
1998	0	0	01	02	01	0	04
2012	0	0	0	0	0	0	0
2013	0	0	0	02	0	0	02
2014	0	0	01	03	0	0	04

HMCO

	Jun	Jul	Aug	Sep	Oct	Nov	Total
1996	0	0	0	01	0	0	01
1997	0	0	0	02	0	0	02
1998	0	0	02	0	0	0	02
2012	0	0	0	0	0	0	0
2013	0	0	0	04(01)	02	0	06
2014	0	0	0	02	01	0	03

HMC

	Jun	Jul	Aug	Sep	Oct	Nov	Total
1996	0	0	0	0	0	0	0
1997	0	0	0	0	0	0	0
1998	0	0	0	0	0	0	0
2012	0	0	0	0	0	0	0
2013	0	0	0	03	01	0	04
2014	0	0	0	05	0	0	05

CG

	Jun	Jul	Aug	Sep	Oct	Nov	Total
1996	0	0	0	02	0	0	02
1997	0	0	0	01	0	0	01
1998	0	0	0	0	0	0	0
2012	0	0	0	01	0	0	01
2013	0	0	0	02	0	0	02
2014	0	0	0	0	0	0	0

NDTC

	Jun	Jul	Aug	Sep	Oct	Nov	Total
1996	0	0	01	02	0	0	03
1997	0	0	0	02	0	0	02
1998	0	0	02	0	02	0	04
2012	0	0	0	04	0	0	04
2013	0	0	02	01	01	0	04
2014	0	0	0	06	0	0	06

AC

	Jun	Jul	Aug	Sep	Oct	Nov	Total
1996	0	0	03(01)	02	0	0	05
1997	0	0	02	04	0	0	06
1998	0	0	0	03	02(01)	0	05
2012	0	0	01	04	01	0	06
2013	0	0	02	02	01	0	05
2014	0	0	0	05	0	0	05

Appendix 3: Pup births, Land's End v North Cliffs: 1996–1998

1996	Aug	Sep	Oct	Nov	Total
Land's End	0	8	6	0	14
North Cliffs	11	12	0	0	23

1997	Aug	Sep	Oct	Nov	Total
Land's End	0	3	2	0	5
North Cliffs	3	17	0	0	20

1998	Aug	Sep	Oct	Nov	Total
Land's End	1	4	1	4	10
North Cliffs	10	8	5	0	23

Appendix 4: Pup births, Land's End v North Cliffs: 2012–2014

2012	Aug	Sep	Oct	Nov	Total
Land's End	0	8	6	0	14
North Cliffs	1	9	1	0	11

2013	Aug	Sep	Oct	Nov	Total
Land's End	1	10	6	0	17
North Cliffs	2	14	5	0	21

2014	Aug	Sep	Oct	Nov	Total
Land's End	0	10	7	1	18
North Cliffs	2	25	4	0	31

Almost nothing has been written anywhere about seals using Devon sites:

Grey and harbour seals at South Devonshire sites

Contents

Summary

In south Devonshire, grey seals occur almost always in small numbers at isolated sites. Especially since about 2005, numbers have been increasing steadily. At these relatively few sites, they are at the eastern limit of their current breeding, moulting and regular haul-out range on the Channel coast of England. These are also among the southernmost sites regularly used by the grey seals in the east Atlantic.

The three most important haul-out sites are the (Dart) Mewstone archipelago, just north of the entrance to the estuary of the Dart, on floating pontoons anchored in the River Dart mainly north of Dartmouth and at the Peartree Point archipelago, just west of Start Point. Both archipelago sites are used during the hours around the time of low water, although some individuals remain close by in the sea through the remainder of the tidal cycle. The River Dart site use is not influenced by the tide and is used more heavily in the winter and spring months.

Satellite-tagged seals have been recorded travelling from Brittany to southwest Devonshire after release from veterinary care in France (Vincent, 2001) as well as in 2008 (Liret, pers. comms). These results, as well as results from photo-ID studies, indicate the likelihood — impossible to confirm without identifying and tracking individual seals — that some seals using Devon sites are visiting from other localities.

Between 8 and 15 pups are born annually, currently, primarily at three sea cave and on one rock and sand beach near Bolt Tail. Beach sites are also used irregularly as nursery sites. These include Newfoundland Cove (Dart river-mouth, east shore), Froward Cave (at the south end of Froward Cove), Shinglehills Cove (Dart river-mouth, south shore), the west end of Great Mattiscombe Sands (west of Peartree Point), Rickham Beach and Inner Hope Cove.

The lone moulting site is situated on the main beach deep inside a sea cave in the vicinity of Bolt Tail.

Seals occur daily in the estuary of the Dart through the year, especially on the high-water half of the tide cycle and as far upstream as the weir, above Totnes. They use the estuary primarily as a resting place, sleeping in the water but also hauling out. Since 2006, especially during the winter and spring months, they have used mainly floating pontoons at the entrance to Old Mill Creek, in an area used for Admiralty moorings. Currently they use a larger number of floating pontoons farther upstream.

More occasionally, although over a longer span of time, they haul out on the Anchor Stone, a midstream islet situated just south of Dittisham, and on the floating pontoons of the Dolphin boatyard on the south shore of Galmpton Creek.

Occasionally, during the summer season, they identify a particular moored boat upon which they haul out. Usually, the boat has a cover that proves attractive as a resting place, but their main requirement is to be able to surge up out of the river waters on to it. Therefore, the gunwales of such favoured haunts are typically low-slung.

Grey seals take fish in the estuary, especially in the late summer. There was a considerable conflict between the salmon netsmen and the seals until the first decade of the 21st century. This has subsided since that time due to the near-cessation of netting on the estuary due to the very low numbers of salmon now returning to the river to spawn and because most licenses were bought out by representatives of the rod-and-line men.

It is impossible to estimate the number of seals in Devonshire waters from annual pup production figures. This is due to the phenomenon of seal circulation around sea areas — in this case around the western Channel and the Celtic Shelf area (implied by the Breton tracking studies). For example, records from the 1950s through to the 1970s (e.g. Johnston, 1959) show that some pups born at sites in West Wales follow a track that brings them to Devon, Lundy, Cornwall and Scilly coasts after leaving their nursery sites. Therefore, some moulted pups found on Devonshire shores today most probably originate from natal sites outside the region. By the same token, it is likely that some moulted Devonshire pups are found at least as far afield as the shores of Cornwall, Scilly, Lundy, Brittany, Wales and Eire.

Small numbers of seals from Brittany wearing coloured plastic tags bearing 'registration' letters glued to the top of their heads were observed on the coast of south Devonshire in 1998 and 1999, and later off Godrevy Point near St Ives in west Cornwall. These tags were applied at Océanopolis, Brest, where they have accumulated much data from sightings made by members of the public of hat-tagged seals.

For at least 25 years from the 1988 summer season, pleasure boats from Dartmouth and Torbay harbours took passengers to see the grey seals hauled out on the Mewstone. Variable amounts of disturbance were caused by these trips, as well as by visits made by local boats. A partially respected voluntary exclusion zone exists for the lagoon area at the Mew Stone, intended to protect seals from disturbance and the too-close approach of boats following such events. This area is overlooked by the Froward Point National Coastwatch Institute Watch Station. Some of the Watch Station personnel have recorded disturbance events.

The main threat to seals at south Devon sites today comes from human disturbance at the archipelago and pontoon sites on the estuary. At this time, the sea cave sites remain largely secure against human intrusion, especially as they are only lightly used during the summer months, when such events are most likely to occur. This is principally because those sites remain little-known even locally.

A site-based database for seals and a small catalogue of seal images captured at Devon sites is held by Stephen Westcott.

South Devon Seal Sites: Grey Seals (Dart) Mewstone

The Mewstone archipelago is situated ENE of the northern entrance to the River Dart in Devon less than 400m from the mainland shore. It consists of the main island (the Mewstone), a number of smaller rocks (Shooter Rock, the Shag Stone, the Cat Stone) and, at low water, reefs that connect most of the greater and smaller rocks. At low water, there is a lagoon largely contained by a horseshoe arrangement of rocks with a main entrance open to the SW under the Shooter Rock and by a narrow channel to the NE. The lagoon has long served as an initial refuge for seals when disturbed from the more south-westerly haul-out rocks and was designated a voluntary exclusion zone in 2000–2001 for that reason.

This site is used exclusively as a resting place by seals.

The sites used as resting places by seals around the lagoon are the Reef, Seal Rock and (rarely) the Shag Stone. The other major resting place is Flat Skerries, situated beyond the NE channel draining from the lagoon. Trickle Skerries, situated on the SW side of the Mewstone are also used. Rarely, but increasingly, seals haul out on rocky sites low along the SE skirts of the Mewstone and at the Eastern Blackstone, usually between the two main islets.

During the spring and summer months, the tidal rocks at the Mewstone appear to be used predominantly by a mixed group of mature male and female seals, with varying numbers of immature seals. However, only the males appear to be sedentary. Unique patterns of pelage markings on the head, chest and neck of individuals (Hiby and Lovell, 1990) indicate that females sometimes, not always, return to the site.

Estuary of the Dart

In the estuary, grey seals are most commonly seen hauled out on floating pontoons at the entrance to Old Mill Creek and at points northward to Long Stream. To a lesser extent, they haul out on the Anchor Stone just south of Dittisham and on floating pontoons at the Dolphin Boatyard on the south shore of Galmpton Creek. Occasionally, they haul out on moored boats.

In the water, they are most commonly seen in the vicinity of the Kingswear Fish Quay, the Anchor Stone, Higher Gurrow Point, Long Stream, Ham Reach, Sharpham Point and the weir at Totnes.

They have been regarded traditionally as a considerable nuisance by some salmon netsmen. Indeed, between 1998 and 2000, at least four seals were shot: 2 in 1998, 1 in 1999 with 1 being seen floating downstream on July 17, 2000. Farther along the Devon coast, in the Tamar estuary, 2 seals were killed in 1999, being found washed upstream by the tide at Gunnislake. Local reports (anecdotal) suggested these killings were due to seals-fisheries conflicts.

Pups are rarely born on River Dart sites. They have been born at three river-mouth beaches in the last 30 years, only on one occasion at each site.

Peartree Point

WSW of Start Point lies the Peartree Point archipelago, among whose rocks Greater Sleaden Rock is the largest and most regularly used. It is almost attached to the mainland at LWST. Little Sleaden Rock is the only other rock used by seals that is not submerged at high water, other than those rocks situated just to the south of Raven's Cove.

The mainland at Peartree Point consists of craggy rocks under which runs the coastal footpath and below which is a grassy sward. Below the grassy sward are mainly quite low cliffs rocks and a small shingle beach, from which it is possible to gain access to Great Sleaden Rock at low tide.

Site specific behaviour saw seals at Peartree often making a 'preliminary' haul out in the lee of Great Sleaden Rock on small skerries, apparently using them as a 'waiting room' before rocks more remote from potential disturbance by people coming from the land became available with the ebbing of the tide.

Halftide Rock, the skerry farthest from the shore on normal spring tides, was the favourite haul-out site at low tide during spring tides when there was minimal wave action.

Seal behaviour through the period of observation was generally quiet, with few aggressive interactions between the seals, the majority of which appeared to be immatures.

Seals may be seen over the period of high tide, often asleep and 'bottling' (upright in the water with head above the surface, snout pointing to the sky) in the sea just offshore, especially just off and to the north of Raven's Cove.

Other seals coming to haul out appeared to come from the (easterly) direction of Great Mattiscombe Sands. Occasionally, pups are born at the west end of Mattiscombe Sands.

During the spring and summer months, the tidal rocks at Peartree Point appear to be used predominantly by juvenile and mature male seals.

The Seal Caves

West of the entrance to the Kingsbridge estuary there are several sea caves used as resting places by grey seals. Only one is used for moulting. At least four sea caves are used for pup production. One cliff-backed beach is also used for pup production.

One sea cave is used as an occasional resting place and an occasional nursery site in Froward Cove, just north of the Mewstone. Close to Durl Head is a cave, accessible with some difficulty from the land, where pup production used to occur (1995, 1998) and may still do, despite lack of recent confirmation.

In addition to discovering seals and white-coated pups, tracks and resting place hollows have been identified on sand and shingle beaches in these caves, some of which delve as far as 100 metres into the cliffs.

Other Observations

Seals haul out sometimes, always in very low numbers, on sandbanks in the estuary of the Exe between Starcross and Exmouth. They occur also in the sea in the vicinity of Sidmouth. Very occasionally, they haul out on the Mewstone under the guillemot nesting cliff at Berry Head and on floating pontoons in Brixham harbour. More regularly, they have been hauling out on the fishermen's pontoon at Salcombe in the Kingsbridge estuary.

Seals are seen in the sea, increasingly 'bottling' at rest, in Brixham harbour or hauling out there on floating pontoons but also at Horseley Cove, Prawle Point and near another Mewstone (near Wembury). They often appear among the surfers at Bantham.

1b. Seal Sites: Harbour Seals

Historically, harbour (previously known as 'common') seals have occurred only rarely in south Devonshire waters, usually as solitary individuals. Nevertheless, one harbour seal pup was said to have been found stillborn at a site on the Erme estuary, Devon, in 1994. This was the only recorded occasion in the 20th century when harbour seal pup production at any West Country site was confirmed (although it is commonplace for members of the public to mistake juvenile grey seals for harbour seals).

Since 2006 and through to the present, always at least one male harbour seal has been present continuously in the estuary of the Dart or at the Mewstone. Its place of origin is unknown. Very few harbour seals are found on the south coast of England, the nearest localities where they are regularly recorded being Poole and Chichester harbours.

Large and increasing numbers of harbour seals occur on the north coast of France, especially in the estuaries of the Somme, estuaries around the SE and SW roots of the Cotentin Peninsular and the Rance. They occur, also, in the Molène archipelago off the west Brittany coast. These are their likeliest places of origin. Indeed, tracking studies of French seals are current and support this contention (while not excluding the alternatives).

In June and July 2019, the harbour seal association with the Dart was strengthened by the birth of two pups at the south end of Long Stream in the Dart at Blackness Rock. Altogether, they plus two adult females and two adult males were present in the lower reaches of the estuary at that time and thereafter. They may prove to be the founders of the first harbour seal colony in SW Britain.

That possibility was reinforced in 2020 when precisely the same number and mix of harbour seals was observed. The precise birth date of the firstborn pup was unknown but the second pup was born on July 17.

In both years, the seals were disturbed into the water on an almost daily basis. Consequently, it remains yet premature to imagine this locality is an established harbour seal nursery site.

Disturbance at Seal Sites

In 2000, an investigation carried out at two south Devon sites, the (Dart) Mewstone and Peartree Point, into whether grey seals using them were subject to disturbance by people, concluded that seals at both sites were subject to considerable (avoidable) disturbance. These are the two easternmost rocky sites regularly used by grey seals on the English Channel (north) coast: a frontier of their range.

Mewstone

At the Mewstone, disturbance was caused mainly by the activity of motor boats and kayaks approaching too close and too fast to the rocks upon which seals were assembled.

At Peartree Point, disturbance was caused mainly by people swimming and snorkelling in the sea or by people clambering over rocks close to the seals, as well as — to a much lesser extent — by boat activity.

Recommendations designed to mitigate disturbance levels and reduce them to the barest minimum for the Mewstone were agreed, having been discussed by all affected or interested parties (including representatives of the fishing community, pleasure and private boat operators, the police, the Dart Harbour Navigation Authority and conservationists). The agreement was widely publicised, on television, radio and in regional and local newspapers. A voluntary exclusion zone was established in the lagoon area and it was further agreed that boats would approach no closer than 25 metres from the seal rocks.

In 2006, the study was repeated at the Mewstone only and elaborated to review whether the recommendations were working or required refreshment, as well as to gauge the views of the public.

Seals used precisely the same sites as were being used in the 2006 survey. At the Mewstone, a high incidence of 56 disturbance events was recorded in the 60-day study, the largest proportion of which occurred in late May and June. 39% of these events occurred as a result of boats entering the lagoon exclusion zone, very similar to the 37% of events recorded for 2000, suggesting either that people were not aware of the status of the lagoon or that they elected not to observe it, which was known to be the case in a number of the events. As in 2000, seals showed absolutely no tolerance for the proximity (sometimes as far away as 100 metres) of kayakers or divers. Their presence close by deterred seals from hauling out on that tide.

15 of the 54 disturbance events were initiated by the only wildlife cruise operator who had undergone training for a national accreditation scheme (the WiSe scheme). Other cruise operators (who had not undergone accreditation) initiated 2 such events.

The individual seals using these sites varied little over the 3-month survey period. A lone harbour seal was also present throughout. The maximum low water count was 11 seals.

In 2018, grey seal behaviour was studied again for 40 consecutive days at the Mew Stone. Boat activity within 200m of the site was studied simultaneously using the same methods employed in the previous studies (2000 and 2006).

Daily haul-out counts revealed an average of 15 seals hauled out per day, ranging from 0 – 30 per day — an increase on past numbers. The average period between the first seal hauling out and the last one re-entering the sea was 240 minutes (143 – 312 minutes). The main 2 sub-sites used by seals were the same as previously observed although one sub-site previously well-used on spring tides was this time hardly used (Seal Rock). There were 41 disturbance events that caused 135 seals (0 – 12 per day) to abandon their haul-out sites and re-enter the sea, the largest number of events being caused by the close approach of kayak flotillas but with slightly more seals (48 v 45) being disturbed by the close and occasionally aggressive approach of open motor boats. The lagoon area, agreed in 2001 to be designated a voluntary exclusion zone as it functioned as the principal place of refuge for seals disturbed from the rocks, was repeatedly entered/abused.

This and the previous studies, along with anecdotal accounts reporting seals biting people at SW England sites including near the Mewstone, show increasing habituation to people and their water craft by seals. This suggests a discussion needs to take place so that avoidable inter-actions potentially entailing injury to people or seals can be averted.

Peartree Point

Here, disturbance by humans comes from a greater variety of quarters than at the Mewstone because of the (closer) proximity of the haul-out sites to the mainland.

Several boats pass very close to the haul out sites. In some cases, one or two of the local crabbers checking pots close by made clearly aggressive runs close to the rocks upon which seals were resting, notably Halftide Rocks. These actions drove seals into the sea. Immediately after this happened, boats slowed down dramatically. Most of this behaviour was performed by two boats (on 5 of 7 occasions observed).

Where people walked without attempting to conceal their approach over Great Sleaden Rock, seals were always disturbed from small 'waiting room' sites situated around the Rock. However, disturbed seals tended to haul out again quite quickly on Halftide Rocks or other sites farther from Great Sleaden. Boat disturbance tended to cause seals to remain in the water for longer periods.

As at the Mewstone, the non-aggressive disturbance of seals was predominantly unintentional, either because people did not notice them (e.g. jet ski operators) or else they continued to approach seals until they were so close that seals dived into the sea (canoeists, swimmers, snorkellers and motor boats).

No commercial pleasure boat caused disturbance at this site

As at the Mewstone, disturbance occurred on an almost daily basis, at least when observers were present, between 17 July and 5 August, when very quiet sea conditions and fine sunny weather prevailed. The peak period for disturbance was between 13.00 and 15.00.

The importance of this site is that on some days of the year, this is the principal haul out site on the Channel coast of England.

Fisheries Inter-Actions in the Inshore Waters

Occasional violent death resulting from gunshot wounds is not the only problem facing grey seals in south Devonshire. Very occasionally, a seal becomes entangled in fishing nets from which they are always at risk of an unpleasant death. A female seal entangled about the neck and her right flipper by a trawler's tickler net was found on Seal Rock at the Mew Stone in 1993. Despite attempts to liberate the seal from entanglement, supported by the (then) Harbour Master, Captain Moore, who made available a DHNA vessel and team, the seal could not be captured — being highly wary of approach by boats closer than 100 metres. Three weeks later, she was reported to have been shot.

The extent of current fisheries inter-actions in south Devon waters is not known. However, inter-actions between seals and bottom set nets in Cornish waters are well-documented (Glain, 1998; Westcott, 1999). There, it is evident that grey seals (also harbour porpoises, eels, crabs etc.) take fish that are captured in such nets. It is likewise evident that these nets take a heavy toll in seal lives, especially seals in the first year of life — that is, those learning to hunt while being less developed physiologically than older seals.

In the estuary of the River Dart, salmon seine netting is currently mainly suspended after decades of catastrophic decline. Higher upstream, salmon fishing by rod and line has been reduced but still continues, for reasons unclear in the context of the loss suffered by the netters. In 2008, only 3 licences were active, the remainder having been bought out by the rod-and-line fishermen who fish the higher freshwater reaches of the river. In addition, the season was shortened so that it ran only through July and the first half of August. This was a reaction to continuingly very low numbers of salmon returning to the river to breed.

Epilogue

As I conclude this manuscript, everywhere research continues into grey seal biology — if least so in the seal caves. Today resembles yesterday, resembles a decade since, resembles the 1980's in that the barrier of health and safety requirements for would-be seal cave researchers is so exacting as, usually, to be prohibitive. This is understandable in that approaching, entering, exploring and departing the caves *is* potentially mortally dangerous. There is an apparently growing risk of cliff-falls matched by smaller erosion events inside caves, coming to all manner of grief as a result of falling while treading across the often-slippery inter-tidal rocks and becoming stranded due to an un-forecasted deterioration in sea conditions.

Even while I have been writing this manuscript, there has been another significant rock collapse in the North Cliffs district of west Cornwall, obliterating at least three more seal nursery sites.

Finally, there is the risk posed by the changing behaviour of the seals themselves. Evidence indicates seals are becoming significantly less wary of humans, both ashore and in the sea.

There has always been the risk of being cornered in a cave by a seal behaving aggressively and barring the escape route — hence the injunction always when exploring seal caves to ensure you have a clear and secure line of retreat before proceeding deeper into the cave. However, during the last decade, anecdotal accounts indicate seals are more likely to remain in caves when they are being explored, with incidents of cornering increasing.

Hence the wariness on the part of funding or commissioning agencies. However, it was felt when I was seeking funding that my experience of sea cave exploration rendered me fit for funding; or maybe it was simply felt that I was expendable. For my part, when more acutely conscious than usual of the risk of, for example, cliff-falls, I have taken refuge in the fact that catastrophic events are exceptional, less-than-a-needle-in-a-haystack moments: it doesn't mean they will not happen but it is a calming perspective.

Seal cave research will continue from strength to strength. As elsewhere, technology will provide the research tools of the future, supporting researchers across the stepping stones of here, now, and the future. Technology will generate ever more informative insights into the sea cave behaviour of grey seals, ever more safely if never, quite without a modicum of risk — unless hereafter robots and whatever they evolve into place the recording tools in place.

I feel that I have gone as far as an old-fashioned seal biologist, using more or less traditional methods, can go. I carried out my research as a way of life, hoping to serve good ends while living a prolonged adventure calling on body, intellect and also (perhaps most importantly to me) soul. It is an entrancing world of so many moods that the grey seals and all their neighbours inhabit. It is the frontier place where the sea of so many moods meets the land, where sun and icicles visit the cave entrances to adjust atmospheres. Despite the seeming harshness of the seal cave environment, there is rare peace and quiet to be found there, along with a wonderful lack of clutter — even despite the battered deposits of marine debris.

The rare cave visits made during clear nights were magical with the acoustics being more than ever musical: an improvised natural choral song while the crowding stars wheeled on high above the cave entrance in silent accompaniment.

From part way across the seal cave stepping stones, I wish well to those who carry the story ever on.

The End, for now.

Bibliography and References

Anderson, S.S. (1977). The grey seal in Wales. Nature in Wales.

Baillie, C.C. & Clark, N.A. 1974. Brief visits to the sea-level caves on the east side of Lundy. Lundy Field Soc. An. Rep. 25: 59-62.

Baines, M.E., Earl, S.J., Pierpoint, C.J.L. & Poole, J. (1995). The West Wales Grey Seal Census. (CCW Contract Science Report no.131).

Barnett, J. & Westcott, S. (2001). Distribution, demographics & survivorship of grey seal pups (Halichoerus grypus) rehabilitated in southwest England. Mammalia 65, no.3.

Barron, W.H. (1936). Seals on the north coast of Cornwall: Fishery Officer's report. Cornwall Sea Fisheries Committee Report.

Borlase, Dr W. (1758). The Natural History of Cornwall.

Carew, R. (1602). Survey of Cornwall. S.S for John Jaggard.

Chanter, J.R. (1877). Lundy Island: A Monograph, descriptive and historical.

Clark, N.A. 1976. The composition and behaviour of the grey seal colony of Lundy. Lundy Field Soc. An. Rep. 27: 32-42.

Clark, N.A. & Baillie, C.C. 1974. Observations on the grey seal Halichoerus grypus at Lundy. Lundy Field Soc. An. Rep. 25: 57-59.

Clark, N.A. & Baillie, C.C. 1973. Observations on the grey seal, Halichoerus grypus, populations at Lundy. Lundy Field Soc. An. Rep. 24: 41-42.

Craggs, J.D. and Ellison, N.F. (1960). Observations of the seals of the (Welsh) Dee Estuary. Proc. Zool. Soc., London, vol.135, part 3.

Cullen, M.S. (1978). The stock of grey seals (Halichoerus grypus) of Pembrokeshire, Dyfed. Nature of Wales, vol. 16.

Davies, J.L. (1949). Observations on the Grey Seal *(Halichoerus grypus)* at Ramsey Island, Pembrokeshire. Proc. Zool. Soc., London, vol. 119.

Davies, J.L. (1956). The Grey Seal at the Isles of Scilly. Proc. Zool. Soc., London, vol. 127.

Envernus. (1867). Seal hunting in Cornwall. Once a Week.

Fordham, R. and Lewis, D. (1961). Observations of the Grey Seal (*Halichoerus grypus*) in Cornwall. Royal Cornwall Polytechnic Society Annual Report.

Fordham, R. and Lewis, D. (1962). Observations of the Grey Seal (Halichoerus grypus) in Cornwall, 1962. Royal Cornwall Polytechnic Society Annual Report.

Glain, D. (1998). Conservation of the grey seal (Halichoerus grypus) in Cornwall: a study of circulation and inter-actions with fishermen. MSc. Thesis, University College, London.

Hook, O. 1964. Grey seals (Halichoerus grypus) at Lundy, Bristol Channel, 1954-1957. Rep. Lundy Field Soc. 16: 24-25.

Hudson, W.H. (1923). The Land's End. J.M. Dent & Sons, London. 307pp.

Johnson, A.L. (1972). Seal markings. Nature in Wales, vol.13, no.2: 66-80.

Kiely, O., Lidgard, D., McKibben, M., Connolly, N. & Baines, M. (2000). Grey Seals: Status and Monitoring in the Irish and Celtic Seas. Maritime Ireland/Wales INTERREG Report No.3. Coastal Resources Centre, National University of Ireland, Cork.

Lockyer, R. (1955). The Seals and the Curragh. Scientific Book Club.

Lockyer, R. (1966). Grey Seal, Common Seal. Andre Deutsch.

Loyd, LRW. (1925). Lundy: its history and natural history.

Morrey Salmon, H. (1935). Seals of the West Coast. Trans. Cardiff Naturalists Soc., vol.LXVIII.

Neale, J.J. (1896). Notes on a visit to Skomer, 1896. Proc. Cardiff Naturalists Soc.

Owen G. (1603). The First Book of the Description of Pembrokeshire.

Pennant, T. (1771). A Tour of Scotland MDCCLXIX. John Monk.

Pennant, T. (1776). British Zoology.

Pomeroy, P.P., Anderson, S.S., Twiss, S.D. & McConnell, B.J. (1994). Dispersion and site fidelity of breeding female grey seals (Halichoerus grypus) on North Rona, Scotland. J.Zool. Lond., 233.

Poole, J. (1996). Grey seal monitoring handbook: Skomer Island.

Prime, J.H. (1985). The Current Status of the Grey Seal Halichoerus grypus in Cornwall, England. Biol. Conserv. 33.

Ridoux, V., Creton, P. & Allali, P. (1997). Des phoques sur les cotes de Bretagne (in) Mammiferes marins en Bretagne, Océanopolis.

Steven, G.A. (1932). A short investigation into the habits, abundance & species of seals on the North Cornwall coast. Report to the ministry of agriculture & fisheries, 30 December, 1932. J.MBA, vol.XIX, no.2.

Steven, G.A. (1936). Seals (Halichoerus grypus) of Cornwall Coasts. J. MBA. 15.

Summers, C.F. (1974). The grey seal (Halichoerus grypus) in Cornwall and the Isles of Scilly. Biol. Conserv. 6.

Thomas, D. (2003). Net fisheries & interactions with marine wildlife around Wales. Report for the Wildlife Trusts & CCW.

Thomas, D. (1993). Marine wildlife & fisheries in Cardigan Bay. Report for CCW.

Thomas, D. (1992). Marine wildlife & net fisheries around Wales. Report for RSPB & CCW.

Tregarthen, J.C. (1904). Wild Life at the Land's End. John Murray.

Vincent, C. (2001). Bases écologiques de la conservation du phoques gris, Halichoerus grypus, en mer d'Iroise. Thèse de Doctorat d'Université de Bretagne Occidentale. Soutenue le 11.07.2001.

Ward, A.J., Thompson, D. & Hiby, A.L. (1987). Census techniques for grey seal populations. Symp. Zool. Soc. Lond., 58: pp.181-191.

Westcott, S.M. (2010). Procedural guidelines for studying grey seals in SW England. Natural England, Cornwall & Isles of Scilly, Truro.

Westcott, S.M. (2010). The status of grey seals (Halichoerus grypus) at Lundy, 2008-2009. Report to Natural England, Devon & Severn, Exeter.

Westcott, S.M. (2009). Seals at South Devon Sites, 2008. Unpublished

Westcott, S.M. (2007). Year-round grey seal use of sites in the Boscastle locality, north Cornwall, 2006 to 2007. Report to Natural England, Cornwall & Isles of Scilly, Truro

Westcott, S.M. & Stringell, T.B. (2005). Field observations on the disturbance of grey seals in North Wales, 2003. CCW Marine Monitoring Report No.15.

Westcott, S.M. & Stringell, T.B. (2004). Grey seal distribution and abundance in North Wales, 2002-2003. Bangor CCW Marine Monitoring Report No.13.

Westcott, S.M. & Stringell, T.B. (2003). Grey seal pup production for North Wales, 2002. Bangor, CCW Marine Monitoring Report No:5.

Westcott, S.M. (2002). The distribution of Grey Seals (Halichoerus grypus) and census of pup production in North Wales, 2001. CCW Contract Science Report 499.

Westcott, S.M. (2000). The disturbance of grey seals (Halichoerus grypus) at haul-out sites. A report for English Nature & Cornwall Wildlife Trust.

Westcott, S.M. (2000). Seals and Fisheries Interactions in Cornwall and Isles of Scilly Seas. Report to English Nature & Cornwall Wildlife Trust.

Westcott, S.M. (1997). The Grey Seals of the West Country and their Neighbours. Stephen Westcott/Cornwall Wildlife Trust.

Westcott, S.M. (1995). Marine debris and oil pollution impacts upon grey seals in southwest England. Mamm. News: 10.

Westcott, S.M. (1993). The grey seals (Halichoerus grypus) of the West Country. MSc. Thesis, unpublished. University of Greenwich.

Willcox, N.A. 1987. Grey seal pupping on Lundy in 1987. Lundy Field Soc. An. Rep. 38: 47.

Willcox, N.A. 1986. A review of Grey Seal (Halichoerus grypus) pupping on Lundy, and some new observations. Lundy Field Soc. An. Rep. 37: 32-34.

Willis, B. (1716). Survey of St. David's Cathedral. Printed for R. Gosling, London.

A bull seal on guard just below a back-of-the-cave nursery beach